Under the Radar

Under the Radar

Starting Your Net Business
Without
Venture Capital

Arnold Kling

PERSEUS PUBLISHING
Cambridge, Massachusetts

Cataloging-in-Publication Data is available from the Library of Congress
ISBN 0-7382-0468-4

Perseus Publishing is a member of the Perseus Books Group.

Find us on the World Wide Web at http://www.perseuspublishing.com

Perseus Publishing books are available at special discounts for bulk purchases in the U.S. by corporations, institutions, and other organizations. For more information, please contact the Special Markets Department at the Perseus Books Group, 11 Cambridge Center, Cambridge, MA 02142, or call (617)252-5298.

Text design by Heather Hutchison
Set in 11-point Stempel Garamond by Perseus Publishing Services

First printing, August 2001
1 2 3 4 5 6 7 8 9 10—03 02 01

CONTENTS

LIST OF CASE STUDIES

Case Studies

ACKNOWLEDGMENTS

I was as naïve about publishing a book as I once was about starting a business. For example, I had no clue about book proposals. Fortunately, David Miller, my agent, was patient and supportive. He helped define this book. He also pushed me to do extensive interviews with other entrepreneurs, which provided me with new insights and examples.

I once heard the great singing duo Clive Gregson and Christine Collister thank their sound engineer for "making us sound better than we really are." I would say something similar about Jacque Murphy and the editorial staff at Perseus.

I would like to thank all of my various partners at Homefair and TheSchoolReport.com, who helped build a great business. Also, I am grateful to the many entrepreneurs who took time out to be interviewed for this book.

In many respects, this book is a product of the Netpreneur program, an association of Internet entrepreneurs in the greater Washington, D.C., area started by Mario Morino. I have incorporated many insights that I gained by attending Netpreneur events. Many of the people whom I interviewed for this book are Netpreneurs. I especially want to thank Morino Institute stalwarts Cathlin Bowman, Mitch Arnowitz, and Mary MacPherson for connecting me with entrepreneurs for interviews.

I received constructive comments on earlier drafts ofl this book from my father, Merle Kling, and from my wife, Jackie Kling. My daughters—Rachel, Joanna, and Naomi—were skeptical that I could earn a living on line. This book is for them.

I issue the standard disclaimer that any errors or flaws remaining in this work are strictly my own.

The website for this book is http://arnoldkling.com/undertheradar/

ONE

Introduction

Netstrapper: An entrepreneur who bootstraps an Internet business.

My first business, Cosmix Web Design, was built without venture capital. Founded in 1995, we raised our capital via friends and family, around $400K in total. The experience was very interesting and intense—a couple times we had less than $1,000 in the bank. When I sold the company to U.S. Web we had around forty employees and a $3–$4 million run rate.

The core competency that we tried to own was not technical or creative prowess, but adaptivity. Having had no formal training or experience in either business or tech made the experience even that much more challenging—however, there were advantages as well. Since the landscape that we were playing in was unformed and super dynamic, we simply had to evolve more quickly than our counterparts.

—Don Pickering, founder of Cosmix.com

Don Pickering's story is a lot like mine. I also founded my Internet business without venture capital (VC). I also was neither a technical wizard nor a business master. My enterprise was a web site that I started in May 1994 called "The Homebuyer's Fair." It started out as a vehicle for me to develop web calculators and on-line articles to educate consumers about the mortgage process. It evolved into a site specializing in providing data to enable relocating individuals to compare the cost of living, crime rates, and school rankings across cities. As the World Wide Web became mainstream, we renamed Homebuyer's Fair to match its URL, homefair.com. I refer to it here as Homefair.

As Don Pickering points out, there are some advantages to being naïve, or having "beginner's mind." In fact, had I known more about the demographics of the user base of the World Wide Web in 1994, I would probably have been discouraged from starting Homefair. Instead, I blindly plunged ahead.

Although I had a very discouraging first year, I had the good fortune to meet some very dynamic entrepreneurs who became my partners. Together, we were able to build Homefair and two related businesses into a package that was ultimately sold to Internet real estate powerhouse Homestore.com for $85 million in cash and stock.

Consider Scott McLoughlin, another founder of a very profitable business. McLoughlin, like many netstrappers, is an information sponge. He is an avid reader of articles and books on business and the Internet. In fact, his company, the Adrenaline Group, encloses a new book with each monthly billing statement to all of its clients.

McLoughlin obtained many of his ideas about running a business from some classic books on marketing and entrepreneurship. But if he had relied on the magazine articles and books that are on the shelves today preaching gospel about doing business on the Internet, he would not have started the Adrenaline Group. Instead, those articles and books would have told McLoughlin that:

- All Internet businesses are funded with venture capital.
- All Internet businesses lose money.
- The only path to success is to win the IPO sweepstakes.
- The Internet opportunity is tied to the value of the Nasdaq.

In spite of all the attention lavished on the Internet by the media, the truth is that they wound up missing the real story. It went unreported that there are many entrepreneurs who have used the Internet to start successful businesses without venture capital. No, they are not being featured in magazine cover stories, but they have built profitable companies. They have not been involved in high-flying IPOs, but many of them have netted millions of dollars from the sale of their companies to larger firms.

Venture capitalists have many mouths to feed. Typically, an entrepreneur would be very satisfied to create a business that can be sold for $5 or $10 million. In contrast, a venture capitalist needs to see potential valuations of as much as $1 billion. Venture capitalists raise the bar this high in order to compensate for:

- Their risk
- Their time
- The team of executives with gold-plated résumés whom they like to see running the business
- The other venture capitalists they want to participate in order to give themselves comfort and security

Between those two bars—the $5 million that would satisfy the entrepreneur and the $1-billion minimum demanded by the venture capitalists—lies a zone of opportunity. This is the zone that I call "under the radar."

Anyone considering starting an Internet-based business can certainly benefit by studying the patterns that other successful businesses follow. But I'd suggest that you think twice before listening to the "conventional wisdom," which says to put all of your energy into polishing a business plan and a likely-to-be-futile pitch for venture capitalists. There is another way, embodied in the strategies and tactics that have worked for me and for many other founders of thriving Internet companies.

Because I successfully launched a business on the Internet without using venture capital, many people who are interested in starting their own companies ask me for advice. Based on these conversations, my impression is that just about everyone has an idea for a profitable new enterprise somewhere inside of them. However, these potential businesses also appear to me to be buried by misconceptions and improbable hypotheses.

Just as Michelangelo believed that a sculpture was hidden within a block of unfinished marble and the sculptor's job was to chisel away to reveal it, I believe there are many successful Internet businesses that have yet to be fashioned. My purpose in *Under the Radar* is to take the ideas you hold about Internet-based businesses, apply a chisel, and hammer away at them. Various tempting illusions and misleading assumptions will be cut to pieces and knocked aside. But the result will reveal a workable idea, along with the execution strategies that will make it succeed.

Undoubtedly, this hammer-and-chisel process sounds unpleasant. It will be particularly painful for anyone who was taken in by the stories that flourished during the dot-com mania of 1998–1999. The legends of that era made venture capitalists sound like fairy godmothers who appear with their magic wands as soon as you come up with a cool executive summary.

Maybe after reading all of the fairy tales in the business magazines, you wanted to jump up and shout: "I've got the vision! I've got the passion!! *Show me the money!!!*"

Well, sit down. Vision and passion are fine, but they won't put points on the board. You won't find them in my list of characteristics of successful entrepreneurs. Even my favorite passionate visionary, Winston Churchill, wrote in a famous passage that "facts are better than dreams." Winning coaches are passionate about the fundamentals.

As to money, if what you are looking for is a treasure map that will lead you to venture capitalists, or at least to angel investors, then this book is not the answer. I discuss funding strategy and tactics, particularly toward the end of Chapter 3, "Room Under the Radar." However, most of this book is about creating a successful Internet business, as opposed to fund-raising. Fund-raising is for charities.

Forget everything you have ever heard about starting an Internet business. Forget the moon-shot IPOs. Forget Silicon Valley. Forget venture capital. Forget *Forbes, Fortune, Upside*, and the *Industry Standard*. The start-ups featured in those magazines and the ones that fit the venture-capital stereotype represent only one thin sliver of the potential for entrepreneurship unleashed by the Internet.

While the venture capital community has been creating stock market sucker plays, another type of Internet entrepreneur has been achieving success without waiting for the blessing of a venture capitalist fairy godmother. These netstrappers are building successful businesses by combining traditional entrepreneurial scrappiness with pragmatic early adoption of the technologies of the dynamic Internet environment.

Although I believe that facts are better than dreams, I find stories to be more instructive than statistics. Although I will spend some time, particularly in Chapter 3, "Room Under the Radar," providing evidence for the validity of the netstrapping model, most of the lessons in the chapters that follow are illustrated through stories. These come from my experience with Homefair, as well as from my interviews with over two dozen netstrappers for *Under the Radar*.

In each chapter, I illustrate general principles by using specific examples drawn from the experience of entrepreneurs I have interviewed. Then, at the end of the chapter, to provide more background on the entrepreneurs, I present a synopsis of the history of their businesses. Their stories are not as familiar as those of America Online (AOL) or Amazon.com, so the synopses should help you to grasp the context and tell you how they got started, what mistakes they made, and what challenges they overcame.

These entrepreneurs are the "millionaires next door" of the Internet industry. They do not have public relations firms concocting stories about their business genius. They did not foist money-losing companies on the investing public. They have built valuable enterprises by combining Internet technology with old-fashioned business values, such as persistence and profitability.

While as individuals they are diverse in age and ethnic and educational background, their paths to success had much in common:

- They did not have access to venture capital.
- They launched their businesses without having undertaken systematic market research. Most of them began with no formal business plan.
- Success came only after years of effort and adaptation. Some netstrappers went through "early divorces," in which partnerships dissolved. In many cases, early customers were mainly small accounts, and it took time to develop the large accounts that provided major revenue.
- Many of them cashed out by selling businesses to strategic investors.

Their experience bears little resemblance to the Internet start-up stories that make the headlines. But their stories are far more typical, which is why anyone who wants to start a successful business in the Internet environment should get to know the strategies and tactics for operating under the radar.

Case No. 1: Don Pickering

Don Pickering's goals for his first enterprise were to "survive the experience and make a dollar." A freelance photographer and writer, six months out of college (where he majored in sociology), Pickering did not hold extravagant expectations for his foray into the world of Internet start-ups. He saw his web-design company, Cosmix, as an opportunity to learn from facing challenges. "It was my MBA," as he put it.

Unlike many under-the-radar entrepreneurs, Pickering wrote up an extensive business plan—150 pages, in fact. "Major overkill," he now says, laughing. "If we had stuck to our plan, we would have fallen flat on our face."

In fact, the need to adjust and change was so high that Pickering took to using a special term for it—"adaptivity." He believes that adaptivity was the key to the success of Cosmix, as its average contract size grew from $15,000 to $300,000 and the number of employees grew to over forty.

When he founded Cosmix in the fall of 1995, Pickering's core hypothesis was that customers would want a web-consulting firm that could supply skills both in engineering and in design. Therefore, his hires included magazine art directors as well as web programmers.

Pickering also took the view that for an unknown firm to gain recognition in the market, Cosmix would have to bid aggressively for its first customers, losing money in order to build a portfolio. In addition, he spent $10,000 a month in print advertising, in order "to look a lot bigger than we were." To keep the company afloat until it could achieve profitability, he put up his assets of nearly $100,000 and solicited additional money from "friends, family, and fools."

The first contract that Cosmix competed to get was one to design a web site for a local radio station. The company beat out eleven other companies, largely because the former magazine art directors at Cosmix presented a gorgeous, detailed proposal. Although the contract was for $12,000, Pickering chose to take only $3,000 in cash. He took the rest in advertising on the radio station.

Cosmix executed its strategy very effectively, achieving a win rate of over 90 percent in its bids for web-design contracts. The goal of an impressive portfolio was achieved.

Pickering and Cosmix thought that their next step would be to "push yourself up the food chain," getting bigger contracts from larger firms. However, they found at the time that there was no middle market. The only way to increase contract size and achieve profitability was to fight for the big deals.

To obtain larger contracts, Cosmix had to learn to handle more complex web sites. This forced Pickering to reconfigure his staff. He needed to reduce sales development and create more engineering consulting capability.

Another challenge with larger contracts was that the bidding process itself could be very expensive. Cosmix learned that it is often a mistake for a small company to respond to RFPs (requests for proposal) that come from the Dilbert sector—large bureaucratic enterprises, including the government. Pickering adopted a much better strategy, which was to obtain a pre-RFP contract to help develop the specifications for a project. Not only did this earn revenue for Cosmix but it also put the company in a strong position to win the contract for the full development. This is a good example of the tactic I call "charging for the sales presentation," because the write-up of the project specifications creates a powerful sales opportunity. Small companies need to learn this tactic in order to have profitable relationships with customers from the Dilbert sector.

Initially, Cosmix focused on Unix development, and like many early web companies, it thumbed its nose at Microsoft. However, Cosmix was surprised to find that Microsoft outsourced some of its own web development. Cosmix was able to win a contract to help Microsoft develop some of its "push" channels when that technology was in favor. This evolved into a relationship with Microsoft Consulting Services, a division that Microsoft created to help increase the market penetration of its products, particularly web servers.

As an integration partner for Microsoft Consulting Services, Cosmix had to adopt Microsoft's consulting and development methodology. This was yet another example of "adaptivity."

In the spring of 1997, an opportunity arose for Cosmix to be acquired by U.S. Web, a network, or "rollup," of web-development firms. Although Cosmix was now achieving profitability, Pickering felt that the acquisition offered better financial security for himself and his employees.

As with many acquisitions, the terms included an "earn-out." Pickering was to spend another year as head of the Cosmix.com subsidiary of U.S. Web, at the end of which he was paid according to a formula based on that year's revenues and earnings.

For the first six months of the earn-out, Cosmix outperformed the expectations that had been written into Pickering's contract. However, there arose an opportunity to strengthen the company for the long run that involved taking on additional technical overhead. Pickering elected to do this for Cosmix, even though ultimately it cost him almost $1 million in personal equity, based on its effect on the earn-out.

One problem with earn-outs is that they create a short-term focus. We encountered this with Homefair. In 1999, we were in the second year of a complex, three-year earn-out with Central Newspapers, Inc., under which we had an incentive to focus on short-term earnings at the expense of long-term investments in infrastructure and brand awareness. Rather than accept the "win-lose" choice that Pickering encountered, we raised the issue with our parent, who agreed to set up an accounting "bucket" that allowed us, subject to their approval, to make long-term investments without adversely affecting our earn-out.

Pickering has no regrets. "Integrity is everything," he says, and he looks back on his experience with Cosmix with pride and satisfaction. He exemplifies the high rate of recidivism among veterans of start-ups. He has already brought along another start-up, Altrec.com, serving as executive strategist between May 1998 and March 1999. He is now involved with other start-ups as well as with a public-private effort to promote entrepreneurship in his state.

Case No. 2: Scott McLoughlin

When I first met Scott McLoughlin in 1997, he did not strike me as the type who could run a business. He loves computer programming, and because of his visionary approach, he appears to be highly distractible. His instincts run counter to aggressive marketing and salesmanship. Before he formed his company, the Adrenaline Group, the only selling he had done was taking orders for an artificial intelligence product advertised in the back of technical magazines.

I asked McLoughlin point-blank how someone with his personality and background could be successful as an entrepreneur. He replied that he learned from reading books. The books he listed were:

- *Selling the Invisible*, by Harry Beckwith
- *22 Immutable Laws of Marketing*, by Al Ries and Jack Trout
- *Crossing the Chasm*, by Geoffrey Moore
- *Relationship Marketing*, by Regis McKenna
- *The E-Myth Revisited*, by Michael Gerber

Among other things, Beckwith's *Selling the Invisible* argues that companies selling services must focus on keeping their promise to customers. As he puts it, "The core of service marketing is the service itself" (p. 3). Beckwith is adamant that no amount of advertising or promotion can overcome flaws in what you deliver to customers.

In *The E-Myth Revisited,* Michael Gerber insists that businesses must be built on reliable processes, not simply on the technical skills of the founder. To take one of Gerber's examples, a good pie-maker does not have a business until he or she can replicate the pie-making process.

In 1996 and 1997, McLoughlin was a member of the technical team for Freeloader, a company that was developing "push" technology, which was very trendy at the time. However, by May 1997, the "push" fad had imploded, taking Freeloader down with it. Even before they left Freeloader, McLoughlin and his team began to receive solicitations from other companies eager for technical talent. They decided to try marketing themselves as a team and formed the Adrenaline Group.

In assessing the market, McLoughlin took the view that the Internet was turning many ordinary businesses into software companies, meaning that they were going to need to build software applications in order to take advantage of the Net. This implied that there would be demand for the Adrenaline Group to develop commercial-quality software on a custom basis. McLoughlin had spotted what I call a "killer trend," which is a phenomenon that creates promising opportunities for start-ups.

As it turned out, the first few potential clients that had contacted the group did not pan out. Then, an important client appeared to be in financial difficulty. Discouraged, most of the original Adrenaline Group team members drifted away, leaving just McLoughlin and Greg DePertuis.

Based on his early experience and on his reading, McLoughlin became obsessed with two goals:

- Maintaining a steady flow of new clients, in order to avoid "key client risk," whereby the loss of one contract could disrupt the business.
- Creating and replicating reliable business processes, so that the Adrenaline Group would be able to maintain a consistent level of service as it increased its client base and added staff.

The Adrenaline Group succeeded in both of these goals. In their first three years, they attracted sixty-five clients.

The Adrenaline Group ended the year 1998 with six employees. One year later, the company had grown to thirty-five people, all of whom were doing billable work. Finally, in the year 2000, the Adrenaline Group had built a sufficient base of customers and technical staff to warrant adding employees in marketing and business development. As of our interview in August 2000, the Adrenaline Group had sixty employees and was pulling in about $1 million in revenue per month. Its profits were the highest of any company whose founder I interviewed for this book.

Apart from worrying about the flow of new projects, the other main focus was on developing internal processes and ensuring that these processes were understood and followed by the entire team. As part of this indoctrination effort, the Adrenaline Group has an enormous internal web site, or Intranet, with information ranging from the nature of the promise that the company makes to its customers to the format for status reports. There is an "Adrenaline way" of executing projects, and new employees are instructed in this methodology.

McLoughlin is adamant in his belief that in a service business you must have a process that works for the customer. "Most technical firms become frustrated by the neediness of customers," he says. The challenge is to make the customer successful while keeping unforeseen requirements from becoming a source of friction between a technical firm and its customers.

The Adrenaline Group typically starts an engagement with a process geared toward discovering the customer's needs and designing software to meet those needs. The team does not want to start coding on a project before being confident that it will solve the business problem.

The Adrenaline Group's approach works so well that clients have started coming to the company simply to go through the initial brainstorming process. For example, a major company in the emerging "smart card" industry engaged the Adrenaline Group to come up with a product plan. The resulting product concept was sufficiently compelling that Microsoft chose to feature the client in its "road map" for the future.

Neither the focus on maintaining a client flow nor the focus on a business process came naturally to McLoughlin. However, based on the books he read, he came to believe that these were the aspects of entrepreneurship he would need to master in order to succeed.

TWO

My Story

People like to hear my story. There are entrepreneurs who have asked me to tell the tale of Homefair to them more than once.

I think that what makes my story inspiring is how ignorant and unprepared I was for becoming an entrepreneur. The point is that you do not have to get every single decision right or anticipate every contingency. Now that I have had the experience, I would say that starting your first business is like going through adolescence: Nobody is completely prepared for it, but somehow you make it through.

In my case, I was particularly unprepared to launch a business (I think I also was particularly unprepared for adolescence, but that's another story). Some of the lessons I have to offer in this book are examples of the "Don't-do-what-I-did!" variety.

And yet, as you will see, things worked out very nicely in the end. I can afford to write this book, for one thing. (If you're deciding between being an entrepreneur and a writer, my experience is that as far as monetary rewards are concerned, the former sure beats the latter. When my agent told me what I would be receiving for this book, the phrase that first popped into my head was "rounding error.")

To get the most out of reading my story, you might keep the following questions in mind:

- What sort of mistakes did I get away with making?
- How did I find contacts, and how did I make use of them?

- How successful were my initial sales efforts and those of my partners?
- What was the useful life of a typical ownership agreement?

Making the Decision (or, as Tom Ashbrook would put it, "taking the leap")

If you think of the World Wide Web in 2001 as a vast ocean, then when I jumped in, it was a puddle. In the spring of 1994, I left a well-paying job at Freddie Mac, a large enterprise that operates in the mortgage market. I launched one of the first commercial web sites, at a time when there were only about 1,000 web sites altogether, most of which belonged to universities.

Three factors led me to become an entrepreneur. I was pushed, I was pulled, and, in retrospect, there might also have been a "midlife crisis" factor involved.

I was pushed by my frustrations within a corporate bureaucracy. I do not blame Freddie Mac for being what it is. As corporate environments go, my guess is that it's better than most, worse than some. The way it affected me personally was in how my creative ideas were handled. I would spend a couple of years trying to persuade senior management to undertake an innovative major project. Then, after I had done all the hard work of pushing the initiative uphill through the approval process, when it came time for the downhill part of executing the project, I would be booted off. I called this process "handing off the idea to the credit-takers."

In the latter part of 1993, I sensed that it was happening again. I had become involved in a project to try to automate the underwriting of home mortgages. The closer the project came to generating a meaningful product, the more likely it appeared that my role was going to be marginalized. I made a promise to myself that if it worked out that way, I would quit.

Around that time, I first felt the pull of the Internet. In November 1993, I attended a dinner talk that was part of a series sponsored by the MIT Alumni Club of Greater Washington, D.C. The scheduled speaker canceled, and one of the two men invited to fill in at the last minute was Vinton Cerf, one of the founding fathers of the Internet.

Cerf outlined his vision for the Internet, including commercial uses that were unheard of. At the time, even the legal status of Internet commerce was somewhat unresolved. The Internet backbone was still being managed by the National Science Foundation and had not yet been turned over to the private sector. Moreover, the graphical web browser Mosaic, which really served to set off the Internet commerce boom, was unknown outside of a narrow academic community.

Soon, I had immersed myself in the topic of the Internet. In those days, there were only a handful of Internet books, and I read just about all of them. Ed Krol's *Whole Internet Catalog* is probably the only one still in print.

In my reading, I came across a reference to Hal Varian. He had taught one of the basic required courses that I took as a graduate student in economics at MIT in the late 1970s. I renewed our acquaintance by using e-mail. He responded by snail mail, sending me two of his papers on the economics of the Internet. Among other things, the analysis in those papers convinced me that the Internet could support itself once the government subsidy was phased out. A few years later, Varian coauthored (with Carl Shapiro) a valuable book called *Information Rules*.

I also read the first magazine devoted to the Net—*Internet World*. I sent an e-mail to one of its columnists, Christopher Locke, in which I offered praise and commentary on the ideas in one of his columns. That weekend, Locke himself called me, treating me to his four-letter-word-laced hippie-visionary rap about Mecklerweb, his big project at the time. That effort, which was something like what we would now call a portal, died at its premature birth, but Locke has been more successful as a writer, with *The Cluetrain Manifesto* and *Gonzo Marketing*. I finally met Locke over five years after our phone conversation, at a large event in Washington billed as "Live Cluetrain."

The Internet's "pull" on me was quite strong. I bought into the visionary outlook expressed by such partisans as Cerf and Locke. I believed that creativity and forward thinking would be more of an advantage in the emerging on-line environment than in the Freddie Mac bureaucracy. I believed that the Internet was going to advance the power of individuals relative to large corporations.

In addition to the "push" of frustration and the "pull" of a phenomenon in which I had faith, there was the "midlife crisis" factor. My fortieth birthday was coming up, in May 1994. Often, I've said that I became an entrepreneur because it was either that or get a sports car and a bimbo. If you look at it from that perspective, I made the safe, conservative choice.

It's a joke to say that starting an Internet business was a safe thing to do, but it's not entirely wrong. One of my core personal values is learning and growth. I was very close to a plateau at Freddie Mac. I was not going to learn or grow much if I stayed there. On the other hand, even if my new venture failed, I would be exploring the technology of the Internet and learning about the challenges of running a business. From the standpoint of personal development, I saw the move as involving no risk at all.

The final stimulus to leave Freddie Mac came in March 1994, when I located a web-development company called Electric Press. I was surfing the Web using a text browser (no graphics) and looking in the CERN directory of sites (kind of a prehistoric Yahoo!). Under "commercial web sites," Electric Press was one of about three listings (most web sites at that time belonged to academic institutions). What struck me was that Electric Press was located in Reston, Virginia, about a ten-minute drive from my office at Freddie Mac. I made an appointment just to talk with the people there.

I met with Rob Main at Electric Press, and I discussed an idea that would combine information and shopping capability for consumers in the real estate and mortgage markets. The idea was pretty fuzzy, and the meeting ended inconclusively.

However, when I went home, I had one of those sleepless nights that you have when you get a brainstorm. I conceived of a site called "The Homebuyer's Fair," where there would be a booth for mortgages, a booth for new homes, and booths that would have information for consumers. I called Main back the next day, and soon I was ready to pay Electric Press a start-up fee of about $6,000 and to commit to paying $1,200 a month thereafter to host and maintain my site. Main registered the domain homefair.com, figuring that would be easier for users to type.

Maybe it was still a fuzzy idea, but it felt good at the time. Meanwhile, my worst fears had come true about the automated underwriting project at Freddie Mac. Because my best hope of obtaining customers would be to contact mortgage lenders, it seemed to me that there would be at least an appearance of a conflict of interest if I remained at Freddie Mac. I almost welcomed this situation, because it gave me an excuse to quit. In April, I handed in my two weeks' notice.

All the same, I did not burn my bridges. I told everyone at Freddie Mac that what I was doing carried an enormous risk of failure and that I could end up coming back and asking for a job. I wanted to have a fallback position of returning to Freddie Mac if the business did not work out. I figured I would give myself six months, or at most a year.

The First Year

I had no business plan. Even if I had known what an "elevator speech" was, I could not have given one. It did not occur to me to look for venture capital funding, because I was ignorant about that whole scene. It's just as well. In May 1994, the only thing crazier than starting a commercial web site would have been trying to get one funded.

When it launched, Homebuyer's Fair had:

- Articles for new home buyers, on topics such as closing costs and choosing the best mortgage, and reviews of books for home buyers.
- A calculator that you could use to figure out the monthly payment on a mortgage. (This was Main's idea. I figured that no one would be interested in it, since there is a function in any spreadsheet that does the same thing. But I told him the formula and he coded it.)
- Pictures of the rooms in Main's house, linked to a floor plan of his house. The purpose of this was to demonstrate "the future of house listings."
- A comment form, which I called the "checkout counter." On the site, I said, "Don't leave the Fair without visiting the checkout counter and sending me your comments."
- Two paying sponsors.

Traffic for the site was about 100 hits a week, although we had a spike up to about 500 when Main sent an announcement into the "What's New" page of the National Center for Supercomputing Applications, which was the most popular page on the Web at that time. The most popular parts of the site turned out to be Main's house pictures and the mortgage calculator.

I received many comment forms, including one from a guy named Bill Roberts. He said, "Congratulations! You've set up your lemonade stand on the moon. Now you just have to wait for the astronauts to get there."

I rented an office in a shopping center a few blocks from home. My web server was located at Electric Press, but I needed to set up an Internet connection in the office so that I could view my site, make changes to it, and communicate using e-mail. The critical software was something called "Trumpet Winsock," a communication layer that was eventually made obsolete by Microsoft Windows 95™, which included the same functionality in the operating system. (The guy who developed "Trumpet" probably should have hit Microsoft with an antitrust suit. But the fellow was Australian—what did he know?)

I could not get Trumpet Winsock configured properly. Finally, I called my ISP (Internet service provider), a company called US.net, and asked for help. Their founder and president, Dave Stoddard, drove over to my office at 8 o'clock at night during a downpour and got things working.

I should have realized at that point that I was out on a limb. I was hardly a novice when it came to computers, having over the years written programs in BASIC, FORTRAN, Pascal, and C. If someone with my background could not readily gain access to the World Wide Web, how many home buyers or mortgage borrowers were likely to visit Homefair?

In the summer of 1994, I had lunch with Jeffrey Dearth, the founder of Electronic Newsstand (now enews.com). He pointed out the miscalculation that was embedded in my unwritten business plan. I had read that there were 20 million Internet users, and I just assumed that most of them could reach my site. However, Dearth said that most of the 20 million only used e-mail or on-line services that did not provide access to the World Wide Web. His estimate was that the number of web users at that time was probably not over 500,000. A few months later, he and I collaborated on an article for *Information Week* in which we lamented that the Web was a party where most of the guests had yet to show up.

I was worried about revenues and customers from day one. At that time, there was no hint of a future era in which hit counts, growth, or buzz could substitute for profits.

My first sponsors were mortgage lenders. Banner ads had not yet been invented. Even when banners came into vogue, I resisted them, and Homefair always got most of its revenue from non-banner sources.

While at Freddie Mac, when we were trying to pre-sell our automated underwriting concept, I had gotten to know about a dozen lenders. Of these, the companies that had executives most congenial to me were Monument Mortgage in California and PHH in New Jersey. As soon as I resigned from Freddie Mac, I contacted both of these companies.

My marketing brochure consisted of a demo disk. None of my potential customers had seen the Web before, so I created a disk with a copy of the browser software Mosaic that would default to a home page stored on that disk. That page explained how to click on a link; then it provided links to information about Homefair, as well as sample pages from Homefair.

People loved the demo disk, because clicking on links was so new to them. They thought that I had come up with the whole concept of a browser. I had to disabuse one customer who drew up an agreement that began, "Arnold Kling, who owns a product known as the Internet . . . ." Not even Al Gore ever made that claim.

I mailed the disk to Monument, which agreed to become a sponsor and to pay me an $800 setup charge and a monthly fee of $200. I visited PHH, and their people also agreed to the same terms. I asked them to provide me with educational material for borrowers and promotional material about their companies. To this material, I added contact forms to enable consumers to request information or a rate quote and to have this request automatically forwarded to the lender.

After I had signed up Monument, PHH, and two mortgage insurance companies, I had exhausted all of the contacts that I took with me from Freddie Mac. From this point forward, every customer I obtained came from a "cold call" or a referral.

I had never done any selling previously. I assumed that I would not be any good at it. In fact, considering how few of my customers had even heard of the Internet, my closing rate was fairly high and my cost of sale was not bad. I was fortunate that:

- My professorial style was fairly appropriate for what I was selling. By being patient, straightforward, and clear in explaining the Internet and the World Wide Web, which most of my customers had never seen before, I was able to offer reassurance.

- My demo disk gave me credibility. Mailing it out to a potential customer often helped to get me in the door.
- I did not know how to use PowerPoint. Not having a presentation forced me to have conversations with my customers.

What I failed to learn to do was:

- Set a high enough price to make my sales efforts worthwhile (what I now call "standing up to the bear").
- Give the buyer a special sense of enjoyment and pride in having purchased a sponsorship, in other words, make the buyer feel good about the decision.

In pricing my sponsorships, the most I ever asked for was $5,000. That was for a Q&A message board that allowed consumers to post questions, with the answers posted on the site (unless the consumer requested a private response). There were no off-the-shelf web message boards at the time, so it cost me nearly $5,000 in additional development expense with Electric Press. I sold the message board concept to Norwest Mortgage, one of the top two mortgage lenders in the nation. Obviously, the company could have afforded to pay much more.

Within two months, Norwest shut down the message board. The problem was not too few leads, but too many. The Norwest staff did not have time to answer all the questions that came into the message board, and there was no staff in place to convert the inquiries into closed loans. I should have offered to answer the questions myself, told them to treat the project as public relations until they developed processes to handle the leads, and charged them $50,000. But nobody ever told me about standing up to the bear.

Otherwise, I almost never asked for more than $800 up front, and never more than $200 a month thereafter. The result was that if you added up the revenues from all of my customers, they covered my expenses but left me with no net income.

The first big expansion of the site came when we added the *Washington, D.C., New Homes Guide*, which gave us listings of all new housing developments in the metropolitan area, updated monthly.

Unfortunately, I failed to create a strong bond with the *Guide*'s publisher, Charlie Browning. My thoughts on how I might have handled this better are given in Chapter 7, "The Zen of Partnership," where I talk about the need to "celebrate your partnership."

In spite of my regrets about what might have been, my relationship with Browning was indirectly very significant. He introduced me to Jay Minkoff, the publisher of the *Philadelphia New Homes Guide*, and Minkoff became an early mentor of mine. Minkoff had experience in media and business that he was willing to share. For me, Minkoff helped to fulfill the vision that I had adapted from the Beatles of "meeting the right people at critical moments."

By the end of 1994, I had learned that if anyone was prepared to use the Internet in the process of buying a home or looking for a mortgage, it was the relocating consumer. The first mortgage leads that were generated by Homefair were for people from overseas moving back to the United States. The first successful sponsors were apartment locator services, which acquired most of their Homefair leads from people who lived in one city and were in the process of relocating. It was Jay Minkoff who first deduced that the early Internet demographics constituted an apartment market, and he put me in touch with the apartment search services.

Early in 1995, I asked Minkoff whether there were any companies in the real estate industry that focused specifically on relocation. He said that he had an entire book of such companies, and he gave me names and phone numbers for two executives, one at PHH and one at Prudential. PHH proved to be a challenging bureaucracy, but the executive at Prudential, Steve Ozonian, spared me the bureaucracy and instead put me in touch with Rich Ganley, who ran a small relocation services company called FAS-Hotline. Eventually, Ganley's involvement would turn Homefair into a successful enterprise.

Don't Look Back (maybe)

Meanwhile, by early 1995, I was ready to give up on Homefair. I did not realize that I suffered from "pioneer time," which leads many entrepreneurs to overestimate the speed with which their business will take off. We will return to the problem of pioneer time in Chapter 4, "Planning Your Business." Had I known about pioneer time, I would have guarded against unrealistic expectations. As it was, all I knew was that those expectations had not been met.

I made an appointment with Eddie Snyder, the head of my accounting firm, to assess the business and give me advice. I outlined my accomplishments to date and the risks going forward.

Traffic to my site was increasing. The press was becoming fascinated by the Net, and Homefair was enjoying free publicity in various consumer and industry publications. I believed that I had established a leadership position among consumers interested in finding information on-line about buying a home, finding an apartment, or obtaining a mortgage.

However, as of January 1995, the Web was far from established as a medium for business. None of the three major on-line services—Prodigy, CompuServe, and America Online—offered web access to their subscribers. The dominant personal computer operation system, Windows 3.1™, made it awkward to set up and use an Internet connection. The two events that propelled the Internet toward the mainstream—Netscape's spectacular IPO and Microsoft's release of Windows 95™—would not take place until August.

Snyder forced me to stop talking in terms of site traffic and Internet speculation. Instead, he focused on revenues and expenses. Finally, he told me that as of that point, my business was probably worth no more than $20,000. He said that if I kept at it, then in five years in the most optimistic scenario, it might be worth $1 million.

Comparing Snyder's assessment with what I could earn risk-free working at Freddie Mac, I was not encouraged. My threshold for financial pain is extremely low. We were in the process of planning the bat mitzvah of the first of my three daughters. I had noticed already that the inability of Homefair to offset my lack of salary was affecting my attitude about the expenses. That was more pain than I could take. I did not want to have the conversation that went:

"Dad, why can't I have the kind of party my friends had?"

"Because your friends' dads all kept their jobs, but your daddy flipped out and tried to start a business on the Internet."

I think that before I even walked into Eddie Snyder's office, I knew that I had reached my pain threshold. After all, if I had wanted encouragement, I would have picked someone other than an accountant to ask me to help make up my mind.

Having given up on Homefair, I asked friends at Freddie Mac to help me find a job there. Because a hiring freeze there seemed imminent, they said that it was pretty urgent to move quickly.

My philosophy about big decisions is: "Pick your option. Make the best of it. Don't look back." In 1994, when I left Freddie Mac to start Homefair, I gave up a lot of unvested stock options. I have never tried to calculate, even approximately, what those options might have been worth had I stayed. Don't look back.

Now that I had decided that my web business had failed, my "Don't look back" approach meant that I was inclined to break away from Homefair as decisively as I had broken away from Freddie Mac. My intention was to fold the business and forget about it. The "Don't look back" style was to focus entirely on what I would be doing when I returned to Freddie Mac.

My wife, Jackie, cannot understand the philosophy of "Don't look back." She and I agree when it comes to values and priorities, but she approaches decisions completely differently. I say that she likes to engage in post-purchase research. Another term people use is "buyer's remorse."

Once, Jackie bought a minivan. When she drove it off the lot, the first place she took it was to another car dealer. She had already looked at the vans sold at that dealership, but doing sufficient post-purchase research meant looking at the two brands of van side by side. As it happened, the ramp leading to the place the other vans were parked was very steep. As she drove up the ramp in her new car, she noticed that it did not hold its position very well when you moved your foot from the brake to the accelerator. She wound up returning the minivan to the dealer and asking for her money back.

In April 1995, one year after I had left Freddie Mac, I was fortunate to be able to return (the hiring freeze did in fact materialize). At this point, I was prepared to admit defeat and abandon Homefair. ("Pick your option. Make the best of it. Don't look back.")

Although Jackie supported my decision to return to Freddie Mac, she did not see how I could possibly walk away from Homefair. It was not costing us anything, because revenues were sufficient to pay Electric Press for server hosting and rent for my office, which were the primary expenses. She thought I should continue to maintain the site in my spare time. She thought that I could keep it up if I just worked on it during the evening and on weekends.

That's not the decision I would ordinarily make. But for some reason, in this instance, I went with her philosophy of post-purchase research, instead of my philosophy of "Don't look back." Because I did it Jackie's way instead of mine, I wound up in a position to write this book. It goes to show you that my way of doing things is not always right. You need to evaluate my ideas relative to your situation, rather than just blindly follow what I have to say. And you might want to wait for Jackie's book.

Advice from the Beatles: Meet the Right People at Critical Moments

No one ever told me that entrepreneurship is a contact sport. I picked it up from the Beatles.

During the early months of my entrepreneurial venture, to say that my spirits needed a lift would be an understatement. To maintain my morale, I frequently watched a tape of a movie called *The Compleat Beatles,* which tells the story of their career. During the introductory section, after describing how difficult it was for the Beatles when they first got started, the narrator says: "But they were determined. And they were lucky, playing the right clubs and meeting the right people at critical moments in their careers."

Every time I watched the tape, I focused on the phrase, "meeting the right people at critical moments in their careers." I took the view that I was going to need luck to succeed, and in order to be lucky, I would have to meet the right people at the right time.

I consciously decided that whenever I got stuck, meaning I'd reached a point where things were not working well or moving forward quickly enough, I would try to meet new people. I might call a customer and ask for a referral. I might attend a conference. I might attend a meeting of an organization. I did these things to try to improve my luck.

Sometimes, one phone call would cause a chain reaction. I asked Doug Bendt, the founder of a company that provides analysis of mortgage risk, for advice on a public relations firm. He recommended Sirotka and Associates, a specialized PR firm serving the mortgage industry. In addition to helping me get articles in some of the mortgage industry trade publications, Sirotka connected me with Stephen Pizzo, a reporter whose beat focused on the savings and loan industry. Pizzo introduced me to Scott Cooley, the president of Contour Software, a company serving mortgage brokers. Cooley suggested the idea of a mortgage qualification calculator to allow consumers to compute the maximum amount that they would be permitted to borrow based on industry guidelines. He helped fund the development of the calculator, which became a very popular exhibit on our site.

Starting with Bendt, all of these contacts were made over the phone. The only one I ever met in person was Cooley, who took a side trip to visit my office when he was in town on other business.

Sometimes, the opportunity to meet people had to be created from scratch. In 1996, when I needed to find a developer for the Netscape server platform, there was no relevant organization. So I started a local users' group, by posting an announcement on the on-line bulletin board that was dedicated to Netscape server users.

At the first meeting of the users' group, I met Dirk Reinshagen, a developer who became a consultant for Homefair. Reinshagen was a jewel. His design and implementation gave us the power to integrate our site with hundreds of partner sites, including many whose budgets for web development were in the tens of millions of dollars.

As things turned out, both the users' group and our confidence in the Netscape product quickly dissolved. But Dirk continued his outstanding work for us, using more robust technology. He was such a good find that I consider starting the users' group to be one of the best inspirations I ever had.

The Compleat Beatles told me that it is important to be lucky. But even better, it told me that the key to serendipity would be "meeting the right people at critical moments." Today, I know that entrepreneurship is a contact sport.

The Magnificent Seven

Just as I was returning to Freddie Mac, I was making my first telephone contact with Rich Ganley, the founder of a small relocation services firm in Scottsdale, Arizona. His company, FAS-Hotline, worked as a sort of bridge between companies that did head-hunting and firms that provided relocation services. For example, it provided the clients of Management Recruiters International (MRI) with real estate services from Prudential Relocation Associates.

One of the tools Ganley had developed was called the "Cost of Living Report." This report, which was assembled by a subsidiary of FAS called the Center for Mobility Resources, enabled an MRI recruiter to provide a job candidate with factual information that the candidate would need in order to decide whether to take a job in a different city. As the name suggests, the data included a proprietary estimate of the cost of living in each city covered by the report. At the time, there were about 500 cities in the database.

In May 1995, Homefair displayed a sample cost of living report, and it provided a list of all the cities for which reports were available. We provided a contact form that a consumer could fill out to obtain a free report from the Center for Mobility Resources. Ganley wanted to sell the reports, but I relayed to him the sad fact that consumers on the Internet were reluctant to pay for information. So instead, he decided to try to treat consumers who ordered the reports as prospects. The Center for Mobility Resources would call the consumers to try to determine their level of interest in real estate agents, moving companies, and the other relocation services that FAS-Hotline provided.

The program was a disaster. Ganley's company was deluged with requests for reports, but these came mostly from people who were not close to making a decision on moving. The cost of mailing and faxing the reports as well as contacting the consumers was not offset by the revenues from the few cases in which FAS-Hotline successfully was able to refer consumers to real estate agents or other service providers.

In August, I discussed the situation with Ganley. My view was that we needed to offer information to consumers on-line, immediately, in an interactive way. This would make consumers happier and get rid of the cost of mailing and faxing reports. His concerns were:

- He needed to avoid channel conflict with MRI (to whom he was offering the cost of living reports as an exclusive recruiting tool).
- We needed to weed out the "Lookie-Lou's" who were not good prospects.

- We needed a revenue model that did not depend on lead conversion. It is difficult to monitor and collect from companies such as real estate firms. You are depending on them to track which leads they received from you and to pay when those leads close.

Somehow, brainstorming led us to create the Salary Calculator™. This tool restricted the information that we would offer on-line to just the cost of living information. We provided the information in an entertaining format, in which a consumer would enter his or her current salary, choose the origin and destination city, and have our site calculate the salary needed in the destination city to maintain the consumer's standard of living. The information was interactive, customized to the individual's needs, and gave immediate results.

This format became a huge hit. As Ganley later described it, "It's like Homefair is Disneyland, and the Salary Calculator is like the Pirates of the Caribbean."

More important, Ganley came up with a revenue model. We sold real estate companies the right to advertise in a city-specific way on the results page of the Salary Calculator. For example, suppose that as a consumer I chose Allentown, Pennsylvania, as my city of origin and San Jose, California, as my destination. When the site then calculated my required salary, it would also show me ads for an Allentown real estate agent to sell my house and a San Jose real estate agent to find me a house.

Ganley's pitch to real estate agents was that we would charge them an annual fee to be listed for their cities. We would create their ads, which would include contact forms. We assumed that the "Lookie-Lou's" would not bother filling out the contact forms, but we advised real estate agents to offer additional information about their cities as a way to encourage consumers to fill out contact forms. The contact forms were sent directly to the real estate agents. Since many of them did not have Internet access, we offered them the choice of receiving leads by fax or by e-mail.

We collected nothing in referral fees. Any commissions that the real estate agents earned from our leads were theirs to keep. From the agent's point of view, with one transaction per year, the ad could easily pay for itself.

Ganley calculated that if we could sell 500 cities for an average of $500 apiece, we would have $250,000 in revenue per year. We realized, of course, that some cities would be worth more than others, so that we would have to use a tiered pricing structure. For cities that we could not sell, leads would go to FAS-Hotline, which would try to generate referral fees.

Ganley had recruited Bryan Schutjer, a former marketing executive with Bekins Van Lines, as a partner. In 1996, to supplement the Salary Calculator, we came up with the Moving Calculator, a tool that could estimate the cost of interstate moves based on the distance of the move and the number of furnished rooms in the consumer's home. Again, we used a local advertising model, allowing moving companies to have their ads appear based on the consumer's city of origin.

In May 1996, I dissolved my original business and joined with Ganley, Schutjer, and their other partner, Steve Ziomek, to form The Homebuyer's Fair, LLC. I contributed the web site, including the minimal revenues that still came in from apartment relocators and the Housing Guides of America. The partners from Scottsdale contributed their business expertise, contacts in the real estate and moving industries, and so forth.

We split the ownership of the new business four ways. It was a simple, equal agreement. We did not worry about how to value my previous effort to create the web site or their previous effort to create the cost of living database and their industry contacts. Ganley, whom we all agreed should be CEO, wanted us to focus on building a partnership going forward, leaving behind whatever baggage that we brought with us.

In 1996, we earned a profit of $200,000. Divided four ways, this was not yet enough to support us as well as we wanted, but it was sufficient for me to be willing to cut back my time at Freddie Mac to three days a week. My guess is that if Freddie Mac had not accepted that arrangement, the other partners would have been willing to have me go full-time and take out a salary.

Toward the end of 1997, one of our partners, MapQuest.com (they supplied us with the distance calculations for the Moving Calculator), was undergoing turmoil, with the loss of a key executive. Ganley swooped in on Bill Sedgwick, MapQuest's VP of marketing. Ganley had added up our "inventory" of page views and decided that banner ad revenues were too much to resist. He brought in Sedgwick to try to capitalize on this opportunity. Although Sedgwick struggled initially trying to implement our intended approach for selling banner ads, after a while he was able to develop a better sponsorship model that included additional advertising techniques.

At this point, Ganley and Schutjer started talking about *The Magnificent Seven*. In the movie of that title, each member of a team of Old West fighters has a specialty (one is a knife thrower, one is quick on the draw, and so on). At Homefair, with Ganley's sales skills, Schutjer's experience in the moving industry, my knack for web design, the development talents of our consultant, Dirk Reinshagen, and now Sedgwick's web ad-sales expertise, we were starting to feel like a Magnificent Seven for the Internet. With our Magnificent Seven team, we built up tremendous momentum in 1998.

Cashing In, Phase One

One of our strategies was to "co-brand the world," as Ganley put it. In 1996, Ganley had struck a deal with *USA Today* Online to create a version of our site that would consist of our content embedded in a design that leaves consumers with the impression that they remain on *USA Today*'s web site. This method of content sharing, called co-branding, came to be widely used on the web, and we were fortunate to be in the forefront of it. We developed a system for co-branding that would allow us to set up a co-brand site in minutes. Even years later, other sites were bragging that they could complete a similar process in "only" two weeks.

By March or April 1997, we thought we had a valuable franchise, and we wondered what we might be able to obtain if we were acquired. We were thinking in terms of getting some money up front while retaining some potential from future growth of Homefair. That summer, Prudential expressed some interest in purchasing our company on such terms.

One of our co-brand partners, to which we licensed content, was Central Newspapers, publisher of the *Arizona Republic*, the largest newspaper in Arizona. (In 2000, Central Newspapers sold itself to Gannett.) Ganley mentioned to his contacts at Central Newspapers that we were considering a sale of Homefair, and they said, "Maybe we should acquire you. We're doing that sort of thing now." In fact, they had recently purchased an on-line job-search site, and they were happy with how that acquisition was proceeding.

Central Newspapers initially proposed to purchase Homefair for a multiple of seven times earnings in the twelve months following the purchase. We would receive some of the money up front, and the rest after twelve months.

We were somewhat concerned about betting everything on a single twelve-month period, so I suggested that we base the purchase price on a multiple of four times the first year's earnings plus three times the second year's earnings plus two times the third year's earnings. Because Internet usage was growing rapidly, I thought that this would lead to a larger total payout. What appealed to Central Newspapers about this schedule was that it would encourage us to build a growing business rather than go all out for one year and then quit. They liked the "4-3-2" formula, and that became the basis for the buyout.

The way such "earn-outs" work is that you get a payment up front, and then additional money based on the earn-out. For the purpose of the earn-out, the base payment is like a debt. Up to a certain threshold, your earnings are used to repay the debt. After that, you get the earnings. If you never meet the threshold, you get to keep your initial payment, but you look pretty bad.

For example, suppose you had three partners, each of whom received $2 million up front, and you used a 4-3-2 formula for the earn-out. The total base payment is $6 million ($2 million times three partners).

This base payment of $6 million is the threshold that is your debt against the 4-3-2 formula. For example, if in your first year your profits were $1 million, you would get credit for $4 million against your base payment, because of the multiplication factor of 4. However, you would not yet get any money, because you had not met your threshold.

Next, suppose that in your second year, profits were $1.5 million. Then you would get credit for another $4.5 million, because of the multiplication factor of 3. This would be added to the $4 million from the first year, for a total of $8.5 million. Because $8.5 million exceeds the $6-million base payment, you then would receive $2.5 million, split among the three partners. Continuing this illustration, if your third-year profits were $1 million, you would be entitled to $2 million, because of the multiplication factor of 2. With your base payment already covered, this $2 million would be split among the three of you.

The definition of profits used in the formula was EBIDTA, which stands for "earnings before interest, dividends, taxes, and amortization" expenses. As partners, our goal was to average over $2 million a year in EBIDTA during our "earn-out," and we were on pace to beat that.

We never got to find out what would have happened under the formula. In 1998, we mentioned to Central Newspapers that we thought that some kind of merger between our company and TheSchoolReport.com would be advantageous, because both of our sites catered to relocating consumers. Both companies had revenue sources in the real estate industry.

Central Newspapers was only too happy to have other potential acquisitions brought to their attention. In retrospect, we should have been more aggressive about this. For example, we looked at MapQuest.com at a time when it might have been acquired for about $30 million. We stayed on the sidelines, and subsequently MapQuest went public. Later, it was purchased by America Online in a transaction valued at $1 billion.

Central Newspapers gave us the money to buy TheSchoolReport.com in the fall of 1998, "resetting the clock" for our 4-3-2 formula to begin on January 1, 1999. The cost of acquiring TheSchoolReport.com was combined with our up-front payment, so that our earnings had to reach a higher threshold before we could receive money.

To mitigate our risk that the acquisition might not benefit the original Homefair principals, we structured the transaction to put relatively more of the risk on the principals of TheSchoolReport.com. Our new EBIDTA formula gave TheSchoolReport.com a bit more leverage in the company than we had. We added up the expected profits in the combined business plans of Homefair and TheSchoolReport.com. Our payout formula then said that if the actual total profits turned out to be less than planned, the principals of TheSchoolReport.com would receive a smaller share of the EBIDTA payout. However, if profits turned out higher than planned, they would get a relatively larger share.

1998–1999

Neil Rosen, the founder of TheSchoolReport.com, who joined us with the merger in the fall of 1998, was the first to notice a flaw in the EBIDTA formula. It forced us to focus on short-term profits as opposed to maximizing the value of our company.

The years 1998–1999 were the period of Internet mania in which consumer web sites, like ours, were being evaluated by investors based on their site traffic, not on profitability. The theory was that the web properties that could aggregate the most "eyeballs" (visitors to the site) in their "space" (business category) would be the winners. Web sites that finished second or lower in the ratings race would be losers.

As owners of Homefair, we did not buy into this "eyeball aggregation" strategy, but we had to be mindful of how businesses like ours were being valued in the market. For one thing, the stock market infatuation with dot-coms was leading venture capitalists to pour money into enterprises that competed with ours. We were sobered by the news that VirtualRelocation.com had received $14 million in venture money. That company now had a big budget to play with, while we were funding our business out of revenues that were slightly less, and meanwhile trying to control expenses in order to maximize EBIDTA.

We took this issue to our parent company, Central Newspapers, and we proposed that we be allowed to allocate a portion of our budget to long-term investments in marketing and product development. The idea was that we be allowed to amortize these investments over time, thereby reducing their impact on EBIDTA in the near term. Our parent company agreed, pointing out that the "A" in EBIDTA stood for "amortization." They encouraged us to draw up a list of projects that were designed to improve our long-term position. They approved most of these projects, some of which they counted only partially against EBIDTA and some of which they agreed not to count at all!

Much of our efforts were focused on increasing consumer traffic, which seemed to be the metric of most concern to the stock market. We had long since seen the growing futility of "search engine placement" tactics. These tactics—of designing the site to maximize its chances for showing up when a web surfer typed a particular "keyword" into a search site such as AltaVista.com or Infoseek.com (now Go.com)—had worked well in 1996 and 1997.

However, as the major search sites morphed themselves in "portals," the significance of their automatic recommendations declined. Instead, we could see that they were trying to control traffic by responding to search requests with a list of recommended or suggested sites. The web sites that showed up in these menus of recommendations often had partnership arrangements with the portals. Accordingly, we developed our own portal strategy, and Schutjer was assigned to work full-time on negotiating deals with portals.

We did not think that we could afford the extravagant prices that were being paid to portals at that time. Companies were paying AOL and other major portals tens of millions of dollars to direct traffic their way. Instead, what we tried to do was offer revenue-sharing arrangements with portals. They would direct traffic to our site (often to a co-branded version that kept the consumer within the portal's navigation scheme). We would agree to split advertising revenue into three equal parts. One part would go to the portal, for providing the traffic. One part would go to us, for supplying the content. The third part would go to whoever sold the advertising.

Another strategy that we had was to seek out partnerships with web sites that were "higher up in the food chain" than ours. These sites were not portals, but they nonetheless were destinations for people with an interest in relocation. Most notable among these were the major job-search sites, such as Monster.com. We gave away co-branded versions of our content to these sites for free.

Most of the revenue on our site was generated by leads, either directly or indirectly. For example, on the Salary Calculator and the Moving Calculator, we continued to encourage consumers to fill out contact forms that would go to service providers. One inducement that we offered was that anyone who filled out a contact form was entered into a quarterly drawing for $1,000 toward moving expenses.

Although we did not charge service providers on a per-lead basis, we did use the volume of lead traffic as an important justification for the rates that we charged real estate agents and moving companies to advertise with us. Leads that came from co-branded sites were just as valuable to our advertisers as were leads that came from our main web address.

We came up with several other lead-generating tools. TheSchool-Report.com offered its reports to consumers by using a "coupon" model. If you wanted to order a set of reports about schools in a county, you were presented with a list of advertisers from which to choose. Whichever sponsor you selected would receive your contact information. Alternatively, if you did not want to be contacted by any sponsor, you could pay cash for the report. Nobody wanted to do that. Everyone wanted reports for "free."

Our biggest revenue came from "free" city reports, which people could order to receive all the information we had, including cost of living data, crime statistics, and information on tax rates. However, people could not receive the reports unless they filled out a contact form that they knew would be sent to Prudential, which then might try to sell them real estate services, mutual fund services, insurance, or other products.

Returning to our traffic strategy, other sites that we treated as "above us in the food chain" included the high-traffic news sites, such as *USA Today*. Another important partner was the on-line career site of the *Wall Street Journal*, which combined the ability of a major newspaper to generate traffic with the relevance to us of consumers who were active in the job market.

We also set up co-brands for sites that were "below us in the food chain." Primarily, these were low-traffic sites belonging to newspapers, management recruiters, and real estate companies. Their goal was to expand their content and make their sites more "sticky"— meaning that consumers would stay on their sites rather than leave to go elsewhere.

We earned little or no advertising revenue from these "lower in the food chain" co-brands. In some cases, the deal precluded our including ads or generating leads. Our revenue model for these smaller co-brands was to charge the partner for our work in setting up and maintaining the co-brand. While our profits from this activity were low, it also helped to spread our brand name, because every co-brand page had a logo indicating that it was "powered by homefair.com."

Bill Sedgwick, our executive in charge of advertising and sponsorship, was on a roll. We set up links on our navigation bar to features such as "Find a Job," "Find a Home," "Find an Apartment," and "Find a Mortgage." We did not have extensive content in these areas, but we set up tools with which consumers could enter pertinent information and jump to the relevant parts of other sites. For example, in "Find a Home," after you entered geographic information and other preferences, you were presented with links to the relevant listings in two major real estate sites.

We could generate a lot of traffic to the destination sites in Sedgwick's "Find a . . ." sections. In 1998 and 1999, traffic was so important to the value of web companies that Sedgwick could charge very high prices for listings in these areas. In effect, these sites were paying us for the same reason that they paid portals. For our sponsors, the deals with us were more cost-effective than portal deals, because the sponsors received much more traffic at less cost.

My job was to mesh all of our co-brands (over 1,000) with the various revenue models. This was a challenge from the standpoint of site design, because we needed to balance the requirements to continue to satisfy consumers with the attempt to steer them toward sections in the site that generated income. Moreover, it was a challenge to create systems that could handle the various permutations that emerged from our revenue strategies. I discovered that concepts like "version control" and "data modeling," which I had associated with old-fashioned information technology (IT) bureaucracies, had relevance for the Web, at least once a site became as demanding as ours.

Cashing In, Phase Two

As the year 1999 unfolded, the Internet bubble continued to inflate. I described the impact this had on us as the "Guffy effect."

When I was young, my father was given a book on poker strategy, in which the author seated the reader at a fictional poker table with characters whose names were meant to suggest their playing style. One of the fictional players, Guffy, overplayed every hand. "You will be annoyed with Guffy when you lose a lot of money by finishing second on a pot where he bets heavily and comes in third," warned the author.

We saw a number of Guffys in 1999. VirtualRelocation.com, with its $14 million in VC funding, was one. That company secured a valuable exclusive relationship with Yahoo!, from which we were not able to dislodge them.

Another Guffy was a company that did nothing but take demographic data on neighborhoods from the U.S. Census—information nearly ten years old—and resell it to individual web sites. Some sites took their offering instead of our city reports. We feared really intense competition from them when they announced that they had gone public. As it turned out, however, we could not find them on the Nasdaq or on any of the other exchanges that you can find in the newspaper. They had issued their stock in the obscure "over-the-counter" market ("the Yugoslavia stock exchange," I called it), a futile gesture of desperation.

The Guffys were driving up our costs as we tried to compete, but they were also calling attention to our value. They were sweetening the pot in the real estate and relocation segment of the Internet.

Our parent company asked its investment bankers for advice on how to maximize the value of its Internet properties. We did not really fit the profile of companies that were going public. We were profitable, for one thing. More important, we did not have the growth plans or "story" that could be sold to Wall Street.

However, we had some assets that looked valuable to other companies that were considering public offerings. Two assets were particularly compelling:

- Site traffic. We were the leading site on the Internet for relocation and one of the top five in the hotly contested real estate category.
- Revenue. We had perhaps the best-developed revenue models of any non-porn web site on the Internet. Thanks to the sales efforts of Ganley and Sedgwick, our site was pulling in over $60 per thousand page views. This was far beyond that of any other site for which I could obtain data at that time. For example, Yahoo! consistently reported just $4 per thousand page views.

Another asset was the data that was used for many of the tools on our site. However, this belonged to FAS-Hotline. For this reason and others, it made sense for Central Newspapers to buy FAS-Hotline from Ganley, Schutjer, and Ziomek, adding it to the package with Homefair.com/TheSchoolReport.com.

In the summer of 1999, two web-based companies with ambitions in the real estate and relocation market were considering going public. One was Move.com, a subsidiary of Cendant, which owned two major "brick-and-mortar" real estate franchises as well as other businesses. The other was Realtor.com, the leading site for real estate listings, with ties to the National Association of Realtors. For the purpose of its IPO, Realtor.com was changing its name to Homestore.com. Both the Cendant spin-off and Homestore.com seemed like potential buyers.

Our EBIDTA payout formula had no provision for allocating proceeds from the sale of Homefair. However, our contract from 1997 included a provision that gave the four minority partners the right to veto any transaction along the lines of a sale of our company. Therefore, the first step in any deal was for Central Newspapers to come to terms with the four of us about how we would share the proceeds.

We agreed that before our partnership could receive any money, Central Newspapers would be repaid for the funds it had spent to acquire the various companies and to contribute to the "buckets" for expenditures that had not counted against our EBIDTA payout. Everything after that was "profit." We agreed to split these profits 50-50 between Central Newspapers and our partnership, which included four principals from TheSchoolReport.com as well as the four of us from Homefair and FAS-Hotline.

For a variety of reasons, Homestore.com emerged as the leading buyer for our businesses. However, it was about to enter its "quiet period" prior to going public, so nothing took place beyond an initial feeler from our end. Once the IPO was complete and the company had reached the date where it was legal to speak with us, negotiations began in earnest.

The final sales price to Homestore.com for all of our properties came to $85 million. The transaction took place in October 1999. Homestore.com paid us in a combination of cash and stock. Recipients of stock in this sort of transaction are typically restricted from selling their shares for a year. Therefore, our principals and the Central Newspapers executives were adamant that a large part of the payment had to be in cash. We were not willing to put all of our accomplishments at risk by exchanging them for a huge bet on the continuation of Internet stock mania. We figured that no matter what happened to the Internet bubble, cash would retain its value.

As it turned out, before the restrictions on the sale of our stock were lifted, the stock went on quite a ride. The stock was priced at $50 for the purpose of our transaction. It proceeded to soar well over $100 before the market correction in Internet stocks took place in March–April 2000. It then bungee-jumped into the teens before recovering to near $50 in early September, then plummeted again during the bear market at the end of the year.

Out of the proceeds paid to the principals, we also paid bonuses to key staff, including Sedgwick. A lot of this was very complicated and almost arbitrary, because it was difficult to relate to our original EBIDTA formula. There was a lot of analysis of the sort: "Assume that it had happened this way. Then this would have been X, and that would have been Y, so we can take this ratio and come up with Z." Fortunately, nobody raised a fuss, probably because there was so much money to go around and none of us understood enough about the calculations to make anything an issue. Schutjer, whom everyone trusted, put together the spreadsheet that determined the payouts. As I wrote to friends at the time, "My share in Homefair was pretty dilute by this point. But a couple percent of $85 million is still real money."

Don't Look Back—For Sure

Acquisitions are funny things. When you combine companies, it's never clear how you are going to get the executives to adjust to working with one another. Even before Homestore acquired us, some personality conflicts had started to emerge within our team. Now we were in a completely new environment, and it was inevitable that some of us would adapt better than others.

The night that our deal became official, I happened to be having dinner at an MIT Alumni Club seminar—the same type of seminar at which I had heard Vinton Cerf's vision of the Internet six years earlier. I told my story at the table, and someone who indicated that he had done many acquisitions in the past said that it was really important to tie down the principals in the acquired company with strong handcuffs.

But my handcuffs were not strong at all. I was given a modest salary and a promise of stock options. My main motivation for staying on was that I did not want to be accused of just wanting to take the money and run. I was supposed to hand over the web-site design duties gradually to David Gray in Scottsdale. That way, I did not have to be the one to implement all of the changes that our new parent company made in the look of the site. Other than that, I was supposed to stand by and await further orders, as it were.

In November, I flew to Los Angeles to meet with executives from Homestore.com for the first time. I had a lot of negative reactions to the situation:

- I didn't like their plans for integrating their web properties. I was expecting them to focus on reducing duplication and filling holes in existing content. Instead, they were in the process of launching an ambitious new project, which everyone at Homestore described as "a cross between Yahoo! and Amazon."
- I didn't like the strategy of the company. My thinking was that they should move toward becoming an application service provider for real estate agents. Instead, they were trying to become a shopping portal ("everything for the home").

- I didn't like the fact that they were trying to run a company with nearly 1,000 employees without an organization chart.
- Although I didn't talk with the CEO, I was introduced to him when he happened to be eating at the same restaurant as the group with which I was having lunch, and I didn't like his pouffy Los Angelino hair.

For me, this is about par for the way I evaluate situations in which I am not in charge. Whether or not I've got what it takes to be an entrepreneur, I certainly was not cut out to work for someone else. I don't think you should jump to any particular conclusions about Homestore based on my inherent disrespect for authority.

I certainly don't mean to imply that I think I could do a better job of running such a company. I've never had more than five people report to me. I don't have the first clue about what to do with a corporation of that size. All those employees. All those shareholders. It's almost inconceivable the number of mouths you have to feed. (No doubt the breadth of their strategic objectives has something to do with all those mouths.)

In spite of what I had heard at the MIT seminar, it is rather common for founders to leave when their companies are acquired. I was not surprised or sorry when it turned out that there was no meaningful position for me with Homestore. I was quite comfortable financially and ready to move on to my next gig.

I never look at the Homefair web site any more. The last time I went to it, they had made so many changes that my mental jukebox started playing Joni Mitchell's "Big Yellow Taxi." That parking lot used to be paradise.

Ironically, the day that I separated from Homestore, a letter arrived in the mail at home. Jackie called me and started to read:

"Enclosed are option agreements . . . "

"You can throw that letter out," I said. "None of those stock options are going to vest. Don't even bother looking at anything else in the envelope. Just toss it."

"I know," she said. "Don't look back."

Case No. 3: Rich Ganley

Most people think that you stop selling once the buyer makes a purchase. But when Rich Ganley closes a deal, his sales process has only just begun. After the sale, he continues to convey his enthusiasm for his products and his concern with your success. He wants to make sure that the services you obtain from him make you a star in your organization. He wants to learn from you how your business works, so that he can develop even better products for you going forward.

Ganley, who became my partner and CEO of Homefair in 1996, launched several companies without raising outside funding. He has a hard time thinking in terms of using someone else's money to start a business. Ever since his father threw him out of the house at age fifteen, Ganley has placed a high value on being self-sufficient.

In 1987, he was an independent agent working with Prudential to sell life insurance and other financial products and services. While playing volleyball, an executive recruiter said to Ganley, "Hey, you're a financial planner. I need your help. I've got an executive who doesn't want to change jobs because he's afraid of what will happen to his pension plan." Ganley explained that by doing a rollover, the executive could maintain his retirement assets without suffering a tax penalty.

Ganley thought that there might be a larger market in the executive recruiting industry for financial advice for job candidates. He launched a company called FAS-Hotline, with the "FAS" standing for "financial analysis service." The idea was to help recruiters to close transactions, and in return to receive referrals from recruiters to whom FAS could sell life insurance and other financial products.

Ganley's first customer was Dunhill Personnel, a chain of recruiting franchises. After six months of sluggish business, Ganley obtained a place on the agenda for their national convention. Expecting 300 people for his presentation, Ganley instead gave his pitch to an audience of three.

By this point, Ganley had been so focused on FAS that his insurance sales had fallen off. He had lost his savings and had maxed out on credit cards. He was eating macaroni and cheese every day, and he could afford to go on a date only once every few weeks.

At the Dunhill convention, a man in red suspenders walked up to Ganley and said, "Why aren't you taking your pitch to Management Recruiters International?" The man gave Ganley a contact at MRI.

When he started FAS, Ganley had not done any research about the recruiting industry. He did not know that Dunhill had very little credibility with its franchises or that MRI was the leader in the recruiting field.

The trip to Cleveland to visit MRI was a do-or-die occasion for Ganley. By this time, he was so short on cash that he could barely manage to obtain a plane ticket and a suit to wear. Fortunately, he got along very well with the MRI executives, and he was given the green light to test FAS for six months with fifty of the 600 MRI franchises. The test worked well, and he signed a long-term agreement with MRI.

Ganley worked very closely with the MRI organization. He noticed that many of the firm's clients needed relocation. Often, job candidates would be most of the way through the recruiting process before they understood the full impact of the relocation. For example, they might be making a preliminary house-hunting trip to the new city, and suddenly they would realize that the cost of living there was too high to make the job change worthwhile. Then they would decline the job offer. Ganley saw that this raised the costs and frustrations of the recruiting process.

He asked a local librarian how one might go about comparing the cost of living in different cities. She gave him books with data on the cost of food, housing, and other factors. The data were scattered in different sources, with much being out of date. Ganley saw an opportunity: What if he could gather all of the data, replace the information that was stale with current updates, and put it all on one piece of paper? This was the inspiration for the "Cost of Living Report," another product that FAS could provide to MRI.

What really delighted MRI about the cost of living reports was that Ganley offered them exclusively to MRI offices free of charge! They could use them as a recruiting tool (it became the most popular service that MRI offered) at no cost. Ganley could make this arrangement because of the value of referrals from MRI.

Individuals who are relocating to take a new job need many services, including real estate transactions, mortgages, moving companies, and financial services. With its ties to the recruiting process, FAS was in a position to be the first company to contact the relocating individual with an offer to organize and simplify the relocation process. FAS in turn earned referral fees from the service providers.

By the time Ganley received a call from me, early in 1995, he had nearly ten years' experience in the relocation business. He understood the management recruiting business. He had built a large referral network of real estate agents and other service providers. He had the data for the cost of living reports. Most important, he had an experimental and inquisitive mind, along with good business experience and judgment. Prudential's Steve Ozonian, the man who referred me to Ganley, once told him, "Out of every person I know, you have the best ability to sniff out a deal and make it work."

When we came up with the idea for the Salary Calculator, with individual real estate offices owning the rights to advertise in their local cities, Ganley had complete confidence in his ability to sell. Even though at that time most real estate agents had not heard of the Internet, he knew that they understood the value of leads from consumers who are relocating. Most important, he knew that they trusted him on the basis of many successful past transactions.

Ganley makes a strong effort to bond with every company with which he does business. When he would take me around the corporate offices of MRI or Central Newspapers, he seemed to know the entire staff, from secretaries to the highest levels of management. He is genuinely happy to meet anyone and everyone. Phil Marcus of Rent.net dubbed him "Group-Hug Ganley."

However, Ganley's charm is based on more than superficial friendliness. He practices what I call "doing the role reversal." He constantly asks himself questions like "What would make a management recruiter look good to a client?" or "What can I do to make Steve Ozonian look like a hero to the other executives at Prudential?"

You might not expect Rich Ganley and Arnold Kling to show up on the same team. Ganley is outgoing, optimistic, and earthy. I am introverted, pessimistic, and nerdy. Both of us are emotional and strong-willed.

Personality differences are the cause of many business failures, including those of netstrappers. Ganley has an approach for handling these differences, called the "integrity agreement." He got the idea from John Goodson, an attorney who found in his estate planning practice that he needed a process to cope with the bitter battles that often erupt among siblings who become heirs following a death.

As applied by Ganley in his businesses, the integrity agreement says that when one of your colleagues does something that makes you angry or upset, you will not hold it inside you and let it fester. Instead:

1. Within twenty-four hours, you will talk to the person about what he or she did and how it affected you.

2. If talking about it does not resolve the issue, you will write the person a note saying that you are still not happy about the situation.
3. If writing a note does not lead to resolution, you will bring in a neutral third party and discuss the issue in the presence of the third party.

We used the integrity agreement a few times over the course of our partnership from 1996 to 1999. It worked every time.

Any start-up is going to undergo stress. I recommend adopting something like the integrity agreement as a way of making sure that your people work constructively as a team.

Case No. 4: Robert Main

Visionaries see the world the way they believe it ought to be. They are distinguished by their reluctance to compromise with reality. Within a typical bureaucratic organization, visionaries can win many strong admirers. However, their fate seems to rest more in the hands of their enemies.

Rob Main was part of a small team of visionaries at the National Academy of Sciences (NAS). Their ringleader, Duffy Mazan, ran the information technology group. In the late 1980s, Mazan's team had a vision of giving everyone at NAS a PC linked to a local area network and to the Internet. This would facilitate communication with the scientific community, which constituted the main early adopters of the Internet.

It took several years of fighting bureaucratic obstacles. In particular, managers thought that personal computers were beneath them in that they were used by secretaries for word processing. However, in the end, even the top executives of NAS were happily using e-mail and other functions of their networked PCs.

In terms of achieving their vision, the information technology team at NAS was a success. However, this is not a tale from *Fast Company* magazine, in which the "change agents" are hailed as heroes. It is a more typical example, in which the determination to accomplish something creates so much friction that it becomes career limiting for the individuals within the bureaucracy. If you want to get ahead in a large organizational setting, it is better to accept things as they are than to envision what ought to be.

In 1993, when Mazan was about to be fired, he and Main got together with two other teammates, Ron Linehan and Peg Dawson, to
conspire about their future. Earlier that year, as part of their mission
to evaluate emerging technologies, Mazan and Main had visited the
National Center for Supercomputing Applications at the University
of Illinois in Champaign. There, NCSA official Larry Smarr introduced them to a student named Marc Andreessen, who had created
Mosaic, the first graphical browser for the World Wide Web.

After seeing Mosaic, the conspirators realized that every business
now had a potential communications infrastructure to reach the market, complete with a graphical interface. This led them to develop
business plans for three possible ideas. They rented a house on remote Chincoteague Island to evaluate the concepts.

An idea for Internet printing—letting you send an order in
Phoenix for 500 copies of a document to be printed in Seattle—required too much capital. It would have been expensive to buy high-
speed printers in every city. An idea to offer Internet service to consumers and small businesses—what has become known as an Internet
service provider, or ISP—was also too capital intensive. Moreover,
looking ahead, the conspirators saw Internet service turning into a
commodity, with vicious price competition.

Main, Mazan, Linehan, and Dawson decided that the best opportunity was to create an on-line publishing company for businesses
that wanted to use the new medium of the World Wide Web. They
agreed to work for six months without salary and to contribute
$90,000 in funds from savings to pay for equipment and advertising.
By January 1994, all four were working at their new enterprise, Electric Press.

Mazan was CEO, and Main does not remember what titles the
others had. "All of us had sales responsibility," he points out. At a
time when there were only a few hundred web sites in existence, primarily belonging to universities, sales were a challenge.

The Electric Press team used the list of web sites published on-line
by NCSA to identify seventy private companies with web sites. Then
they called the competitors of these companies and tried to goad
them into matching their rivals.

Another tactic that Electric Press used was local radio advertising.
While today the airwaves are saturated with "dot-com" ads, at the
time this was a highly original and effective tactic. Many of the com-

pany's early customers first heard about Electric Press through advertisements.

Electric Press had not planned to go after the government market, because of the long sales cycle, but one of the companies that heard an Electric Press radio commercial was Computer Sciences Corporation, which had just won a contract with the U.S. Treasury that included building a web site. CSC subcontracted this work to Electric Press.

This led to a contract with the Internal Revenue Service. To the surprise of the client, and not without some subterfuge, Electric Press put up a searchable database of every tax form, in printable format. This instantly popular application continues to run, with taxpayers downloading and printing tens of millions of forms a year. Electric Press charged $2,500 for this project.

Pricing is a very tricky problem for start-ups. Because the product or service is new, there is no established market. Consumers do not know what they ought to pay, and in fact they are doubtful about buying at any price. As a seller, you have so many objections to overcome that you worry about creating a problem with a high price. Thus, it is easy to fall into the trap of pricing for a small profit and congratulating yourself on simply getting some business in the door. That is what Electric Press did with many of its early customers. Clients such as the IRS, which might have been charged $250,000, were given relatively small markups.

In spite of an inability to "stand up to the bear" on price, Electric Press came close to meeting its six-month objectives, and the company was able to repay the initial founders' loans, including their forgone salaries. This is a remarkable achievement for a start-up. It testifies to the value of joining a killer trend at the right time.

The Electric Press radio commercials moved one man to tears. Vinton Cerf, one of the most important architects of the Internet and its governance structure, reportedly had to pull over to the side of the road and collect himself after hearing an advertisement. He was moved because he heard the ad as a validation of the vision for the commercial Internet that he had championed.

Cerf introduced his colleagues at MCI to Electric Press. At the time, MCI had conceived one of the most ambitious projects on the web, which was an early shopping portal called MCImall. Cerf and MCI approached Electric Press about working on the project.

True to their nature, the Electric Press team told the executives from MCI that they were going about their project all wrong. Once again, the founders saw what ought to be, and they refused to give in to the MCI bureaucracy. As visionaries, the Electric Press team was vindicated—MCImall was a total failure.

As entrepreneurs, however, the Electric Press founders were not vindicated at all. When Electric Press put them off, MCI turned to Raul Fernandez, the founder of another fledgling web-development company called Proxicom. Even as of June 2000, on Proxicom's web site, the MCI contract is described as a crucial early win for that company.

Proxicom went public in April 1999, and by June 2000, it had a market capitalization of over $3 billion. When Michael Jordan became an executive with the Washington Wizards basketball team, he was photographed next to Fernandez, who was cited as one of the power brokers that helped bring Jordan to Washington. These were the rewards that might have gone to Mazan, Main, and company, had they only been more willing to compromise with the MCI bureaucracy.

Having muffed their opportunity to turn Electric Press into a big winner, in the middle of 1997 the founders took a step back to regroup. They determined that profit margins were not growing in the web-development business, and they decided to try to form a product company.

Once again, they brainstormed and came up with three ideas. However, this time, they decided to attempt executing all three. Mazan took Internet publishing, Linehan took an e-commerce product, and Main took something called eFed, which was a company that would focus on the "B2G" (business-to-government) market.

Main and new partner John Lee built eFed in the fall of 1997. Originally, it was designed as a portal to bring together NASA and its vendors. However, the business model has evolved to a point where eFed can be provided to any agency, and instead of a large up-front setup fee, eFed earns a share of revenues from transactions.

Early in 1999, Main and Lee noticed the same thing that we did at Homefair, which was that the IPO market was creating new competitive threats as well as new financial opportunities. They decided that it was time to seek a buyer for eFed. They hired a major consulting firm, which was quickly able to find companies to present term sheets. However, at the last minute, National Information Consortium (NIC) indicated an interest. NIC, which developed commerce solutions for state and local governments, was in the quiet period prior to its IPO and so it could not suggest terms. However, when Main read the company's S-1 filing, he said it seemed "like they were in our heads." Once the public offering was priced and NIC could talk freely, the match turned out to be as good in person as it was on paper.

NIC has a very interesting business model. The company will set up a government agency so that it can do business with consumers on-line. The Department of Motor Vehicles, usually the poster child for a frustrating bureaucracy, can now be accessed on the web in many states, for services such as license plate renewals. NIC will do this setup for free (!), in exchange for a share of the ongoing cost savings to the agency from the web-based transaction processing. NIC's new eFed subsidiary had been headed in the same direction, moving toward a usage-based revenue model rather than a fee-for-setup revenue model.

For Rob Main, after several years as an entrepreneur, the sale of eFed meant that he had finally achieved success. According to the National Information Consortium web site, the total purchase price for eFed was approximately $29.5 million. Roughly half came in cash, with the other half in NIC stock. The cash retained its value.

THREE

Room Under the Radar

Out of the Park

Venture capitalists look for spectacular returns. As Scott Frederick of FBR Technology Partners put it:

> A lot of people don't understand the kinds of returns we are looking for. Our goal is 10x returns or higher ... We get business plans from people who say they have a guaranteed 2x return. Philosophically, even if I believed that it was 100% guaranteed at 2x, I don't think we could do that deal because that's not what our limited partners want from us. They hired us as an alternative asset class. They want us to swing for the fences, and the sure thing 2x just isn't it. They want home runs that go out of the park, into the parking lot and keep rolling down the street.
>
> "Science, Art, or Sorcery?" *Netpreneur,* December 15, 1999. Available: www.netpreneur.org/events/doughnets/121599/transcript.html

Scott Frederick and other venture capitalists would say that what might appear to be a good business opportunity to an entrepreneur often will be too small for a venture capitalist. Entrepreneurs and venture capitalists tend to have different perspectives on what constitutes an acceptable target valuation.

What Is a Target Valuation?

In the normal life cycle of a successful business, between approximately the fourth and the tenth year, it is typical to trade away much of your equity. You do this in order to cash in some of your chips and reduce your risk. You may sell the business completely. You may accept a partial buyout. You may become a subsidiary of a larger company.

Many of the founders interviewed for this book have been through this process of liquefying their business assets. In 1997, the four partners in Homefair sold an 80-percent interest in our business to Central Newspapers, Inc., a large media company. For the purchase, Central Newspapers valued our business at $15 million, but we only received some of the money up front, with the rest based on an "earn-out" formula.

One of the exercises that you want to go through before you start your business, particularly if you have partners, is to decide what target value you are looking for when you liquefy your successful business. For example, suppose you started the business with the following:

- Two partners
- No outside investors
- $100,000 total cash invested in the business
- No salaries for the first twelve months, and only minimal salaries thereafter

If you were to sell the business in five years, how high would the valuation have to be in order for you to feel satisfactorily compensated for your initial investment, forgone salaries, risk, and so forth? The answer is your **target valuation**.

Not all entrepreneurs would have the same target value. It depends on your "opportunity cost" (how much you think you could make working for someone else), your tolerance for risk, and other factors. However, I would guess that if you took a survey of entrepreneurs and potential entrepreneurs, the median target value would be around $5 million. Maybe your target would be $2 million or $10 million or $50 million. But I think that $5 million would seem reasonable or more than reasonable to most people.

Of course, in setting a target for valuations, $5 or $10 million is not real money to a venture capitalist. However, you might assume that a venture capitalist would think that $200 million or $300 million is real money. That would be incorrect.

Venture capitalists are looking for target valuation with three commas. As one venture capitalist put it,

> To gain venture financing, a company typically has to have the potential to achieve a market capitalization of $1 billion or more.
>
> **(Source: Vincent M. Occhipinti, managing director of Woodside Fund, writing in Upside, August 2000.)**

Observe the differences between the two points of view. One side—the entrepreneur—might be content with a target valuation of $5 to $10 million. The other side—the venture capitalist—is not even willing to consider a business with a target valuation of less than $1 billion. Do you notice a gap here? That gap is the region that I refer to as "under the radar." There is a lot of room under the radar.

When entrepreneurs first find out about the gap between their targets and those of the venture capitalists, they are surprised. Their typical reaction is to return to their business plans and massage their spreadsheets until they reach a bottom line of $1 billion, figuring that this will get their idea onto the venture capitalists' radar screen. If you want to try that approach, be my guest. But I think I can help you figure out a better plan, based on the successes of many netstrappers—entrepreneurs who have bootstrapped their Internet businesses.

By now, some questions may have occurred to you about the "under-the-radar" approach, or "netstrapping." The rest of this chapter will address some questions that will probably occur to you about netstrapping and about trying to compete under the radar.

A. Does netstrapping really work? Doesn't it put me at a tremendous disadvantage in a competitive environment that includes large enterprises and venture-funded firms?

B. What about the Internet shakeout that has taken place? Does the drop in the Nasdaq mean that only large, well-capitalized companies can make it?

C. Why can't I convince a venture capitalist to fund a business with a target valuation of less than $1 billion?
D. Even though my business is in the under-the-radar zone for target valuations, I think I will need an outside investment of $500,000 in order to get the business to work. What can I do?

A. Does Netstrapping Really Work?

This section will show how bootstrapped firms fit in an environment with other types of businesses, including large enterprises and companies funded by venture capitalists. It turns out that the Internet creates a relatively advantageous environment for agile entrepreneurs.

It is only natural to think that a bootstrap-funded business is handicapped when compared with a venture-funded business. After all, venture-funded businesses enjoy tremendous advantages, including:

- Funding to develop systems and implement a marketing strategy
- Top-tier executives, because venture-capitalist-backed firms can lure high-priced talent
- Board members with powerful connections
- Outstanding advice from experienced entrepreneurs associated with the venture-capitalist firm
- Instant credibility with customers, suppliers, partners, and investors

These advantages are compelling. To see this, imagine that we have two businesses, one with venture-capital backing and one bootstrapped, that are alike in all respects, including:

- Trying to meet the exact same market need
- Defining the size and scope of the target market in exactly the same way
- Offering the same type of solution to the customer
- Following the same marketing strategy
- Using essentially the same technology

- Starting from the same level of market penetration

In this situation, you might expect the company backed by venture capital to win. I am not questioning that assumption. I am willing to concede that a bootstrapped firm cannot beat a venture-funded firm in a fair fight.

Avoid a Fair Fight

But who says you have to fight fair? Who says that you have to attack a business funded by venture capital on its own turf, in a large market with the potential for a $1-billion valuation? Once we drop the "fair fight" assumptions, we can see that there are plenty of opportunities to compete under the radar. Here are just some of the tactics netstrappers are using to succeed:

- Define a market need that does not appear to have three-comma potential

Trevor Cornwell's Skyjet.com (Case No. 6), which attempts to address inefficiencies in the charter-jet business, may have the potential to generate profits "only" in the tens of millions of dollars per year.

- Define a market of smaller size or scope

Layla Masri (Case No. 21), founder of Bean Creative, a web-site design and development company, is not trying to make her company a national name. She is happy to obtain business through referrals and to have a concentration of clients in the Washington, D.C., area. ResourceCompany.com's Leif Johnston (Case No. 12) is willing to focus on small business for his web-based software to help manage operations. Don Britton (Case No. 8) is also willing to forgo the large corporate market for his full-service computer service outsourcing company, Network Alliance.

- Offer a different type of solution

Michaela Conley's hpcareer.net (Case No. 5) offers specific placement services for the health promotion industry rather than a generic job-search site. Because of her focus and knowledge of her field, she provides a better solution with which the large web sites simply cannot compete.

- Follow a different marketing strategy

Mike Covel (Case No. 16), founder of Turtletrader.com, markets training and educational software for speculators. He uses an information-rich web site that encourages close interaction with customers. Most other sites that cater to investors offer either impersonal broadcasts or unfiltered message boards with a cacophony of rumors.

- Use a different technology

If you have a system that can do something unique, you can compete against larger companies. Bill Baker (Case No. 24) of Hire Right.com is doing that with his employment prescreening application.

- Achieve market penetration early

One advantage of starting Homefair when it was a "lemonade stand on the moon" is that by the time competitors came along, we had thousands of links from other sites on the Web. Furthermore, our co-branding strategy helped us lock up most of the desirable partners in our specialty. Some really high-quality sites came along with financial calculators and neighborhood information, but they could not get any traction due to our overwhelming market penetration.

Professor Amar V. Bhide: Sorting Out Five Types of Businesses

One of the most knowledgeable scholars in the field of entrepreneurship is Professor Amar V. Bhide, author of *The Origin and Evolution of New Businesses*. Although his studies cover a period that largely predates the commercial Internet, Professor Bhide's theoretical model and statistical evidence clearly show the validity of the under-the-radar approach.

Bhide distinguishes five types of companies. He argues that each type of company has a particular niche in which it is

TABLE 3.1   The Five Types of Businesses and Their Niches

Type of Company (Bhide's original terminology)	Type of Company (my preferred terminology)	Capital Niche	Ambiguity Niche	Overall Niche for starting new businesses	Examples
Large public companies	The Dilbert sector	High	Low	Corporate initiatives	Intel, AT&T
VC-backed start-ups	VC-backed start-ups	Medium	High	Founders with exceptional qualifications and ideas	DrKoop.com
Revolutionary Ventures	Convoys	High	High	Large corporations collaborating to fend off smaller, faster innovators	Covisint
Marginal businesses	Small proprietors	Low	Low	New franchises based on proven models	restaurants, hair salons
Promising businesses	Netstrappers	Low	High	Under the Radar	Homefair.com

suited to starting a new business. The niches are based on different combinations of **capital requirements** and **tolerance for ambiguity**. The five types of businesses and their niches are shown in Table 3.1.

Bhide points out that capital requirements vary for different types of initiatives. A new fabrication plant for a chip manufacturer or a new accounting system for a mutual fund company could cost millions or even billions of dollars to develop. On the other hand, a new web site may cost only thousands of dollars to develop.

The other dimension along which initiatives vary is ambiguity. In statistical terms, I believe that one can characterize an initiative with low ambiguity as having a distribution of outcomes that is unimodal. It looks like the normal distribution, in that there is one peak in terms of probability of outcome. The most likely return on investment will typically be in a moderate range (say, a 15- to 50-percent rate of return). It is relatively unlikely that the return will be either extremely low or extremely high.

With an ambiguous initiative, the distribution of outcomes might be bimodal, meaning that there are two very different outcomes that have a high probability of occurring. There is a significant probability that the return on investment will be close to zero. However, there is also a significant probability that the return on investment will be very high, in excess of 300 percent.

Ambiguity tends to be related to the maturity of the market. In a mature market, ambiguity is low. In a turbulent market, ambiguity is high.

An example of a mature market would be the market for automobiles or the market for microprocessors. With mature markets, demand can be estimated and extrapolated based on existing behavior. This makes it possible to limit the uncertainty in a forecast of the rate of return from investing in a new plant or a new design.

An example of a turbulent market would be the market for smart cards. While everyone would agree that there is considerable potential in cards that you can use that might carry personal identification, financial information, and other data, at this point we cannot predict the ultimate shape of this market or the pace at which this technology will be adopted. Any company that enters this market today could earn either a very high return or close to no return at all.

Each of the five types of businesses employs a system of strategies and processes for dealing with new initiatives. Each system is optimized for a different combination of capital requirements and market turbulence.

Large established corporations and government organizations in the Dilbert sector use decisionmaking processes that deal effectively in situations with low ambiguity and high capital requirements. They can afford to fund new initiatives that require heavy investments of capital. However, they cannot handle initiatives in turbulent markets that have ambiguous returns. The corporate bureaucracy is designed to protect the interests of shareholders, who have the most at stake when the firm undertakes risk. The goal is to strengthen the existing franchise rather than to engage in projects with uncertain outcomes.

Venture capitalists can handle turbulent markets, but they can invest only moderate amounts of capital. They do not have hundreds of millions of dollars to commit to a single initiative. However, they can fund new projects with capital requirements in the $2 million to $50 million range. They expect to be dealing in the realm of ambiguous returns. As we have seen, they want the positive outcome of the bimodal distribution to represent an extremely high rate of return, often described as a "ten-bagger," meaning a return of ten times the amount of investment, or 1,000 percent.

Revolutionary ventures, or convoys, are designed to cope with highly uncertain projects that take heavy capital investment. They are separate ventures funded by consortiums of large corporations. As of this writing, one prototypical convoy is Covisint, a business-to-business Internet enterprise sponsored by the major automobile manufacturers. Another example is Orbitz, a plan for an on-line ticketing system to be run by the major airlines.

Marginal businesses or small proprietors are firms such as hair salons, restaurants, or lawn care services. In this sector, new initiatives require modest capital investment with low ambiguity. The rate of return on investment is unlikely to be terribly low or spectacularly high. In the Internet economy, there are not yet any businesses that fit the small proprietor model. There is a potential for porn sites to emerge as an example of a business with relatively low risk and low return. The service of designing web sites for small business could also evolve into a small proprietor model.

Finally, we have the businesses that Bhide called promising businesses. They fill the niche of undertaking new initiatives where ambiguity is high and capital requirements are low. As with small proprietors, these businesses require relatively little capital investment to get started. However, that is where the similarity ends. Small proprietors enter established markets with proven customer demand. Promising businesses enter ambiguous markets with unproven demand. Small proprietors tend to have limited upside potential. Promising businesses can earn rates of return that would impress a venture capitalist, although on a much lower capital base.

How Netstrappers Fit In

In the Internet environment, I use the term "netstrapper" to refer to what Bhide calls a "promising business." The term is meant to suggest an Internet business that is bootstrap funded, at least initially. It also is synonymous with firms that operate in the region that I call "under the radar."

All five types of businesses may play a role in your environment. They may be potential customers, partners, or suppliers. Therefore, it is useful to understand how the five types of businesses differ from one another. Assuming that you are a netstrapper, some of these businesses will be ideal customers, and some will not. Some will be ideal partners, and some will not. It helps to think in terms of the following questions:

- How do they make decisions about new initiatives?
- How do they react to new technology?
- How do you want to position yourself?
- How you want to avoid positioning yourself?

The answers to these questions are summarized in Table 3.2. Following the table, I describe each type of business in more detail.

The Dilbert Sector. The Dilbert sector includes government and large corporations. These organizations are notoriously bureaucratic. They stifle many initiatives, particularly those that deal with immature markets. However, they excel at managing and setting priorities among large, expensive projects in mature markets.

The function of the bureaucratic process is to filter out mistakes. Avoidance of risk and aversion to error are not accidental qualities of the bureaucracy. They are its reason for existence.

For large capital projects, planning is critical. It may take years to complete a project, so that the forecasts made at the time the project is initiated must be as accurate as possible. These projects are also complex, so that coordination is a major challenge.

As controversial economist and social theorist John Kenneth Galbraith pointed out in the 1960s, enterprises that undertake these large projects abhor market turbulence. He argued that in addition to using careful planning in order to forecast market demand, firms use modern advertising and marketing to ensure that forecasts for demand

TABLE 3.2   How a Netstrapper Should Deal with the Five Types
of Businesses

Types of Business	Decision Process	Reaction to Technology	How You Want to Position Yourself	A Position You Would Want to Avoid
Dilbert sector	Bureaucratic	Analyze first, invest later	As a supplier who can help with research and testing	As a partner
Convoy	Constrained risk-taking	Invest aggressively	As a supplier who can offer a way to speed implementation	As an irrelevant competitor
VC-funded firm	Fast but firm	Market-driven	Either as an irrelevant competitor or as an acquisition target	As a competitor that the VC-funded firm must destroy
Small proprietor	Pragmatic	Afraid of costs and impact	As a supplier who will leave existing business processes alone and provide immediate benefits at low risk	As someone who is insensitive to the small proprietor's challenges and needs
Another netstrapper	Quick and pragmatic	Willing to try anything that might give them an edge	As a partner who can provide complementary services	As a supplier

come true. In 1995, for example, Microsoft invested $250 million in promotion to ensure that Windows 95™ was launched successfully.

The Dilbert-sector bureaucracy is adapted to identifying, prioritizing, and managing very expensive projects that fall into known marketing channels. Examples would include building a plant to manufacture the next generation computer chip or creating a new customer billing system for a large telephone company.

Many middle managers in large corporations have difficulty understanding or accepting this fact about the Dilbert sector. They complain that there are too many bureaucratic impediments to innovation. They believe that they should be punished less for failure and that they should be rewarded more for successful risk taking. They draw inspiration from books by management gurus or magazines such as *Fast Company* that claim that better companies are encouraging their middle managers to become risk takers and "change agents."

The fact is that netstrappers and venture-funded firms are much better suited than large corporations to deal with turbulent markets and innovation. If large companies allowed their employees to take significant risks by committing the firm to ambiguous projects, the results would probably be catastrophic for shareholders.

The reality is that controls on risk taking are absolutely essential in large corporations. Compared with an entrepreneur, a middle manager bears very little risk from the failure of a new initiative. Middle managers do not put up any of their own capital. Even the worst outcomes—a bad performance review or being let go—can often be avoided by adroitly spreading blame.

If large enterprises were to increase the rewards while reducing the punishments for risk taking, then middle managers would have the incentive to take gambles that are extremely unwise. For example, suppose there is a project that could gain or lose $10 million for the company but has only a 20 percent chance of success. If the middle manager is going to be rewarded for success and forgiven for failure, he or she is going to undertake that project, even though it is a poor bet from the shareholders' point of view.

The Dilbert sector must provide institutional checks on individual risk taking, particularly in the case of an ambiguous project with a bimodal distribution of outcomes. The implications of this view of bureaucratic filtering in the Dilbert sector are as follows:

1. For managers working inside large corporations, the initiatives that are likely to be rewarded are large projects that serve existing market channels. Such projects tend to have less ambiguous outcomes. However, even these projects will still require considerable time and effort to persuade the various constituencies and decisionmakers in the corporation to back them.

2. Inside large corporations, other initiatives will meet seemingly irrational levels of resistance. These include small initiatives that nonetheless require interdepartmental coordination or initiatives of any size where the market channel is not established.

3. Entrepreneurs who are starting businesses in unproven markets do not need to fear immediate entry by large enterprises in the industry. Of course, they do need to prepare for such competition once the market becomes established.
4. The Dilbert sector places a high value on research and analysis, particularly for decisions regarding new technology. This represents both an opportunity and a challenge for the netstrapper trying to sell to such a company. This will be discussed more in Chapter 5, "Feeding Mouths and Minds."
5. Netstrappers and Dilbert-sector companies are incompatible as partners. Netstrappers need partners who are quick and informal. Dilbert-sector companies are slow and obsessed with legal protection. This will be discussed more in Chapter 7, "The Zen of Partnership."

Convoys.   Professor Bhide found that there are instances in which large companies will form partnerships with venture capital firms to create what he calls "revolutionary ventures." With the Internet, we see coalitions of established companies forming these convoys, particularly to create on-line marketplaces for trading within an industry. In addition to Covisint and Orbitz, mentioned above, I have seen other convoys discussed in the press. For example, several large banks have joined a consortium to develop tools for on-line banking. Major mortgage lenders have joined a consortium to try to enhance efficiencies in the lending market.

The advantages to large companies of forming convoys are:

- They hope to avoid fragmented standards.
- Manufacturers and other companies that are in the fulfillment part of the value chain believe that they can benefit by reducing marketing and distribution costs and instead conducting business directly over the Web.
- By forming a new venture, they hope to bring the project to fruition faster than would be the case if one of the companies were to try to develop a system on its own, using internal resources.

Although convoys are intended to operate more quickly than corporate bureaucracies, they often fail to do so. They can struggle to deal with the challenge of getting executives from different companies to agree on issues where their strategic interests are not necessarily aligned. For example, Orbitz, the convoy formed by airline companies to sell tickets on-line, was forced to postpone its launch date, and as of this writing it still was unclear whether it would get off the ground.

As a netstrapper, when you see large firms in an industry get together to form a convoy, you would rather be positioned as a supplier than as a competitor. As a competitor, you are going to have a number of disadvantages.

For example, suppose that you had set up an on-line marketplace for ball bearings, and the major manufacturers announced that they had formed a partnership with a venture capital firm to do the same thing. One consequence would be that you would have a hard time getting attention from the manufacturers. Their interest in electronic commerce would be focused on their new convoy.

On the other hand, if you had already developed some industry-specific tools for electronic commerce, you might be able to evolve into a subcontractor for the convoy. That would be a solid revenue opportunity.

Even if you cannot position yourself as a supplier, you should be alert for the likelihood that some firms will not participate in the convoy and others will drop out quickly because of a dispute. These dissident firms may be eager for your alternative solution.

VC-Funded Firms. Venture-funded firms are focused on growth. Explosive growth. Unbelievably fast growth. Total-domination growth.

Growth can be measured in a variety of ways, but the most common metric is revenues. The management team will be told to "grow the top line," which means that the objective is to maximize revenues. The assumption is that if revenues can be shown to be growing dramatically, then the next round of funding can be obtained readily.

There was a period in 1998–1999 when a venture-funded firm did not even need to show growth in revenues. Joseph Murgio (Case No. 15) found with FamilyPoint.com, a site that facilitates communication among family members, that his investors only cared about the number of registered users. Having found an effective way to attract users with on-line advertising, Murgio poured nearly his entire budget into marketing. He did not even have to be concerned with the top line. In that euphoric environment, every dollar he spent served to raise his company's market value by increasing user registrations.

This period of Internet euphoria was one where venture-funded firms followed what I call the McKinsey business plan. In my experience, no matter what question you ask a McKinsey consultant, the answer always comes back: "Sacrifice short-term profitability to expand your market share." Translated into the Internet environment, in books such as *Net Worth*, the McKinsey business plan justified large investments in companies with no profits.

The McKinsey business plan rests on the hypothesis that there are important network economies. Network economies are situations where customers increase the value of the network to one another. For a comprehensive description of network economies, see Shapiro and Varian's *Information Rules*.

An example of a concept that involves network economies is Swati Agrawal's FirmSeek.com (Case No. 11), a web-based referral network for attorneys, accountants, and other business service firms. For consumers to want to participate, they must see large numbers of firms involved. For firms to want to participate, they must see large numbers of consumers. Increasing the number of customers will increase the willingness of firms to participate, which in turn will add value to customers.

Where true network economies exist, the business may not be successful until the customer base reaches a critical mass. This in turn can require significant capital investment, which makes such businesses unsuitable for netstrapping. If your business concept requires network economies in order to succeed, you might do well to come up with a different idea.

Indeed, this appears to have occurred to Agrawal. She has been looking instead into developing products that she can sell as stand-alone systems to enable large firms to manage referrals more effectively. For example, a major accounting firm might have two of its units bidding on the same proposal, unless it has appropriate tracking systems in place. Agrawal's company could develop software to address this problem.

Venture-funded firms are willing to use their capital to attempt to capture network economies. The investment in market share is as meaningful to them as an investment in physical plant would be to an industrial firm.

As a netstrapper, do not look for venture-funded firms to share the market. The venture-funded firm wants the entire market, not just a share. Even if your services are complementary to those of a venture-funded firm, chances are that unless you are acquired by that firm, the company will compete against you. Your strategy is to try to go as long as possible without being noticed by the venture-funded firm. By the time you are noticed, your hope is that the company will see that it is cheaper to acquire you than to try to dislodge you.

I am not saying that you should panic whenever a venture-funded firm enters your market. Often, venture-funded firms make announcements that reflect their ambitions but do not yet have any basis in reality. If your customer base is established, the venture-funded firm will find that even with a large marketing budget there is little it can accomplish. When VirtualRelocation.com obtained venture funding to come after us at Homefair, the only major partner they were able to obtain was Yahoo!, and even that was not because VirtualRelocation had a bigger marketing budget but rather because we failed to adapt our content to meet Yahoo!'s needs.

Small Proprietors. Small proprietors, such as restaurants and real estate brokers, tend to have profit margins that are reliable but narrow. Their approach to making decisions is risk averse and pragmatic.

Small proprietors are threatened by change, particularly change that involves new technology. A small manufacturing firm, retail franchise, or service business has plenty of headaches and day-to-day challenges. When approached with "revolutionary" ideas, small proprietors tend to see threats rather than opportunities. As we will see in Chapter 5, "Feeding Mouths and Minds," the challenge for a netstrapper is often to convince small proprietors that a new product or service can be adopted at low cost and low risk.

The ideal position for a netstrapper to adopt vis-à-vis a small proprietor is to serve as a bridge between the small proprietor's industry knowledge and the technologies of the Internet. For example, with Homefair, my partners Rich Ganley and Bryan Schutjer already had credibility with the owners of local real estate companies, moving companies, and management recruiting firms around the country. Ganley and Schutjer approached these companies on their own terms as friends, rather than as threatening revolutionaries.

Other Netstrappers.   Other netstrappers are different from VC-funded firms in that they are eager for partners. When a netstrapper finds a company that offers complementary services, it is typically only too happy to share the market with another netstrapper. Connie Mazur, of the web design firm CyberVillage Networkers, was introduced to one of her most helpful partners when a client used both companies to work on a project. Other netstrappers make ideal partners, because they are nimble, flexible, and willing to share opportunities.

VC-funded firms are less oriented toward partnership with other firms. They are reluctant to share a market, because this would mean forgoing precious revenues.

There are many ideas for products and services that might be sold to netstrapper companies. However, neither netstrappers nor VC-funded firms are a desirable target market. They can be very demanding, with a need to squeeze as much as they can out of their budgets. Their needs and their fortunes can change quickly. Many advertising-supported web sites discovered this in 2000. Suddenly, they were scrambling to obtain reliable advertisers from brick-and-mortar industries, after the fortunes of the dot-com stocks declined and their advertising budgets withered.

B. What About the Internet Shakeout?

Now that many Internet stocks have collapsed and some famous companies backed by venture capitalists have gone out of business, you might be wondering whether small netstrappers can be successful. Are we headed into a phase where only large, well-capitalized companies will survive? In fact, the mood among netstrappers continues to be optimistic, because they have been focused all along on building solid, profitable businesses.

It may help to draw a distinction between two processes. One process, which I will call **consolidation**, will be defined here as a reduction in the number of firms in an established market. For example, airline mergers and banking mergers constitute consolidation.

The other process, which I will call a **shakeout**, will be defined here as the disappearance of companies that either failed to execute properly or never had a tenable business model in the first place. For example, the closure of Pets.com in November 2000 represents the failure of that company to demonstrate a viable business model.

For netstrappers, it makes a very big difference whether we experience a consolidation or a shakeout. When a market is consolidating, winners swallow losers. Strong capital resources are a necessity. One could argue that Homestore's ability to buy Homefair in late 1999 was an example of consolidation.

Instead, what happened in the Internet market in the latter half of 2000 looks to me like a shakeout. Investors grew tired of subsidizing unprofitable companies. Netstrappers, who never relied on such subsidies, find the new playing field more to their liking. For example, Mike Covel (Case No. 16) can now pursue his HomePharmacy.com on-line drugstore without facing competitors with $100-million advertising budgets.

You will hear pundits predict consolidation on the Internet. These prognostications are for winners to emerge in every major category, with everyone else dropping out. I have been hearing these forecasts since 1995, and I fully expect to continue to hear them in 2005. But I doubt that the consolidation theory will come true.

The pundits will argue that consolidation is a natural process. They point out that until the 1920s, there were dozens of auto manufacturers in the United States, but by the 1950s, there were only five. The same phenomenon occurred in many other industries of the industrial age.

In the industrial economy, with its reliance on plant and equipment, scale matters. Therefore, consolidation makes sense. However, Internet businesses do not rely on plant and heavy equipment. Because capital requirements for an Internet business are extremely low, there will always be easy entry. New netstrappers are going to be able to pick off profitable niches that are not well served by large companies.

The venture capital industry has a strong interest in promoting the consolidation theory. If you do not believe in consolidation, then you may not have confidence in the stories that venture capitalists are telling about their companies. Your faith is needed in order to bolster the share prices of these firms when they go public.

Venture capitalists are likely to confuse a collapse of Internet stock prices with a collapse of the Internet opportunity. A stock market collapse adversely affects the ability of venture capitalists to market their wares on Wall Street. It does not mean anything like a consolidation of the entire Internet industry. In particular, it does not reduce the ability of netstrappers to establish themselves.

An alternative to the consolidation theory is the frontier settlement theory. According to this theory, the Internet is comparable to the American West in the latter half of the nineteenth century. For the first pioneers, land is ample and fortunes are up for grabs. Over time, however, all the land gets staked out, and new settlers have to carve out smaller areas for their ranches and farms.

When the frontier was thinly settled, a single general store had to serve people for miles around. As more settlers arrived, stores became more specialized and more localized. While localization in the geographic sense will not be as pronounced on the Internet, my guess is that as the information space becomes more crowded, businesses will have to serve narrower markets with smaller overall revenue opportunities.

The frontier settlement theory predicts that the companies that face the biggest challenge are not the netstrappers. It is the venture capitalists who ought to be concerned. As more of the land gets fenced in, you are not going to be able to build another ranch the size of Yahoo! or eBay. The opportunities that exist are in smaller, niche markets.

I believe that the evidence supports the frontier settlement theory. The total number of Internet businesses continues to grow. Some industry leaders have pulled away from their closest competitors, but they are unable to shake the Lilliputian netstrappers.

For example, consider the proliferation of Internet sites catering to employment and job search. The consolidation theory is that one site such as Monster.com will drive all the others out of business. However, data on traffic show that no single employment site has been able to achieve a market share of more than 25 percent in the job-search category.

The frontier settlement theory is that smaller sites that focus narrowly on specific occupations, locations, or other niches will be the survivors. Michaela Conley's career site for health promotion professionals (Case No. 5) represents the future, in this view.

Another example of the failure of the consolidation theory is in the health care industry. The high-profile would-be giants, such as WebMD, Neoforma, and DrKoop.com, are struggling. Smaller companies that target more specific constituencies are much more likely to prove successful. I told the founder of one start-up in this field, "You are the type of niche submarine that is going to sink the big aircraft carriers."

The consolidation theory predicts that in the area of providing web-development services, a few large firms will come to dominate. However, the scale economies in web development are not evident. Web development may emerge as the restaurant industry of the Web, except that it will be less receptive to fast-food chains. My guess is that when it all shakes out, the large, publicly traded web-consulting firms will have more difficulty staying in business than the small mom-and-pop operations.

The lack of consolidation in the web-development services category is evident in the study conducted by the *Industry Standard* ("The State of the Start-Up," June 5, 2000.) Based on a survey of executives of Internet start-ups, the researchers found that web-development service was the leading start-up type, accounting for 20 percent of the businesses in the survey.

Many other findings from the study also appear to contradict the consolidation theory, including these:

- Twenty percent of the firms had been launched within the six months prior to the survey, and over half had been launched less than two years prior to the survey.
- Although only 22 percent had annual revenues of over $1 million, 41 percent reported that they were profitable.
- Sixty percent of the firms had raised less than $500,000 in financing.
- Fewer than one-fourth of the companies had an exit strategy of going IPO.
- Fifty-seven percent had fewer than ten employees.
- Seventy-two percent had five job openings or fewer

Overall, this study paints a picture of companies that are smaller and more likely to be profitable than their venture-funded counterparts. What the statistics show is that among Internet start-ups, there is a lot of activity that is taking place under the radar.

The Internet is an outstanding environment for bootstrapped businesses. Professor Bhide says that such businesses are suited to turbulent markets with low requirements for start-up capital. The Internet fits that model.

The Internet is a turbulent market. Innovations emerge suddenly, and you have to decide whether it is a trend, a fad, or something irrelevant. For example, "push technology" made the cover of both

Business Week and *Wired* in the same month early in 1997. The idea was that web sites would send automatic updates to the user. At Homefair, we had to determine whether we needed to develop such a capability. In the end, we decided that it was not important, and eventually the market decided that "push" was a fad.

On the other hand, when we encountered the concept of "co-branding" (sharing content with another site, with both sites getting branding benefits), we decided that this was a good idea. We developed a generic co-branding capability that proved to be a significant source of competitive strength.

As technology evolves, the constant stream of decisions and choices with which you are presented is one of the things that makes the Internet fun for an entrepreneur. On the other hand, established businesses, such as Dilbert-sector organizations and small proprietors, find that their decisionmaking processes are stupefied by this complex uncertainty. The phrase "deer caught in the headlights" is frequently and aptly used to describe the way established businesses react to the ambiguity that arises on the Internet.

C. So Many Mouths to Feed: Why Venture Capitalists Won't Settle for Target Valuations Under $1 Billion

Most people think of venture capitalists as being very rich. In the conventional sense, this is true. Partners in VC firms often live in expensive houses, drive nice cars, and have plenty of money to spend. However, if you are an entrepreneur trying to predict their behavior, it helps to think of them as being a poor family with many mouths to feed. Indeed, the fact that the bar is set at $1 billion for target valuations would suggest that venture capitalists are practically trying to feed an entire Third World country.

Assume that you start out with a business plan that requires $2.5 million in funding. The mouths that the venture capitalists need to feed include:

- Partners who could earn high salaries elsewhere as executives or investment bankers
- First-tier executives whom the venture capitalist will insist join the management team
- Investors who are seeking a high rate of return on capital

- Risk premium (failed companies in the venture capitalist's portfolio)
- The next round of funding

Suppose that a venture capitalist partner values his or her time at $1 million per year. If the partner is going to have to spend one-tenth of his or her time with your company for three years, that is a $300,000 mouth to feed.

The venture capitalist wants to have a high-caliber management team. You may already have some of these people. However, there are many executives, often including the CEO, who will be recruited in conjunction with funding or right afterward. This process will add more mouths to feed, say, $2.2 million worth. With the additional mouths to feed, your company now needs $5 million in funding.

For the fund as a whole, investors would like to see a hefty annual return, say, 50 percent. Ignoring compounding, this means that over three years, they need to see their $5 million become $12.5 million.

Next, we have the risk premium. Venture capitalists do take risks. Many companies in their portfolios will fail. The successful companies have to make up for the failures. Assume that nine of out ten of the companies in the portfolio will fail. Nine failures at $12.5 million per failure represent $112.5 million in mouths to feed. (One could say that you are not feeding their mouths but are instead feeding the investors' mouths. It makes no difference.) Adding this to $12.5 million for your company gives you a total of $125 million worth of mouths to feed.

Finally, we have the fact that it is impossible to grow quickly enough to feed all the mouths if you only have $5 million to work with. So at some point you are going to need another, larger round of funding, for a total of, say, $40 million. That means eight times as many mouths to feed. Multiplying $125 million by eight gets you to $1 billion.

In other words, a $1-billion target valuation makes perfect sense from the standpoint of the venture capitalists. Once you understand how many mouths they have to feed, you can sympathize. It's almost enough to make you want to organize a charity walk on their behalf.

Sarcasm aside, there is a point to be understood about the venture capital process. It is a system in which all of the pieces fit together. That system is designed to produce big winners. It is suited to markets that are broad and rich. Instead, opportunities on the Internet are getting narrower and more focused. The venture capital process is structurally committed to swinging for home runs, regardless of whether the environment is conducive to that strategy. The Internet is offering many opportunities for singles and doubles. Netstrappers have a clear shot at these opportunities, which the venture capital system is unable to address.

D. Obtaining Funding: Plan B

Suppose that you have a business idea to which you really are attached that requires $1 million in funding to execute. Plan A is to obtain $1 million right away, perhaps from venture capitalists. However, after making a few attempts to pitch your idea to them, you realize that Plan A is not going to work. It is time to try Plan B.

Plan B might be to raise $200,000 now and attempt to reach a point in nine months where the company can be valued at $2.5 million for purposes of raising the remaining $800,000. Here are some possible specifics:

Objective: achieve operational milestones (such as completing a working prototype and signing initial customers) that enable the firm to be valued at $2.5 million.

Initial Capitalization: 2.5 million shares of common stock, valued at $1 per share. No shares issued; 800,000 shares reserved for future investors; 400,000 shares reserved for preferred stockholders.

Financing: 400,000 shares of preferred stock at a cost of $0.50 a share, for a total of $200,000. When common stock is issued in nine months, each share of preferred stock will convert to one share of common.

If all goes according to plan, in nine months our company will find new investors willing to buy 800,000 shares at $1 apiece. These investors will be impressed by the reception that customers have given to our working prototype as well as the soundness of our marketing strategy. Our original investors will have a profit on paper of $200,000 (a 100-percent return in nine months), because their 400,000 shares of preferred stock will convert to common stock that has a value of $400,000. The expectation is that the original investors will stay invested to try to earn even more. With the additional $800,000, we can execute our marketing strategy and build a business that will be earning millions of dollars in profits within a few years.

The chances are that not everything will go exactly as planned. That is why we used the device of convertible stock, instead of issuing 400,000 shares of common stock on day one to the initial investors. Preferred stock, which is not voting stock but which carries special privileges, gives us more flexibility in our initial funding than either common stock or a loan.

For example, suppose that it takes eleven months rather than nine months to obtain the first round of funding. This means that the initial investors have had their money at risk longer. To compensate them for this, we could have the preferred stock designed to pay a dividend of, say, 2 percent per month for each month beyond the nine-month period. This dividend could be payable in common stock when the next round of financing is complete.

Another possibility involves the issue of voting rights and control. Suppose that four months before the end of the nine-month period, another investor becomes interested in our company. This new investor would eventually like to invest $1 million in exchange for 40 percent of the company. For now, she might be willing to put in $150,000 at month four, but she does not like the original investors. If they held common stock, they would have more voting power than she would with her proposed $150,000 initial investment. However, if they hold preferred stock, this is not a problem.

These examples illustrate a very important issue in setting up a company. Agreements need to be flexible, because circumstances can change. This issue will be discussed in Chapter 8, "Making a Clean Getaway."

The best funding strategy will show investors a plan to increase the value of their initial investment. The plan will show the projected value of the company as each operational milestone is reached. Of course, investors have to agree that the market values associated with achieving these operational milestones are realistic. As each operational milestone is reached, the value of the company should increase. As the value of the company rises, the investors can see an increase in the value of their stake.

Getting the Money

Plan B still requires you to find $200,000 in capital up front. Where do you get this initial $200,000? There are many funding sources to which you can turn. The generic term is "angel investing." It refers to individuals or groups of investors who will provide initial capital to a business before it is able to attract institutional venture funding.

In order to maximize your chances of receiving angel funding, do the role reversal. That is, imagine that you were an angel investor, and think about what you would be looking for. When you do the role reversal, the following points become fairly obvious:

- The goals of the angel investor matter

As an entrepreneur in need of financing, your natural instinct is to put all of your energy into the business plan. You write a business plan that is as convincing as possible from your perspective. What you leave out are the goals of the investor.

The most important goal of the investor is to see a clear return on the investment as soon as possible. While you may be focused on the monthly budget, the investor is focused on the overall value of the company. You want to show a path along which the value of your company increases steadily. An example would be a plan that shows the value of a share in the company growing from $1 initially to $2 in six months and $5 in eighteen months.

Not all angel investors are in the under-the-radar market. Many angel investors are nothing more than venture capital wanna-bes. They are seeking the same billion-dollar opportunities as venture capitalists, except that they have smaller amounts of money to commit and are therefore willing to take a chance on a company earlier in its life cycle. For example, they might provide a "seed" round for a company that needs to do a proof of concept. Ultimately, however, they want to be part of the bigger game.

Even genuine angel investors have needs for psychic gratification as well as for financial rewards. Angel investors may want to be valued as much for their coaching and advice as for their money. A group of angel investors may be in the game to have fun, and they might reject a concept or a team that they consider boring. You have to know the specific preferences of different angel investors in order to know whether and how to market your business to them.

- Market your company as an asset

Do not think of yourself as doing fund-raising. Fund-raising is for charities. Angel investors receive plenty of solicitations from wonderful charities. Do not position yourself so that you end up competing for those dollars.

What you are doing is marketing assets for investment. From that perspective, you are competing with people who are offering stocks, bonds, collectibles, and real estate. Think of your business as an asset that the investor is buying with the goal of seeing appreciation in value.

Present your business in terms of its assets, including systems already developed, customer agreements already signed, and so forth. Your concept by itself is not a significant asset. Unless you have a valuable patent, your intellectual property is not worth much.

- Do not take a salary

Chances are, the most valuable asset that you have to offer is your personal effort to build the business. That is why one of the most counterproductive things you can do is pay yourself a salary. Asking for a salary from an angel investor who is providing your initial funding is like asking someone both to purchase your house and pay you rent. When you ask for a salary, you are undermining the value of your assets.

- Angel investing is a contact sport

You will not find angel investors walking around with big signs around their necks that say "Hit me up for money." The typical angel investor is somebody you already know within your industry. The person who hired you five years ago when you first came out of school and is now an executive vice president with vested stock options would be an excellent angel investor.

Apart from people who know you, there are people who will react to you favorably because you are part of the same religious organization, alumni group, or other association. Use these affiliations to try to meet potential angel investors.

If things get really desperate, you can try to meet angel investors with whom you have no natural affinity. You need to identify the clubs, social events, and business organizations that provide opportunities to meet potential investors.

You can try to find people who can introduce you to angel investors. Being introduced tends to start you off on the right foot more effectively than introducing yourself. Often, lawyers or accountants know people in the investment community. Ask your attorney or accountant to help introduce you to angel investors.

- Do not send your executive summary

There is a general consensus that it is not a good idea to send an executive summary of a business plan "over the transom," meaning that it is unsolicited by the angel investor. I would argue that this advice should also be applied to cases where an investor asks to see the executive summary.

It should be fairly obvious that sending an executive summary unsolicited is a mistake. The angel investor will assume that you know nothing about his or her idiosyncratic needs. You are demonstrating that you fail to understand the basic principle that it is the goals of the angel investor that matter.

On the other hand, what if an angel investor asks you for an executive summary? When you meet an angel investor at a party, seminar, or networking event, the investor may say, "Send me your executive summary." If I were you, I would take this as a polite brush-off. Even if the investor says, "I'm really interested," do not kid yourself. Being interested is not the same thing as being ready to invest.

If an investor asks you for an executive summary, try saying this: "Look. We do have an executive summary, but our real asset is our team. If you're going to invest in our business, I want it to be because of our team. Would you let me take a few minutes right now to describe who we have on board and what we bring to our business?"

If the investor says that he or she is too busy at the moment and asks you to take the initiative to try to set up a meeting, then you should reply, "I understand. I'm busy myself. I'll tell you what. Here is my card. Give me a call if you want to talk further." This shows investors that you are as concerned as they are about avoiding meetings that waste time.

Many entrepreneurs consider it a great privilege just to be able to present a plan to an investor. There are those who will tell you that they considered this a positive experience even though they were turned down. They say that they learn something from it. That sounds good to me. But then I ask them what they learned, and they say, "I got some ideas to make the business plan look better." In other words, back to square one.

To me, valuable learning would be the knowledge you can gain by test-marketing or building a prototype. If I were you, I would not confuse wallowing in your business plan with making real progress in learning how to execute your business.

The exception to the rule that you should not send your executive summary is a case where someone who is trying to help you says, "I talked to so-and-so, and they said to send them an executive summary." In that case, you should send the executive summary, even if it is unlikely to result in an investment. Failure to follow through would embarrass your friend.

- Create urgency for the investor

Marketing your assets to angel investors can be one of those frustrating situations in which your desire to make the sale is urgent but the buyer believes that the decision can be delayed. Until the angel is as anxious to invest as you are to receive the money, you are not finished making the sale.

When Brandon White (Case No. 22) was looking for investors in WorldwideAngler.com, he sent an unsolicited proposal to an angel investor whom he had seen pictured with a fishing rod. Luckily for White, the connection with fishing worked, and the investor actually called him back. However, although the investor expressed an interest, he never made a commitment.

Finally, another potential investor advised White to send an e-mail to the angel, saying: "Here are my wiring instructions. Wire me the money by the end of the week, or you lose the deal." The potential investor understood the importance of creating urgency. Also, he stiffened White's backbone by telling him, "If they won't fund you, my friends and I will."

Competition is the most effective device for creating urgency on the part of investors. Faced with the prospect of losing the deal, they realize that they either have to put up or shut up.

In the absence of competition, some other means must be used to create urgency. One approach may be to demonstrate that the value of the business will be higher if it is begun sooner. You should try to quantify the cost to the investor of waiting to make a commitment.

- Markets determine value

Founders often ask, "How should I value my business?" They want to know what is "fair." As a student of economics, I do not believe in fairness. I believe in markets. If you have two or more term sheets from investors, then you can use competition among those investors to arrive at a market value for your business.

On the other hand, if you have only one term sheet, then you have no competitive forces working for you. With one term sheet, you are doing fund-raising, and fund-raising is not for businesses. Fund-raising is for charities (I promise I won't say that again).

Some investors will offer you a term sheet with a "no-shop" clause. That is, you are supposed to stop marketing your assets for a period of thirty days or so, while everyone makes up their mind about the term sheet. On the face of it, this would keep you from learning the market value of your company.

If someone were to give me a "no-shop" clause, my instinct would be to come back with a "No, thanks" clause. Maybe if I had done my due diligence and had learned that other founders who had worked with this investor were very satisfied, I would feel differently.

- It's the people, not the terms

When you receive a term sheet, your temptation is to analyze the numbers to death. Instead, my recommendation would be to focus on the people. Ask these sorts of questions:

A. Do you feel that there is good "chemistry" between you and the investor?
B. When you talk to other founders who have worked with this investor, do they give you a positive feeling about the investor's business acumen and ethics?

I have not participated in enough deals to be an expert. However, based on my limited observation, my hypothesis is that there is no such thing as a bad term sheet from a good investor. By the same token, there probably is no such thing as a good term sheet from a bad investor.

Case No. 5: Michaela Conley

The theory behind the big-spending venture-funded businesses is that they will scare competitors away. But Michaela Conley is not intimidated. "I've come in under the radar," she says proudly. (She did not know that I was planning on using that phrase for the title of my book.)

Conley is in the health promotion industry, a field that combines public health, health education, and wellness. A typical job would be working to promote health programs within a human resources benefits area or in a health-related nonprofit organization.

When Conley moved to the Washington, D.C., area six years ago, she found the job search process to be difficult. Positions that might be available were nonetheless hard to find. At a conference in 1997, she had what she calls a "light bulb experience," where it occurred to her to create a mechanism to enable people in the health promotions field to find relevant jobs more easily.

The employment/recruiting sector of the Web is crowded and competitive. Some of the sites are very well established in terms of traffic and funding. Nonetheless, Conley felt that she had something to offer within her narrow specialty of health promotions. "I don't know how Monster.com (one of the largest employment sites) can be all things to all people," she says.

Conley had no prior business experience. She had no mentor. Afraid that she could not start a venture alone, she turned to a friend, who was very supportive.

Unfortunately, Conley's friend was not a good choice for a partner. Although the friend enjoyed talking about the business, she was unwilling to roll up her sleeves and share in the grunt work. Finally, after a year of spinning her wheels, Conley ended the relationship and instead turned for help to organizations that provide information and networking for entrepreneurs. Examples included the entrepreneur center at George Mason University and the Netpreneur organization in the Washington, D.C., area.

In the entrepreneurial arena, early "divorces" are very common. The unique pressures and requirements of starting a business can expose personal weaknesses that are not visible when your experience with someone is as a friend or as a colleague in a large company. Conley was actually rather lucky in that she and her friend had formed no legal partnership or equity arrangement. Legally and financially, it was a clean break, even though for Conley it was emotionally traumatic.

If you include a partner in your start-up, my advice is to take into account the possibility that the relationship may not work. Rather than immediately making a long-term commitment, consider starting with a trial period of a few months. Regardless of whether you use a trial period, include in your agreement a process that will allow you to dissolve the partnership and divide the assets fairly should a breakup be necessary.

Finally, on September 1, 1999, Conley was able to launch her web site, hpcareer.net. Her initial goal, which she had nearly achieved within one year, was to gross $10,000 a month in advertising from employers. Nearly all of this is profit.

Conley says that promoting her web site to her target audience was easy. She contacted universities with programs in the health promotions field, finding professors very motivated to help their students obtain jobs. Also, she attended conferences for health promotions professionals, where she could reach a large part of her target market. Most important, as people began to find jobs through her site, the word-of-mouth traffic soared. What author/consultant Seth Godin would call her "ideavirus" spread rapidly.

Less than a year after launch, Conley had 10,000 users receiving e-mail updates of job opportunities. For this, Conley partnered with programmer Charlie Arehart to develop a database application that allows the job opportunities to be targeted by type and location.

As of our interview in August 2000, Conley was thinking in terms of taking her successful model and expanding it to other specialty areas. She was getting ready to add her first employee, her husband, who will handle the bookkeeping and help cover conferences. Traveling to conferences is a challenge for Conley, because her eyesight is so poor. When she uses a computer, she has to wear embarrassingly thick glasses and sit with her nose next to the monitor. But on the Internet, no one knows that you're legally blind.

Case No. 6: Trevor Cornwell

Of all the business ideas I encountered in my interviews, Trevor Cornwell's Skyjet.com was the one that made me say, "I wish I'd thought of that." However, as with any netstrapped business, the idea would have gotten nowhere without execution.

Several years before he came up with the idea for Skyjet.com, Cornwell started a business in Budapest, Hungary, that involved radio programming. Although he was proud of what the business offered, its earnings did not feed the mouths of the investors sufficiently well. He got out of the business in 1995, and he learned from what he calls "a very difficult experience" to be leery of putting someone else's money at risk.

In May 1997, Cornwell had a temporary assignment to work with technology companies for America's Promise, the nonprofit organization headed by Colin Powell. Cornwell happened to notice that Ray Chambers, the principal financier for America's Promise, flew on a private plane that spent a lot of time on the ground in between trips.

Cornwell did a little research, and he found that there were nearly 1,500 charter jets in the United States, which represents enough capacity in the aggregate to constitute a major airline. His idea was to utilize this capacity to create an on-demand airline, which would allow business travelers to book charter flights as easily as commercial flights.

For the business traveler, Skyjet.com offers a much more convenient way to book a flight. Traditionally, booking a charter flight meant taking a day to call individual charter companies to inquire about availability of the desired type of aircraft. With Skyjet.com, the flyer can enter information on a web form and complete the reservation process in minutes.

For the charter companies, Skyjet represents a way to increase demand and utilize capacity more efficiently. Skyjet books the trip, collects the money from the traveler, and pays the charter company, after taking out a booking fee or commission.

Cornwell drew up a detailed business plan for Skyjet.com, and he spent a year raising $100,000. He did much more than just fund-raising, however. He drove around New England to meet with charter operators, went to a trade show for charter operators, and used his contacts in Hungary to obtain a web developer.

The Hungarian programmer charged $5 an hour, so that the web site for Skyjet.com cost just $3,000. Later, when Skyjet.com was purchased, the buyers thought that replicating his site would have cost them over $1 million.

The biggest challenge with executing Skyjet.com was working with the charter operators. The industry is highly fragmented, with 1,500 planes disbursed among about 250 operators. Charter operators have a small-proprietor mindset, meaning that they are risk averse and slow to adopt computer technology.

In order for Skyjet.com to function, Cornwell needed to be able to capture the availability of charter planes in a database. Many of the charter operators did not have the know-how or equipment to update this information via the Web. Furthermore, they wanted to see immediate results in terms of bookings. Otherwise, they might not bother to continue updating their schedules into the system.

To overcome this problem, Cornwell partnered with Air Charter Online, a company that was putting together a database of charter-jet availability for intra-industry use—to enable operators to share capacity and leads with other operators. However, as of our interview in August 2000, Skyjet had switched to a different data source and was moving to obtain the information directly from operators.

Skyjet.com went on-line in May 1998, and its first transaction was booked in August. Cornwell says that in that three-month interval he was not at all concerned about whether travelers would buy the concept. His confidence was based on site traffic and consumer interest.

Skyjet.com could not rely on web-based marketing. It needed to reach its target audience of business executives and their travel assistants by advertising in business publications such as the *Wall Street Journal*. Another expense for Skyjet.com was customer service. There was a large human component to ensuring that the service went smoothly and business travelers were satisfied.

In February 1999, Craig Hall, a real estate developer and investor in seed-stage companies, provided $300,000 in funding. "The day before his check cleared, we had $300 in the bank," Cornwell recalls. Hall subsequently put in another $150,000. Eventually, Hall put in another round of funding, bringing his total investment to $1.8 million.

With Hall's investment, Skyjet.com was able to grow. After doing $600,000 in bookings in 1999, it was on track to do ten times that amount in 2000.

In July 2000, Bombardier, the Montreal-based company that is the largest manufacturer of business aircraft, purchased Skyjet.com as a strategic investment. Bombardier paid off the early-stage investors and gave Skyjet's management a package that included an up-front payment and a deferred payment, with the latter based on performance over the next two years.

I asked Cornwell whether the strategic factor or the human factor was more important in making him comfortable with the acquisition. He said that going into the transaction, he gave them equal weight. However, after the first month and a half, he decided that the human factor is much more important. He says that he is very lucky that Bombardier has an executive team that understands entrepreneurs. They are giving him the right combination of autonomy and support.

When I asked Cornwell what mistakes he made, he said that he thinks he should have bootstrapped the company longer. In retrospect, he does not feel that the $100,000 he raised in the first year was worth the trouble and the dilution that was required to obtain it.

FOUR

Planning Your Business

[T]he lack of research and planning that we find in many promising start-ups has a sound economic basis. Capital-constrained entrepreneurs cannot afford to do much prior analysis and research. The limited profit potential and high uncertainty of the opportunities they usually pursue also make the benefits low compared to the costs. In lieu of extensive planning, we will also see, entrepreneurs have to rely on adaptation: They start with a sketchy idea of how they want to do business, which they alter and refine as they encounter unforeseen problems and opportunities.

—Bhide, *The Origin and Evolution of New Businesses*, **p. 53**

One difference between playing the venture capital game and net-strapping is that you do not need a formal business plan to start a business under the radar. You tend to do more learning by trial and error and less by research.

It is insightful of Professor Bhide to notice that the textbook approach to starting an enterprise does not describe most bootstrapped businesses. However, I believe that it would be a mistake to infer that netstrappers do not plan their businesses. It is true that many netstrappers do not create formal business plans. Also, they tend to resolve many issues by trial and error rather than through research.

As a netstrapper you do want to go through a planning process. However, you use planning to anticipate problems, not to produce a term paper.

Mario Morino, a successful software entrepreneur who went on to found the Netpreneur organization to promote Internet entrepreneurship, says that a business plan is like a résumé. When someone reads your résumé, he argues, they are looking for an excuse to turn you down. Similarly, a venture capitalist will read your business plan looking for holes (see Mario Morino, "Do You Need a Business Plan?" Available: www.netpreneur.org/events/doughnets/10points/default.html).

Trying to obtain venture capital funding without a business plan is like trying to get into college without filling out an application. Ironically, however, even venture capitalists are skeptical about business plans. Any venture capitalist will tell you that a first-rate team with a second-rate business plan is preferable to a second-rate team with a first-rate business plan. In fact, when I listen to venture capitalists describe how they make their decisions, the process often sounds highly intuitive and almost romantic—like the scene in the movie *Jerry Maguire* where his girlfriend says, "You had me at 'Hello.'"

Venture capitalists often complain that the business plans they see are ridiculously optimistic. I believe that this is due to an inherent bias that affects entrepreneurs, as captured by novelist Wallace Stegner.

Pioneer Time

That does not mean he was foolish or mistaken. He was premature. His clock was set on pioneer time. He met trains that had not yet arrived, he waited on platforms that hadn't yet been built, beside tracks that might never be laid. Like many another Western pioneer, he had heard the clock of history strike, and counted the strokes wrong. Hope was way out ahead of fact, possibility obscured the outlines of reality.

—**Wallace Stegner**, *Angle of Repose*

Pioneer time is a distortion in perception on the part of the entrepreneur. It means that you set unrealistic expectations about how quickly you will be able to obtain customers, establish partnerships, and acquire funding.

Because many netstrappers are visionaries, pioneer time is the leading occupational hazard for Internet entrepreneurs. The good news is that you manage to come up with your idea early. But as soon as you get your idea, you expect everyone else to "get" it as well. What you fail to realize is that the flip side of being early is that it is going to take time for customers and potential investors to catch up with you.

Nearly every netstrapper that I interviewed underestimated the time it would take to make the first $100,000 in revenue. This tendency is particularly acute for entrepreneurs who lack sales experience.

Pioneer time also distorts your expectations concerning funding. Those netstrappers who sought funding from angel investors usually found that this process took far longer than they had anticipated.

The impact of pioneer time is that many businesses run out of cash before they can succeed. When that happens, you are faced with a terrible dilemma. One option is to go past your limit. The other option is to give up. Neither choice is pleasant.

The option of going past your limit is illustrated by Tom Ashbrook in his book *Taking the Leap*. Many people who have read it admire Ashbrook for his courage. While I share their reaction to a degree, my admiration is tempered by my strong belief in self-discipline and a concern that he might have gotten carried away.

The other option is to give up. I very nearly did this with Homefair in early 1995. I do not fault myself for lack of courage. My problem was an acute case of pioneer time.

The danger of pioneer time is that it leads you to set unrealistic limits. For example, when I started Homefair in May 1994, I gave myself six months to see whether I could realize $100,000 in revenues. Given that hardly anyone in the real estate and mortgage lending community had heard of the Internet at that time, this was an impossible objective.

Considering how new the Internet was to the business community and that I had no prior sales experience, I should have been rather pleased with the revenues that I actually did bring in during the first six months. Looking back on it, I am amazed at what I accomplished in terms of developing a customer base. However, early in 1995, relative to my pioneer time expectations I had failed to hit my target. In 1997, Internet mania hit, and soon the whole concept of setting expectations for profits was forgotten. But I was two years ahead of that.

Given that my revenues did not meet my goals, to continue to pursue Homefair full time would have meant going back on my commitments to myself about how I would deal with a failure to live up to my unwritten business plan. It was not in my nature to allow my self-discipline to break down in that way. So I went back to Freddie Mac, and I nearly gave up Homefair altogether.

Had I given up completely, you would not be reading this. What I ended up doing was a compromise, going back to work for Freddie Mac while continuing to maintain Homefair on evenings and weekends.

Fortunately for me, pioneer time was not fatal to my business. It caused me to make the mistake of going back to Freddie Mac, but I avoided (just barely) making the decision to shut Homefair down altogether.

Pioneer time is extremely dangerous. To avoid the pitfalls of pioneer time, I recommend taking the following steps when you start your business.

1. Come up with a reasonably conservative estimate of the length of time it will take for your business to obtain the first $100,000 in revenue.
2. If you have never closed a sale of any kind, then double the estimate in step 1.
3. If you need seed funding, then come up with a reasonably conservative estimate of the length of time it will take you to obtain such funding.
4. Double the estimates that you make in steps 2 and 3.
5. When you draw up a budget for the first year of your business, use the estimates from step 4.

If you make these sorts of adjustments to protect yourself against pioneer time, you are more likely to have enough room in your budget to get your business off the ground. You may still fail to meet your objectives. However, if that occurs, at least you can know that it was a failure in the business execution, rather than a case of distorted expectations.

Before You Write a Business Plan

In the textbook model for starting a business, the first step is to write down a business plan. However, the textbook process is inappropriate for netstrapping. In reality, if you were following a sound, systematic approach to starting an enterprise, the business plan would not be the first step, or even the second or third step. In fact, here are the steps that I recommend that you follow. The rest of this chapter will elaborate on these steps.

1. Choose your initial team
2. Conduct a "no-baggage" exercise (imagine the business as a total commitment)
3. Identify trends
4. Brainstorm ideas
5. Diagram your business
6. Create an organization chart
7. Identify critical operating ratios
8. Test-market your offering
9. Identify operational milestones
10. Develop a budget
11. Develop your funding strategy
12. Find a coach

1. Choose Your Initial Team

> "I'd rather not talk about it."
> "Can you *not* quote me on that?"
> "Don't use this in your book."

There is one subject that netstrappers are reticent to discuss, even though it is very widespread. The awkward topic is what I call "early divorces," situations where the founding partnership broke up before the business really got going. It happens a lot, and even though my interviews were limited to people who kept at it, my guess is that in many instances an early divorce ends the entrepreneurial career of everyone involved. Regardless of whether the business continues, an early divorce is a debilitating and traumatic experience.

Many new companies have to make early changes to their business concepts, also. However, adapting your strategy is much less costly and painful than dissolving your partnership. It is more important to have a solid team than to have a solid business concept.

First-time entrepreneurs tend to overrate the value of business concepts and ideas. Rarely does an idea by itself represent a significant asset. Instead, you will find that the value created by entrepreneurial activity comes from unleashing the potential of talented individuals on your team. That is why choosing your team is the first step in the process.

The initial team is the core group of founders for a business. It might be one person. More often, it is two or three people. Assuming that it is more than one person, you must have a lot of confidence and trust in one another. Look around at your team. If your business were a deserted island, are these the people with whom you would like to be stranded?

You have to value spending time with one another, because that will certainly happen if you proceed to establish a business together. Nonetheless, the general opinion about starting a business with a friend is mixed, at best. There are plenty of entrepreneurs who will tell you that partnering with a friend is the worst mistake you can make. Michaela Conley (Case No. 5) would take that view, based on her early divorce. (Keep in mind that I use the term "early divorce" as a metaphor for the dissolution of a partnership, not as a comment on someone's actual marital status.)

In a crisis, having a friend as a partner can add significantly to the stress. Trying to start a business can expose shortcomings in a person, and discovering someone else's weaknesses can be a particularly traumatic experience if that person was your friend prior to launching your enterprise.

Be wary of getting involved with people who provide a high ratio of ideas to commitments. Many people fail to appreciate that in order to get a business to work, the founders need to commit to accomplishing tasks. Instead, coming from a corporate environment or school, they may be used to having other people do things for them. In a start-up, nothing gets done unless one of the founders commits to taking care of it.

When you and the other founders get together while you are still at the brainstorming stage and your business has not been formed, you will typically generate a "to-do" list. Your action items might include a list of people to contact, some software to try, some books or magazine articles to check out, some web sites to research, or some documentation to develop, such as a budget or a project plan. If there are tasks on this list that no one will commit to performing, your team has a problem. If all of the tasks are assigned but some of the team members are not really pulling their weight, then those team members may be a problem.

Of course, commitments are valuable only if they are kept. If everyone seems to have trouble delivering tasks as expected, you probably need to introduce some project management discipline to your team. If only one person seems to fail to keep commitments, then that issue needs to be confronted as soon as possible.

There is nothing wrong with testing one another during the stage when you are brainstorming your business. Giving everyone tasks and evaluating one another's performance is a good way to try to prevent future problems. A little due diligence can go a long way.

2. Conduct a "No-Baggage" Exercise

For a brief period, I allowed people to approach me as an angel investor. This turned out to be a bad idea. Any investor has to say no most of the time, and I do not enjoy doing that.

One start-up concept with which I flirted came from two people whom I will call Bob and Sally. At one point, we had put together terms for an investment. I was going to put up $X for 20 percent of the company. Therefore, the implied valuation of the company was $5X. The plan was that they would use the money to build a working prototype within six months and then use the working prototype to convince new investors to come in and provide full funding. It was what I call a "Plan B" financing strategy. "Plan A" would have been to get full funding from a venture capitalist right away, which only a really impressive, veteran team could have obtained.

Before I signed the term sheet, I asked to see a budget. I was surprised to see that a significant portion of the budget consisted of salaries for three of the principals. Although the salaries were modest, I had assumed that Bob and Sally were planning to work without any compensation at all for the first six months, until we could raise the next round of funding.

Bob and Sally had no patents or proprietary processes to constitute assets. The only chips they had to put into the business were their work efforts. From the perspective of an investor, paying them salaries considerably reduced the share of the company to which I felt they were entitled. At the very least, I would have felt compelled to reduce my valuation to $2X, meaning that my investment would have entitled me to 50 percent of the shares in the business.

Another problem I had was that $X was more than really should have been committed to the business at that point. They wanted enough money to build a working prototype, even though I was not sure that the market would embrace their service. The more logical approach would have been to spend a smaller amount to test-market the concept, and then decide whether to proceed to build the prototype. You might call this initial test-marketing phase "Plan C."

The commitment to Plan B rather than to Plan C was derived not from the needs of the business but from the needs of Bob and Sally. At that time, they worked for a large corporation. They wanted the salaries and the large commitment in order to feel comfortable with leaving their jobs.

Bob and Sally had built their budget and plan around their personal needs. The baggage that Bob and Sally brought with them was the overriding factor in the decision to take salaries and to commit to building the prototype without doing any test-marketing.

You need to lose your baggage. When you start a business, the new enterprise does not care where you came from. It is not obligated to match your salary. It does not owe you protection from the risk of abandoning your 401(k). All your new business knows is that it is starving for cash, fighting for its life, and hoping to provide you with such large rewards that salaries and your 401(k) will look like chicken feed.

When your founding team gets together, you should conduct a "no-baggage" exercise.

A. Think of your new business as a self-contained entity, perhaps represented by a circle on a piece of paper.

B. Assume that each founder will devote full time to the business.

C. "Empty your pockets" onto the piece of paper that represents your new business. That is, have each founder write down his or her financial net worth and make this available to the business.

D. Next, empty your pockets of nonfinancial assets, such as patents, unique ideas, prototypes, customer leads, and valuable industry contacts. List these as assets of the business. Discuss the value of these assets with one another. It is not important that you arrive at a precise value for these assets. However, the conversation will provide useful insights into how an investor might view your team.

From the "no-baggage" perspective, you realize that until the business is profitable, salaries make no sense. The money you take out as salaries has to come out of the assets that you put in as investors, which makes it pointless.

Of course, when you actually start your business, you are under no obligation to empty your pockets into the company. Typically, it would not be prudent to do so. You need to establish your pain threshold, which is based on the way that you trade off risk and return. The next two steps in the exercise address these critical issues.

E.   Ask each member of the founding team to write down how much time and money he or she is willing to lose before abandoning the enterprise.

F.   Also, write down how much money you will eventually be looking for from a successful sale of the business.

Try to solicit honest answers rather than allowing intimidation or peer pressure to factor in. If the answers are honest, then you will have an idea of how your baggage will affect your business.

In the case of Bob and Sally, I think that a no-baggage exercise would have led them to realize that they were not ready to launch a start-up. As founders, they were not prepared to put many chips into the business. Investors are rarely willing to back founders, particularly first-time entrepreneurs, on those terms.

First-time entrepreneurs need to be prepared to launch a business without a large nest egg from investors.

- You need to accumulate enough savings and adjust your lifestyle so that you can go at least six months without a salary.

- You need to think of ways to earn revenue while you are developing your business. In Bob and Sally's case, they could have done consulting for companies that would have been potential partners for their ultimate product.

- You need to be willing to take a small amount of funding now and use your ability to achieve milestones to obtain more investment later. In Bob and Sally's case, they could have asked for enough money to do test-marketing. Had this proven successful, they could have asked the same investors or new investors for funding to build an initial system.

The "no-baggage" exercise can have value beyond helping to determine whether you are prepared to start an enterprise. If there is wide variation in the pain thresholds of different members of the team, then this issue must be addressed. For example, if one person can only go three months without a salary but the other two are prepared to go a year, the latter two are going to have to pitch in and pay the first person some salary after three months.

One of the reasons that "early divorces" are so frequent in start-ups is that the founders only come to grips with differences in pain thresholds when there is a crisis. It is better to try to confront these issues before you start.

Another issue on which founders can differ is target valuations. If I want $2 million out of the business and you want $50 million, then we will not be on the same page when the first buyout offer comes in. We need to prepare for this contingency in our partnership agreement. See Chapter 8, "Making a Clean Getaway."

Part of the value of the "no-baggage" exercise is that it starts the process of putting you in the right frame of mind to run a business. The exercise helps you to think in terms of a team, rather than as individuals. Also, it helps you to think as owners, rather than as employees. As an owner, you think in terms of building assets and shareholder value. As an owner, you need to be willing to accept risk. This in turn makes you more aware of the need to earn a decent return.

3. Identify Trends

Often, you have some initial idea for a business. What trends lead you to believe that this is a good idea? What other trends relate to the skills and interests of your team?

Trends are very important to an Internet start-up. I like to use the analogy of hitting a baseball on a field where there is a wind blowing at thirty miles an hour. If the wind is blowing toward right field and you try to hit to left, you have to connect perfectly just to have a chance at a single. On the other hand, if you go with the wind and hit toward right, just getting your bat on the ball may be sufficient to drive one over the outfielder's head.

Many people rely on business and technology magazines to spot trends. While these periodicals have some value, they are not completely reliable. Promotion and hype often seep into magazine coverage. Technology vendors and venture capitalists plant stories as part of their public relations efforts.

I find that the most reliable analysts for evaluating trends are writers who focus on the consumer experience. My favorite news filter is Lawrence Lee's web site, called Tomalak's Realm (www.tomalak.org). Lee seems to have an eye for the on-line columnists who focus on the consumer experience, including Clay Shirky (www.shirky.com) and Jakob Nielsen (www.useit.com).

Another key to understanding trends is to realize that business adoption often lags personal adoption. This is particularly true in the small business sector. Many doctors, dentists, hairdressers, and other small proprietors use the Internet at home for recreation and shopping. Relatively few of them use the Internet in their business.

As a result of this adoption lag, it seems reasonable to suppose that there is a wind blowing thirty miles per hour behind anyone starting a business that:

- Uses the Internet to organize a fragmented industry consisting of small proprietors. One example is Trevor Cornwell's Skyjet.com (Case No. 6), which allows business travelers to check availability of charter jets from most of the companies in the industry, rather than requiring the traveler to check availability one company at a time.
- Uses the Internet to make software available as a service. One example is Leif Johnston's ResourceCompany.com (Case No. 12), which provides software for operations management.
- Uses the Internet to reduce costs and enhance efficiency. One example is Don Britton's Network Alliance (Case No. 8), which is designed to eliminate the need for small companies to hire network administrators and to worry about software upgrades and installations.
- Uses the Internet to enhance efficiency in transactions between the government and its contractors or consumers. One example is Raj Khera's GovCon.com (Case No. 17) or Rob Main's eFed.com (Case No. 4).

If the timing and execution of these businesses is right, then enough small proprietors can be encouraged to try the new approach to enable the enterprises to succeed. On the other hand, if adoption continues to be a challenge, the wind will feel pretty still, and start-ups in these markets will struggle.

Another phenomenon to watch out for is a trend that is growing stale. For example, banner advertising on the Web seems to be increasingly disappointing to consumers, sponsors, and web sites. The only people who seem to like banners are advertising agencies, which can earn fat commissions by placing banners, apparently without having to waste much time thinking or evaluating their decisions. It could be a big mistake to start a business today under the assumption that the banner advertising model is viable.

Companies are finding that advertisements placed in targeted e-mail newsletters are more effective than banner ads placed on web sites. This is an interesting phenomenon to watch. Will it continue as a trend, or will consumers tire of newsletters as they become saturated with ads?

4. Brainstorm Ideas

Many entrepreneurs start out with a very specific idea, but then they have second thoughts when they attempt to execute their plans. I believe that it would be better if more teams were to conduct open-ended brainstorming sessions before they choose their ideas, as Rob Main (Case No. 4) and his partners did before starting Electric Press, an early web-design and hosting company. By conducting such a brainstorming session, the members of the team would go into a business with a better understanding of why they chose the idea. When the business encountered roadblocks, they would have a clearer rationale for choosing whether to plow ahead or to reconsider the idea.

When your team is brainstorming ideas, try to put several ideas on the table before you discuss any single idea. Once you have generated a list of ideas, try whittling this list down to three or four for serious discussion.

For each idea, you might want to consider the issues in the rest of this chapter, and indeed in the rest of this book. What would a diagram of the business look like? What would the key operating ratios be? How would you market your offering? What would your web site have to accomplish? What might your exit strategy be?

In addition, I recommend asking the following questions about each idea:

A. Why is this a good idea *now*? Would it have been a better idea eighteen months ago? Could it be a better idea eighteen months from now?

   I am surprised to see entrepreneurs continue to introduce new mortgage or real estate sites on the Internet. They do not seem to notice how crowded those categories already are on the Web. The timing for such sites is very poor, in my opinion.

   Maurice Boissiere's CustomerInsites (Case No. 7) was an example of good timing. He saw the trend of companies wanting to measure customer satisfaction with their web sites. Had he started earlier, the concept would have been too far ahead of its time, and his potential customers would not have understood the need for his offering. Had he started later, he would have been late to the market.

B. Why are we the right team for this idea?

   Several years ago, I met a woman who was trying to develop an on-line service for consumers to order groceries. To me this sounded like a business that required expertise in logistics and delivery. Her background was not related to those critical operational functions. Although the idea may have some validity—a lot of capital has since gone into businesses in the on-line grocery category—I did not see how she had any chance of success.

   Mark Matassa (Case No. 18), with his background in journalism, is the right person to try to execute PersonalReader.com, a service to provide edited news links to consumers. Michael Smith (Case No. 9), fresh out of college, is the right person to try to build Firebox.com, a web site aimed at "young blokes."

C. What challenges may have prevented others from solving this problem, and how will we overcome those challenges?

   Some entrepreneurs based in India came up with an idea called dealwala.com, which was a comparison-shopping site for consumers in their home country. It would allow consumers to evaluate televisions, motor scooters, and other products. Once they

were informed about the various products, consumers would proceed to contact local dealers.

Among the challenges that this type of business faces is the fact
that India's commercial infrastructure is not developed in a way
that is suited to the Internet. Credit card approvals and long-distance shipping are much more difficult to deal with in India than
they are in the United States. This limits the potential for an Internet-based shopping service.

Challenges should not necessarily deter you from starting a
business. If you can overcome the challenges, this can be a competitive advantage. For example, Trevor Cornwell faced a challenge
because the charter jet operators he wanted to participate in his
reservation system were not comfortable with using the Internet.
Once he had overcome this challenge, their inertia became a valuable barrier to entry by potential competitors.

D. What excites you the most about this idea, and what concerns you the most?
   The purpose of this question is to get your team members
   to articulate their biggest hopes and worries about each
   possible idea.

No idea is perfect. The point of brainstorming is to help you understand more about the challenges of your idea before you try to
turn it into a business.

As an experienced entrepreneur, I find that many people come to
me for advice. Although I will not sell my body as a consultant, I am
very easy about letting people pick my brain for an hour over lunch.
Here are some examples of ideas that people have brought to me. To
illustrate the brainstorming process, I can indicate how those ideas
might be evaluated using the questions about timing, team capability,
challenges to overcome, exciting features, and concerns.

Condom Sales.   Gary, a friend of mine who is an attorney, asked
himself, "What would people be willing to buy on the Internet? How
about something that they are embarrassed to shop for in a store?
Something that they would prefer to buy in private. Condoms!"

First, concerning timing, this would probably have been a better
idea several years ago. I would expect that by now there are many
sites on the Web that offer condoms for sale.

Second, I do not believe that my friend is the right person to execute this idea. To be successful, you would need to be outstanding at web-site design and promotion, and you would also need someone with a good grasp of the distribution process for condoms.

Third, the fact that people are embarrassed about purchasing condoms creates a challenge for promoting your business. Most good Internet businesses benefit from strong word-of-mouth traffic. However, if customers are embarrassed about purchasing your product, they are not likely to be outgoing in sharing with their friends their favorable experience with your web site.

To overcome this challenge, you might try to partner with a web delivery service such as Kozmo.com, which delivers to consumers on short notice. Your hope would be that reporters writing stories about the delivery service would get a kick out of telling their readers, "You can even have condoms delivered right to your door, right when you need them!"

Overall, what I like about the idea is that people in fact might prefer to buy condoms in the privacy of their own homes. They might also like an opportunity to read about different types of condoms and make an informed decision prior to purchase. However, what concerns me are that there are major logistical challenges with delivering the product as well as marketing challenges, and an attorney does not have experience that would be useful in addressing those challenges.

Apartment Community Portals.   Three students in a class I taught at the business school at American University came up with an intriguing idea. The concept is a portal for an apartment community. As Internet service providers wire large apartment buildings for the Net, they might set up their residents with a start page that provides news, classified advertising, and shopping information relevant to that apartment building.

The timing for this idea appears to be excellent. In 1999, not many apartment buildings were being wired in this way. Over the next few years, it should become commonplace.

New graduates of a business school might be a good team to execute this idea. They could design a portal that would appeal to apartment residents, who tend to be young people.

A challenge for the apartment portal would be to obtain advertisers. Other web sites have had difficulty getting a model of "on-line

Yellow Pages" advertising to work. My guess is that local businesses would not be willing to pay for advertising on an apartment portal without any proof of benefits. To overcome this challenge, you might have to offer free trial periods to advertisers.

What excites me about the idea is the fact that it takes the portal concept to a niche level, which is consistent with my view that people are "settling in the frontier" of the Internet. It is plausible to me that in the long run more people will be served by specific, targeted portals than by traditional portals such as Yahoo!. I believe that apartment residents would appreciate convenient access to neighborhood information as well as the opportunity to become closer as a community.

What concerns me about the idea is whether the economics really work. Would you be able to obtain enough advertising revenue to cover the cost of sales as well as the cost of keeping the site up-to-date?

Commerce and Community Site for Dental Laboratories. I met an entrepreneur, Dave, whose main business was selling educational videos to dental offices. He had an idea for a new business, which would use the Web to enable dental laboratories to engage in on-line commerce more readily. These small proprietors that provide false teeth and other made-to-order products could provide their dentist customers with on-line order tracking and payment capability. The web site for dental labs could also facilitate communication among the different lab owners, including making it easy for owners to advertise labs for sale.

The timing of this idea seems reasonable. Certainly, awareness of the Internet is high among dentists and dental lab owners. However, it may still be the case that many of them view the Internet as something for home entertainment as opposed to something that can be used in their businesses.

Dave has strong qualifications for carrying out this idea. He has been doing software sales in the dental industry for many years. His existing business involves sales to people in the dental community. Clearly, he knows the market and how to sell there.

One challenge with the idea is that it requires a large number of participants in order to be effective. Dentists will not use it unless the labs are using it, and labs will not use it unless the dentists are using it. An entrepreneur could burn through a fair amount of money trying to reach critical mass.

Overall, what excites me about the idea is that it is an under-the-radar niche. I do not see venture-funded firms going after dental labs as a specific market, even though there is probably plenty of money in it from the typical entrepreneur's perspective. What concerns me is that it may take a long time to sign up enough customers and develop enough revenue-generating services to make the business profitable.

Competitive Intelligence Delivered over the Web.   Karmen Carr, a former colleague from Freddie Mac, launched a business to provide competitive intelligence by using the Web. The idea is that a corporation will sign up with her company, and she will set up a custom, secure web site that will contain information and updates about the competitive environment for that corporation.

The timing of the idea seems excellent. Historically, companies have undertaken a competitive assessment no more frequently than once a year. However, with the recent emergence of business-to-business on-line marketplaces and other Internet-based efforts to change the way industries are organized, companies need to monitor their competitive environment on a constant and continuing basis.

Carr has an excellent grasp of the issues of strategy and competitive intelligence. However, she may not be in a strong position to market her offering. The high-level executives who would be interested in competitive intelligence would be inclined to use established consulting firms for this type of service.

My guess is that a big challenge with this service is going to be cost. Competitive intelligence that is customized to the needs of a particular corporation is very labor intensive. Until you build up a large practice, it is going to be difficult to find opportunities for efficiency. Furthermore, the cost of sale may be very high. One reason is that ongoing competitive intelligence is not something that companies currently buy, so it will take time to pry open their budgets. Another reason is that the large corporations that might be willing to pay the most for competitive intelligence have decisionmaking processes that are slow and cumbersome.

To overcome the challenges, I recommended to Carr that she follow the strategy that I call "making the company pay for your sales pitch." That is, she should charge a company a fee, say, $25,000, to create a baseline competitive assessment. In the process of delivering the baseline competitive assessment, she can provide a much clearer demonstration of the advantages of obtaining her ongoing web-based competitive intelligence service.

What excites me about this idea is that the upheaval taking place in many markets should lead executives to demand better competitive intelligence. What concerns me is that existing consulting firms are very well entrenched with senior managers. Under these circumstances, a start-up firm may wind up merely setting the table for a feast that will be enjoyed by the McKinseys and the KPMGs of the world.

Once you have subjected all of your major ideas to these sorts of questions and analysis, you are in a position to choose the one idea that you will pursue as a business. Presumably, this is an idea that fits with trends, exploits the strengths of your team, and presents challenges that are difficult for competitors but not impossible for you. It is an idea for which your excitement is high and for which your concerns are not showstoppers. From this point on, we will assume that you have selected a single idea with which to work.

5. Diagram Your Business

How much detail can you get into during the planning process? While it is not possible or desirable to get into minutia, it is also not sufficient simply to provide a high-level vision and leave it totally unclear how you are going to get from here to there. Often, the right level of clarity can be achieved by using a diagram. A diagram will force you to think about key elements of your business, without leading you too far astray into details. If you think of your business as a car, you want your diagram to show how the transmission drives the wheels, without getting into the exact gear ratios.

The appropriate diagrams depend on the type of business and the knowledge that you bring to it. In some cases, you can put a lot of information on a diagram that shows the flow of money from customers through you to your suppliers. On the other hand, in an enterprise that involves complex data architecture, an entity-relationship diagram may be the best way to depict key features of the business.

Diagrams should help you to identify the key factors in your business. You should be able to point to your diagrams and say, "The really critical issues for us are here, here, and here. If we can execute in those areas, we will succeed."

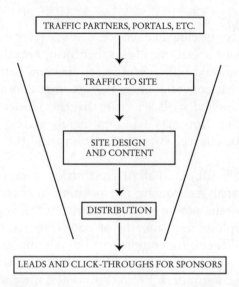

FIGURE 4.1   Diagram of Homefair as a Funnel.

This diagram shows that the main functions of the Homefair business are traffic, content, and distribution. We need to attract traffic to the site, then provide content that satisfies consumers and brings them into our revenue-generating areas. Finally, we need a function that distributes our traffic to sponsors, who provide us with revenue. They pay us when consumers click through to sponsor sites and when consumers become leads by filling out contact forms and sending them to service providers.

For example, with Homefair we had a business model that was a funnel, with traffic flowing into our site and then being distributed to sponsors. This diagram showed us that our critical areas of execution were (1) obtaining traffic, (2) making sure that our site was designed to satisfy consumers and encourage them to connect with our sponsors, and (3) finding sponsors. We called these areas traffic, site design, and distribution.

Consider the examples of the preceding section. Each one could benefit from particular types of diagrams.

For a business to sell condoms from a web site, the critical diagrams would show how you distribute condoms from a manufacturer to the consumer. This would force you to focus on critical issues. Do you partner with existing drugstores? If so, how do you arrange delivery between the drugstore and the consumer? Alternatively if you set up your own warehouse, how much lag can your customers tolerate between order and delivery? How do you control inventory costs?

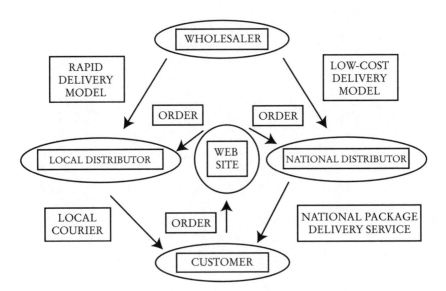

FIGURE 4.2   Diagram of Business for Condom Sales on the Web, Showing Distribution Model.

Inventories of condoms are stored either at local distributors or at one national distribution center. With the national distribution center, our costs are lower, but it takes longer to deliver the condoms to the customer. To be able to deliver rapidly, we must use local distributors, such as a local drugstore or another localized web business, such as Webvan or Kozmo.com

For the apartment community portal, it might be important to diagram all of the critical relationships for the enterprise. Your portal would be in the center, with lines radiating out to apartment managers, Internet service providers, tenants, and local businesses. Your portal will be engaged in transactions with each of these constituencies. What will be the incentives for each constituency to participate? Will you be contacting apartment managers directly, or will you deal with them only indirectly through the Internet service providers? Show this on your diagram.

For the web site for dental laboratories, it might help to configure the home page. What will be listed as the main content sections? You might represent each section by a box. Inside each box, you would want to list the features that would generate traffic as well as the features that would generate revenue.

For the competitive intelligence service, a useful diagram would show the customer's process for evaluating information about the competitive environment. The diagram would show key corporate

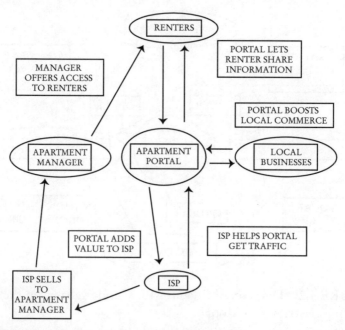

FIGURE 4.3   Diagram of Apartment Portal.

An Internet Service Provider (ISP) provides connectivity for everyone in an apartment building, and we provide a web site that serves that specific apartment community. We do this for many apartment buildings. The apartment portal needs to develop several relationships. We want the ISP to configure our portal as the default home page for renters. We want renters to come to our home page and use our message boards to share information and shop for good and services from local businesses. Our revenue will come from sponsorship from local businesses, which will benefit from exposure on our portal.

executives, research units within the corporation, external consultants, other news sources, and your proposed company. You would want to show how your offering fits into the process. For example, one option would be for your information to be used as input by the corporate research unit, which would then provide reports to senior executives. Another option would be for senior executives to access your custom web site directly, with the research unit serving as consultant on the design of the site. The diagram can depict one or both of these options.

6. Create an Organization Chart

It may surprise you to find me advocating an organization chart for a company in the under-the-radar zone. For many veterans of the Dil-

TABLE 4.1 Diagram of Home Page of Web Site for Operators of Dental Laboratories

Section	*News and Information*	*Classified Advertising*	*Office Efficiency*	*Community Information*
Typical content	Announcements of new products Articles on industry trends Product comparisons	Labs for sale Used equipment for sale Positions wanted Positions offered	Online billing service Online service for tracking orders to and from dentist offices	Trade association news Calendar of upcoming meetings and events
Traffic driver	Timely information	Niche market focus	Usage by dentists	Trade association endorsements
Revenue model	Revenue from sponsors Electronic commerce from catalog sales	Fees charged for placing ads	Monthly subscription fees from dental labs and dentists	Advertising from sponsors

bert sector, one of the most odious symbols of corporate bureaucracy is the organization chart. Your first thought about a start-up might be, "Org chart?!! We don't need no stinkin' org chart!"

In the Dilbert sector, employees perceive organization charts as political tools. An organization chart comes across as a way to distribute power and prestige among executives.

For a netstrapper, an organization chart can be a tool for managing the business in a rational way. Even if you are a one-person organization, you can benefit by listing your roles and responsibilities and assigning yourself a percent of time for each one—for example, 50 percent for sales, 20 percent for web-site maintenance, 30 percent for administrative tasks.

Use the diagrams of your business to identify the key roles that need to be filled in order to execute your idea. Note any instances where one founder has multiple roles or where a role has no one filling it. You do not need to resolve these issues right away, but you should plan to address them.

For example, with Homefair, our "funnel" suggested that we had three major roles:

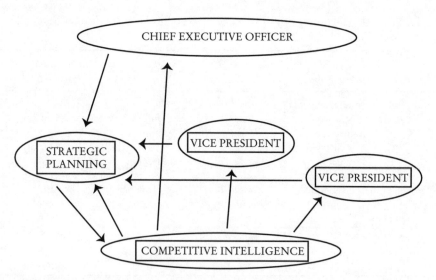

FIGURE 4.4   Diagram of Competitive Intelligence Service, Showing How It Fits into Corporate Structure of a Customer

The strategic planning office works with our Competitive Intelligence service to design
web-based reports. The strategic planning office gets input from the CEO and other top
executives. Our reports then get delivered to the strategic planning office as well as the
CEO and other top executives.

- Maintaining traffic, by partnering with other web sites, including portals. Bryan Schutjer was in charge of this.
- Designing the web site so that it appealed to consumers and
  supported our revenue models. I had this responsibility.
- Obtaining sponsors. Bill Sedgwick was responsible.

Our CEO, Rich Ganley, got involved in each of these areas, but he
was particularly active in helping to close major sponsorship sales.
As our business developed, we began to see areas where we needed
more strength. We needed to add:

- A chief technology officer
- An operations manager to follow through on sales from the
  point of closing to the point where the customer signed off
  on our implementation of the sponsorship or co-brand
- A relationship manager to help deepen our existing partnerships with sites that we were counting on for traffic

We filled all of these positions, hiring a manager of operations and a relationship manager to work in the Scottsdale office and using a consulting firm in Denver as our technology solution.

In the preceding section, I mentioned an idea for a web site for dental labs. The diagram for this business could show a potential for many roles. There would be a classified advertising section. There would be a section for tracking order flow between dentists and laboratories. There would be a section for providing lab owners with informational content, including reviews of the latest products and offers from manufacturers. One of the challenges with assembling this business is that each of these jobs would appear to require at least one full-time person.

The apartment portal concept, also mentioned in the preceding section, is another business that involves many roles on its organization chart. Someone needs to manage the relationships with the Internet service providers, so that they include your portal as the default home page for renters in buildings that they serve. Someone needs to be in charge of selling advertising to local businesses. Someone needs to be in charge of content for all of the sites. One of the issues that would concern me about this hypothetical enterprise is the cost and complexity associated with having all of these critical roles.

One of the reasons I did not fund Bob and Sally (see the "no-baggage" exercise, above) is that I came to realize that their business required a marketing strategist and a technology strategist. Neither of the principals was ready to step into those roles. This left huge gaps in the organization chart.

7. Identify Critical Operating Ratios

Begin by quantifying everything related to how you do business.

> *I mean everything.*
> —Gerber, *The E-Myth Revisited,* p. 123

Gerber's point is that a business is a system that you are constantly trying to refine. He argues that in order for those refinements to lead to progress, you need to measure the results both before and after you introduce a refinement.

At this stage, before we even have done any test-marketing, it is premature to quantify "everything." However, we should identify critical operating ratios. These are ratios that relate revenues and variable costs to their key drivers.

For his FamilyPoint.com community web site, Joseph Murgio (Case No. 15) needed to obtain as many registered users as possible. His key operating ratio was the cost of obtaining a registered user. He calculated this ratio for alternative marketing strategies, selecting the ones that were most efficient.

One ratio that is important in any business is revenue per employee. This is the ratio that will tell you how many mouths your business can feed. However, this is a very difficult estimate to pull out of the air. Until you break down your business into component parts for marketing and support, you are likely to have an overly optimistic view of this ratio.

Two important processes to understand are your sales process and your setup/support process. For example, with Homefair, a key revenue source was selling city-specific ads to local real estate companies. Each ad took about half an hour to set up. Our support costs consisted of answering occasional questions from real estate agents and delivering them quarterly reports on traffic to their ads. Including both setup and support, the cost of an ad in the first year was probably about $75.

Sales were done over the phone. Assuming that one person earning $200 a day could sell ads for five cities per day, the cost per sale was $40. With revenues per city ranging from $250 to $750, we knew that we were making a profit. Setup cost plus cost per sale was only $115.

For web sites that deliver content for free, with sponsorship as the economic model, an important ratio is revenue per thousand page views. With Homefair, our total revenue per thousand page views was around $60. This was remarkably high. Very little of our revenue came from banner ads. Most of it came from sponsors who paid us for contact forms that they received from our consumers. In some situations, we charged a fee per lead, typically between $5 and $10. In other cases, such as the real estate agents, we charged an annual fee, but we tracked leads and used our reports on lead volume to justify our pricing.

When I interviewed Brandon White of WorldwideAngler.com (Case No. 22), I was surprised to find that he did not think in terms of revenue per page view. In fact, when I did a back-of-the-envelope calculation of the total revenue potential for his web site and assumed $50 per thousand page views, he became concerned that this might not feed all of the mouths that were funding his business.

One of the most dangerous "urban legends" about banner advertising is the $35 rate card. That is, if you ask people in the web advertising business about typical rates, they will tell you that most sites have a "rate card" that calls for $35 per 1,000 ad impressions. This is bogus. If you are a buyer and you pay this rate, you are getting ripped off. More important, if you are developing a web site and you think that you can earn this rate, you are seriously mistaken.

Every quarter, when Yahoo! announces its earnings, I divide its revenues by its page views. The range seems to fall between $4 and $5 per thousand page views. Also, in the fall of 2000, I attempted to estimate the ratio of the total on-line advertising budget (reported by one source to be $10 billion) to a rough estimate of the total page views available on the top 100 sites. This came out to much less than $10 per thousand page views. I concluded that the price that will balance supply and demand in the entire banner advertising market is probably no more than $5 per thousand. If you construct your business plan based on $35 per thousand, you will be in for quite a shock when reality hits the fan.

You can come up with critical operating ratios for the hypothetical business ideas that we have been discussing.

For on-line condom sales, if you fulfill orders yourself, then you will need an inventory, and the inventory-sales ratio will affect your costs. You will also want to measure the percentage of repeat orders. Customer acquisition will be costly, and it will be important for you to have existing customers come back and order again.

For the apartment community portal, you are going to have to sell advertising to local businesses. This is probably going to require a combination of door-to-door sales and telephone sales. Revenue per salesperson will be an important operating ratio. Before starting this enterprise, you would want to be convinced that it is plausible to obtain enough revenue per salesperson to support the business.

For the dental laboratories' web site, you will want to know which sections are the most profitable. If classified advertising is a dud, then you do not want to put much effort into it. The ratio of revenue from any given section to total revenue will be an indicator of where to put your focus.

For the competitive intelligence service, there are a number of critical operating ratios. You will need to nail down the time spent per sales call, the closing rate on sales calls, and the number of staff hours needed to support each customer.

As you can see, the critical operating ratios depend on the type of business. The point is that before you launch your enterprise, you need to start thinking about your cost drivers and your revenue drivers. Identify the values of the critical operating ratios that are necessary for viability. These values can provide you with targets to shoot for when you reach the execution stage. If you realize in advance that the value of a key ratio is not realistic, then you have discovered a flaw in the business model. If that is the case, it is better to find out now than to figure it out nine months into the start-up.

8. Test-Market Your Offering

There are some entrepreneurs who have a real aversion to test-marketing. They take the view that if they reveal to potential customers something about their proposed solution, then a competitor will come along and steal their precious idea. Entrepreneurs will say that they are operating in "stealth mode."

If you are in "stealth mode," then I suggest that you do the following:

1. Go to the bathroom.
2. Stand in front of the mirror.
3. Say, "I see a corpse."

Start-ups that are in "stealth mode" are dead. On this issue, I agree completely with the venture capital community, which has no respect for companies that ask them to sign nondisclosure agreements. I'll reconsider my position on this issue as soon as someone can show me a living example of a company that operated in "stealth mode."

But doesn't "under the radar" suggest stealth? Let's take a moment to sort out our metaphors. Regardless of what the phrase "under the radar" may suggest to you, I am not advocating a "stealth mode" strategy. To me, "under the radar" means that you are aiming for a target valuation lower than the amount needed to feed the mouths of the venture capital system. It means that your total market is a small fish that the venture capitalists would throw back. And in my view, "stealth mode" means that you are hiding your offering from potential customers.

As the next chapter will spell out, I believe in learning by selling. The only secrets that "stealth mode" protects are the secrets of what the market really wants. Those are the secrets you need to learn, and "stealth mode" keeps you from learning them.

A valid concern about test-marketing is that you might be accused of selling "vaporware." It is important to manage the expectations of your potential customers so that you do not lose any goodwill.

Many netstrappers will testify to the importance of test-marketing. To them, starting a business without having any evidence that you can sell to customers is crazy. As Brian Lloyd (Case No. 13) puts it, "If you can't line up any customers up front, maybe you don't have a viable business model."

Test-marketing can also lead you to realize that you are not offering the right product. When Derek Scruggs (Case No. 10) test-marketed a Java development tool, he found that what his potential customers really needed was a better way to handle inbound e-mail. He steered his company, Distributed Bits, away from the Java development tool. Instead, he focused his company on building a solution for the e-mail management problem.

The goal in test-marketing is *not* to validate your solution in detail. Your objective is to assess the significance of the problem in the eyes of the potential customer. You want to come away from a meeting with the customer with answers to the following questions:

- Where does this problem rank in the list of the customer's concerns?
- What internal issues keep this problem from being solved?
- How much would the customer pay to make the problem go away?

Most entrepreneurs start businesses in which they have some connection with the industry that is the target market. Usually, you have a friend or former colleague at a company that is a potential customer.

Ask your contacts to arrange a meeting between you and a critical decisionmaker inside the company. Make it clear that the purpose of the meeting is not for you to give a presentation, but to exchange ideas. A meeting over coffee or lunch can help to create an informal atmosphere.

At the meeting, ask the potential customer to list the three most important issues he or she faces. If your offering does not address any of those issues, then either you are talking to the wrong person in the company or you have the wrong idea of what you should be trying to sell.

For example, in the fall of 2000 I met Bernard Brookes, an entrepreneur who is trying to develop web-based software to help mental health professionals manage their administrative functions, particularly billing and filing for claims with insurance companies. I asked him what concerns were most on the minds of his potential customers, such as psychiatrists and social workers. "Being squeezed by managed care," he replied. If this is true, I said, then any software that is positioned to solve some other problem is going to receive a low priority.

Brookes could not promise to make managed care go away. However, it seemed to me that his best chance for selling his product was to position it as a way to reduce the headaches and costs of the managed care system for mental health professionals.

It may turn out that what keeps mental health professionals from solving problems of inefficient claims processing is the fact that regulations and forms are in a state of flux. Errors occur frequently, because both insurance companies and doctors are unfamiliar with new procedures. What Brookes might find in test-marketing is that what doctors really need is someone to stay on top of the rules and regulations and to deal with the clerical errors that come from the managed care companies. If he can address this problem, then his offering will be successful. If not, then his customers will not place much value on the efficiencies of automated web-based processing.

Once Brookes has defined exactly which parts of the managed care "squeeze" problem he can solve and which he cannot, he will need to ask his potential customers how much they would pay to have the feasible part of the problem solved. The way I would approach this would be to say, "Other potential customers we've talked to say that if we were to solve these aspects of the managed care problem for them, they would be willing to pay $X per month to subscribe to our service. Does that seem about right to you? Do you think that a monthly subscription fee is fair, or would you rather have the fee set as a percentage of claims paid?"

Test-marketing really helps a business to get off on the right foot. On the other hand, a well-written business plan that is not based on test-marketing is like a fancy car with a dead battery. It looks great until you try to use it to get somewhere.

9. Identify Operational Milestones

About a month after I interviewed him for this book, I ran into Don Britton (Case No. 8) at a gathering of Netpreneur, a local organization of Internet entrepreneurs. "We've signed our first big customer!" he exclaimed proudly. This is an example of reaching an operational milestone. In this case, a customer had agreed to use the outsourcing service provided by Britton's Network Alliance for all of its computer needs.

In the same brief conversation, Britton told me that he believed that his funding issues were resolved. One of his key team members was also in a position to be an angel investor.

These two events were probably correlated. Just as honey attracts bees, achieving operational milestones attracts investors. Every milestone that you achieve helps to reduce the risk of your business and brings the promise of profitability closer to reality.

Once you have validated your offering by doing test-marketing, you have a realistic picture of what it will take to execute your business. At this point, you can set operational milestones. A number of milestones can be used to chart the success of an enterprise. Possible examples are:

- Development of a prototype
- Fulfillment of the first sale
- The first $100,000 in revenue
- The first $1,000,000 in revenue

It is useful to attempt to forecast the value of the company at each operational milestone. For example, when you have a prototype, the company might be worth $500,000. When you have completed your first sales transaction, the company might be worth $1 million. When you have obtained your first $100,000 in revenue, the company might be worth $1.5 million.

Of course, the true value of your company will depend on how investors perceive the importance of these milestones. Potential investors have to buy in to your estimates of the value of your company as milestones are achieved.

Some self-styled visionaries resist being pinned down on operational milestones. They paint a picture of where they hope to end up, and then they ask investors to give them money so that they can figure out how to get there. You are welcome to indulge in this sort of fantasy, in which an investor comes along who just hands you money and says, "Go off and do something great." However, the reality is that people who invest money care how their money is spent. Operational milestones are a necessity, both for investors and for entrepreneurs.

Even if you do not seek outside funding, it is advantageous to link the estimated value of your company to operational milestones. You may encounter customers, suppliers, or partners who are concerned about the long-run viability of your firm. By demonstrating your ability to achieve operational milestones and by showing a pattern of increasing value of your company, you can help to alleviate their worries.

10. Develop a Budget

One challenge for an entrepreneur is that it can be difficult to assess the degree of success of your business. Rob Main's first business, web-design and hosting firm Electric Press, met its objectives in the first year, but the founders did not prepare well for growth and expansion. In retrospect, it appears to me that Electric Press should have developed a more aggressive budget for the period beyond its initial six months. The founding partners failed to develop a roadmap for a fast-growing enterprise. They achieved relatively mediocre results, because that was all that their budget demanded.

A budget, which includes projections for revenues and costs, is another important tool for self-discipline. It should be designed to take you all the way from launch to big-time success.

It is rare that your actual revenues and expenses will match your budget projections. However, you gain a lot of insight by examining the variances, and over time you will learn to set more realistic goals and to hit those targets.

At this stage, we still are in the planning process. With your operational milestones identified, you should be able to define the steps needed to reach those milestones and the costs of attaining them. You want to develop a budget in which you project out costs and revenues to the point where your business reaches profitability. Make sure that you are not overly optimistic about how quickly you can sell successfully. Be wary of pioneer time.

When I was running Homefair on my own, I never had a budget. It was Rich Ganley who brought that discipline to the business, when I joined with him and the other two partners from Scottsdale. For Ganley, the revenue side of our budget was as important as the cost side. We wanted to be conservative on both. Our goal was to have actual revenues come in higher than the budget, with actual costs coming in lower than the budget.

11. Develop Your Funding Strategy

Smart strategy for funding your business can be a matter of timing as much as anything else. Many entrepreneurs seek funding too soon. Because they have yet to achieve any operational milestones, investors tend to give their proposals a poor reception. Time that entrepreneurs might spend productively by doing test-marketing or developing a prototype instead gets wasted making futile pitches to investors.

On the other hand, it is important to seize the opportunity for growth when it presents itself. For example, Scott McLoughlin of the Adrenaline Group (Case No. 2) was willing to obtain financing in order to achieve rapid expansion of his high-end web-development company.

An example of an overly conservative approach was Rob Main's Electric Press, mentioned in the previous section. Electric Press was one of the first firms to enter the web-site development and hosting market. It attempted to "grow organically," which is the term used to describe a business that uses internal funds to finance expansion. The result of this strategy was that Electric Press was overtaken by competitors that grew faster. In retrospect, I believe that once Electric Press had established the validity of that market, it should have attempted a rapid expansion, using outside funds if necessary.

At the planning stage, your budget should help you to identify the stage at which your business might require external investment in order to expand. This allows you to develop a funding strategy.

For example, the budget may show that you can reach your first milestone without outside funding, but you will have to go $100,000 in the hole to reach your second operational milestone. In that case, your initial funding need is for $100,000. You should start looking for this funding right away, even though you will not ask the investor to write a check until after your first milestone is reached.

As discussed in Chapter 3, the idea is to fund your business in stages. The first stage of funding might enable you to get from one operational milestone to the next. The next stage might take you one step further. You keep doing this until either the business becomes self-funded or you sell the company to a strategic buyer.

Each stage of funding does not have to require new investors and new terms. When you talk to your first potential investors, you lay out your entire funding strategy. At each stage, you show how the value of the firm will increase. Investors who buy into the strategy will carry you through as many stages as they can afford.

12. Find a Coach

A coach is someone who will introduce you to investors. You want someone who will help you because he or she likes you and your idea. You might want to create a board of advisers and include your coach as a member. You might grant your coach some stock for being an advisory board member, which might be as little as 0.5 percent of the company. If you have to pay someone in cash to be a coach, that is a sign of desperation.

Be selective about your coach. Once, an entrepreneur gave me the phone number of someone who was helping him with funding strategy. I called this coach, and I asked him to give me the names of other companies that he had helped. The coach's reaction to that question was hostile and defensive, which was a really bad sign. I then called someone I know in the venture capital community and asked her opinion of the coach. Without prompting, she instantly said, "He's a knucklehead."

Coaches who are known as knuckleheads do not help you. Check out their reputations first. A little due diligence can go a long way.

At this point, after you've selected a good coach, if your coach tells you that you need a written business plan, then do as your coach instructs.

Conclusion

The process I have outlined in this chapter is rather demanding. Keep in mind that many successful entrepreneurs, myself included, have executed some of the steps poorly, even though we might have excelled in other aspects of netstrapping.

Lisa Martin (Case No. 25) was one of those who were held back by an "early divorce" (poor execution of the first step of choosing a team), but she excelled at test-marketing, setting operational milestones, and meeting her budget. Her web-focused marketing company, Leapfrog Solutions, was successful once she got past the early divorce.

I have argued that Rob Main and his teammates could have done better at their budgeting and funding strategy. However, they excelled at identifying trends and brainstorming ideas. Although Electric Press fell short of its potential as an early web-hosting and design service, Main had better luck with eFed.com, a spin-off that focused on electronic commerce for government.

I believe that the process outlined in this chapter will get your business off to a better start than you could achieve by putting all of your initial energy into writing a traditional business plan. I know that my own enterprise would have gone more smoothly had I followed more of the steps I have outlined for the planning process. In particular, I would have benefited from an earlier focus on key operating ratios, operational milestones, and a budget. However, not for one minute have I regretted the fact that I never wrote down a business plan.

Case No. 7: Maurice Boissiere

At first glance, Maurice Boissiere may appear to have achieved success much more quickly than the typical netstrapper. Barely two years after he and partner Leslie Williams founded CustomerInsites in December 1997, TeleSpectrum Worldwide, Inc. purchased his company. Boissiere found himself the CEO of an enterprise, to be called e-Satisfy.com, which TeleSpectrum formed by merging another one of its subsidiaries with CustomerInsites. As of the summer of 2000, the new company already had $10 million in revenues with plans to grow to $100 million in sales over the next two to three years.

In fact, Boissiere's path to success had a few bumps. After acquiring his MBA from Wharton in 1993, Boissiere found himself a couple of years later with a choice of two opportunities in the Washington, D.C., area, each with a company that was struggling to come to terms with the Internet. One was a company that designed games for CD-ROMs; his task would be to provide skills that the company would try to transfer to the web-design market. The other was an on-line service that was under pressure from its users to offer web access. Boissiere chose the game company, Magnet Interactive, and turned down the other opportunity, which was to be a "channel manager" with America Online.

"If I'd done AOL, I'd be a millionaire," Boissiere admits. Still, he has no regrets. Even though his tenure at Magnet Interactive saw the company shrink by 50 percent as it struggled to reinvent itself, it was a learning experience.

In the summer of 1997, Boissiere and Williams evaluated a number of possible opportunities. They decided that developing a formal and systematic approach to measuring customer satisfaction with web sites would be a valuable business. As Boissiere put it, "We felt that with the stakes getting higher for companies on the Internet, people would see the need for traditional approaches to testing usability and measuring customer satisfaction."

At a time when the market was nonexistent, Boissiere and Williams estimated that by 2002, companies would be spending $1 billion a year on customer satisfaction research related to their web sites. Today, with the market already at $100 million a year, industry experts regard this forecast as having been remarkably accurate.

With a single line of code from CustomerInsites on its web site, a company can take a scientific customer satisfaction survey. For a random sample of users, a window pops up that asks the user to participate in a survey. Often, users are given incentives to accept the offer. The survey results are stored and collated by CustomerInsites, and the web-site owner can then log on at any time to view reports.

The first company to sign up for CustomerInsites was The Motley Fool, appropriately enough on April 1, 1998. Other early customers included the *Washington Post* and Fox News.

Boissiere and Williams initially thought that the surveys would be created individually for each client. However, they soon realized that this "project-by-project" approach was too time consuming from a sales perspective. They quickly changed to a model where they offer the customer a set of templates from which to choose for their surveys. The actual content of the surveys (i.e., the questions asked) does vary somewhat from customer to customer, to allow for questions that are specific to an industry or to a web site.

CustomerInsites found that a number of companies could serve as partners. For example, MyPoints.com, a consumer reward service, was a natural partner. Web surfers can collect MyPoints, which work like frequent flyer miles, in exchange for filling out surveys for CustomerInsites. Another partner is Keynote Systems, which resells CustomerInsites services as part of a full-service program to monitor web-site performance, including response time and other technical measurements. It was one of their partners, TARP, which was owned by TeleSpectrum, that led to the strategic acquisition.

In identifying the need for customer satisfaction measurement for web sites, Boissiere and Williams exemplify the importance of being able to spot a "killer trend." They have had to do very little advertising, because companies are so eager for this kind of service that they inquire about where they can find it. As a result, CustomerInsites gets much of its new business by word of mouth. "For some reason, a lot of companies in California know about us," Boissiere says, even though CustomerInsites is based in suburban Washington, D.C.

The new e-Satisfy.com is poised to take advantage of yet another killer trend, the rapid adoption of the Internet in overseas markets. When I first contacted Boissiere for an interview, he was just getting ready to take off for a meeting in their new office in London.

Case No. 8: Don Britton

A very common approach to netstrapping is to start a business in your spare time. Don Britton followed this path for almost two years before making a full-time commitment to his new enterprise, Network Alliance. Late in 1997, when he was working at Beers and Cutler, a local accounting firm, he obtained permission to start his company and work evenings and weekends on it. In 1998, he joined the Morino Group as controller, after first obtaining consent to continue moonlighting on his new business. Finally, in January 2000, he quit his day job and hit the ground running as a full-time entrepreneur.

Network Alliance takes the "netcentric" approach to computing to its extreme. When I interviewed Britton in Reston, Virginia, he connected his laptop to a server in Michigan and ran a word processing program on the server. His keystrokes appeared on his screen as fast as if the program were stored in the laptop itself.

Britton did not invent any of the technology that makes netcentric computing feasible, but he keenly grasps its potential. He believes that he can assemble the components to offer what he calls "subscription computing," with a particular emphasis on the small business market.

For many businesses, such as law firms and small accounting firms, computer systems are a tremendous headache to buy and maintain. For instance, one of Network Alliance's first customers was an accounting firm that had just gone through three network administrators in four months.

Network Alliance is in a position to completely outsource the computer systems for these small businesses. Any software that you now run on a personal computer or a local network can be put instead on the servers at Network Alliance's data center. When you need to use an application, you connect to the Internet and run the application from whatever device you are using, at whatever your location.

This concept will allow small businesses to enjoy much more reliable computing capability than they have today, and at a lower price. Furthermore, this concept will ultimately reshape the computing industry. Instead of having to market their software applications to individual businesses, developers will be able to sell to single purchasing points, such as Network Alliance, which will buy software on behalf of small business users. This will create big efficiencies in the marketing of software.

Although Network Alliance has been self-funded so far, it clearly is a concept that fits the venture capital model. There are genuine network effects to be captured. The more customers Britton obtains, the easier it will be for him to attract software vendors to his platform. Attracting more vendors in turn will enable him to attract more customers. A case can be made that he is trying to become the next Microsoft, but you cannot get all the way from here to there by netstrapping.

Indeed, when I asked Britton to name his biggest mistakes, the second one that came to mind was "moving too slowly." (The first mistake that came to Britton's mind was that he hired some people who later proved to lack the skills that he assumed they had.) Had he obtained funding sooner, he could have been further along in implementing his idea.

On the other hand, it seems to me that because he waited, Britton is in a strong negotiating position. He is showing venture capitalists a working system, not just an idea on a napkin. Also, his ideas seem less strange and far-fetched than would have been the case two years ago, as more of the components of his vision are being adopted and discussed today.

In fact, when I met him in early August 2000, Britton was in the ideal position with venture capitalists. He did not have to go begging to them. Many venture capitalists were eager to fund his company, and his challenge at the time was to choose the investors that would be most advantageous to his company.

Case No. 9: Michael Smith

Michael Smith, co-founder of Firebox.com, gets the award for "Most Unusual Funding Tactic." My first interview attempt was bumped by an eight-hour meeting that Smith had with his attorneys in order to finalize a private placement offering of stock via www.eo.net, a bleeding-edge investment platform based in Europe, primarily the U.K.

However, the Internet-based stock offering is not the most unusual funding tactic that Michael Smith employed. Nor is it that when Smith and his fellow Birmingham University student Tom Boardman started Firebox.com in May 1998, Boardman sold his car and Smith coaxed his parents into investing £1,000 (about $1,500).

What was unique about Firebox.com is that to raise initial capital when they started the company, the founders volunteered to be subjects in clinical drug trials. "We spent one week in hospital. We were able to plan the business, plus get paid about £400 each!" Smith enthuses, adding, "It wasn't as bad as one guy I read about in the States, who sold his bone marrow in order to get started."

The founders came up with the idea for Firebox while students at Birmingham, where they and their friends were avid readers of magazines such as *Maxim*, which targeted eighteen- to thirty-five-year-old "blokes." Smith and Boardman noticed that while these magazines wrote about the latest toys from the United States or gadgets from Japan, there was no one selling these products in the U.K. At first, they thought of creating a catalogue, but by this point (May 1998) they realized that a web site would be less expensive.

Smith and Boardman took on the fulfillment challenge by stocking products in their house. They persuaded suppliers to give them thirty days' credit, because "cash flow was a huge, huge, issue."

At the end of 1998, Smith and Boardman came up with their own idea for a toy. It was a shotglass chess set: Any time you capture a piece from the opponent, you drink a glass. This generated plenty of publicity, as well as profitable sales, which helped to fund growth in 1999.

By the end of 1999, Firebox.com had drawn the interest of venture capitalists, who were impressed at how much the founders had been able to grow the business themselves. They received funding from New Media Spark, the largest incubator in Europe. Smith says that these investors have demanded more reporting and helped to improve company discipline. They helped Firebox.com launch a branch in Stockholm. They are well connected, and they have added credibility with business partners, employees, and journalists. Smith regrets that he did not seek funding earlier, because lack of outside financing inhibited growth.

FIVE

Feeding Mouths and Minds: The Importance of Selling

Effective face-to-face selling is critical for entrepreneurs . . . In my Inc. 500 survey, for instance, only 12 percent of the founders secured their early revenues through intermediaries. The other 88 percent of founders sold directly to end users. And in all but a handful of cases, the entrepreneur (rather than an employed salesperson) was principally responsible for making the sale.
— Bhide, *The Origin and Evolution of New Businesses*, pp. 108–109

Why Sell?

Inexperienced entrepreneurs often think of the product as something that exists separately from customers. I cannot tell you how often I run into people who seem to think that the key steps to launching an enterprise on the Web are:

- Registering a domain name
- Putting up a web site
- Submitting to search engines

If you take nothing else away from reading this book, I hope you get this model out of your head. A domain name, a web site, and an entry in the Internet directories do not constitute a business. A business exists if and only if you have customers who are willing to pay more for your product or service than what it costs to provide.

For netstrappers whose language is computer algorithms, Raj Khera puts it this way:

if revenues > expenses then
    valuation increases
else
    go bust

Do not confuse this issue with the cliché "You should listen to your customers." That cliché applies to established businesses. They have the luxury of choosing which customers they want to hear from and parsing what it means to "listen."

The typical under-the-radar entrepreneur faces a problem that is much more fundamental. You have no customers to listen to right now. Your focus, your obsession, has to be on obtaining customers. Your market does not yet exist, and you need customers to define it for you and teach you how to serve it.

I see too many people who are comfortable pitching to investors for money but are uncomfortable standing up to the bear and asking customers to pay for a product or service. If you have an aversion to selling, get over it before you become a netstrapper.

Learning by Selling

For an under-the-radar business, selling does not just feed your mouths. It feeds your minds. Of all the ways that you can gather information to improve your offering and strengthen your business, the selling process can be the most powerful. From this perspective, selling is a form of trial-and-error learning. If you refrain from selling, then you avoid trial, your errors stay hidden, and your learning is aborted. On the other hand, if you are actively soliciting and listening to input from potential customers, then you are building a knowledge base that will evolve into an enduring source of competitive advantage.

For example, when Raj Khera started GovCon.com, his potential sponsors knew little or nothing about the Internet. He did not know ahead of time what they would need from his company in order to make effective use of his web site. However, once he began talking to sponsors, he realized that to overcome their objections he would have to build web pages for them to enable them to take advantage of sponsorship.

At TheSchoolReport.com, Neil Rosen found that individual real estate agents placed a high value on putting their personal photos on display. Realizing that agents typically did not know how to provide photos in web-friendly formats, Rosen had his company develop the capability to scan in photos and reformat them for the Web. This proved particularly valuable when TheSchoolReport.com created a partnership with Yahoo.com. Telling a real estate agent, "Your picture will be on Yahoo!" tended to clinch the sale.

Bernard Brookes, the entrepreneur whom I mentioned in the previous chapter as developing web-based software to handle billing for mental health professionals, asked me to comment on a draft of a direct mail solicitation for his offering. While I thought that the letter was well written, I encouraged Brookes to make ten face-to-face sales calls before sending a letter. My thinking was that after he had made the sales calls he would have a better idea of which features were crucial to offer initially and which features could be postponed for a later version.

Under-the-radar businesses make major adjustments in order to align themselves with customers. As a result, it often happens that the ultimate business bears almost no resemblance to the initial concept.

As mentioned earlier, Derek Scruggs (Case No. 10) thought that he was creating a Java development tool. When he made his first customer presentation, he realized that what the market was ready for was an e-mail management product. He refocused his business.

In 1998, Homefair developed a system for generating leads from consumers in need of relocation services. Each month, thousands of customers were filling out contact forms that went to companies such as Prudential and Bank One.

We found that the large service providers did not have processes for dealing with Internet leads. Rather than allowing our company sponsors to fail, we developed a program that we dubbed "E-sharp," which trained companies in how to market services successfully to consumers who had contacted them using the Internet. "E-sharp" trained companies to respond quickly, to probe for the customer's needs, and to be prepared for questions and concerns. "E-sharp" became a significant profit center, as more and more companies sought help with managing leads that come in from the Internet.

We developed the "E-sharp" program because of what we learned from trying to sell leads. We discovered that simply delivering leads did not solve the sponsor's problem, because the sponsors' processes for handling leads were not adequate. The sponsors needed help with processing those leads, because Internet users differ from traditional channels in their expectations for technology (use of e-mail instead of the phone), information, and timeliness. Had we failed to address this challenge for our sponsors, they would have become dissatisfied with our service. Instead, we turned it into a consulting service that we could sell to other companies, including firms that were not sponsors on our web site.

Alternatives to Selling

W. C. Fields came up with a joke for his tombstone: "On the whole, I'd rather be in Philadelphia."

Many would-be entrepreneurs are no fonder of selling than W. C. Fields was of Philadelphia. Unfortunately, their businesses are likely to end up underneath tombstones.

In recent years, several alternatives to selling have become popular. If you are considering one of these alternatives, you should know that you are headed for trouble.

Banner Ads

Dirk Reinshagen, whom I got to know when he worked as a consultant for Homefair, developed a web-based collaboration tool called JointPlanning.com. It enables people who are working on projects to share calendars, issue lists, and other information. He reached the market over a year before a site with a similar purpose was launched by Joseph Murgio (Case No. 15). Murgio had only recently launched his OnProject.com when I interviewed him for this book.

Murgio was on track to earn millions from OnProject.com. Reinshagen's JointPlanning.com was more or less a break-even business. The difference was that Murgio was willing to sell, while Reinshagen was trying to rely on banner ads for revenue. Murgio was focused on selling OnProject.com for a monthly fee to project managers and their teams. Reinshagen was trying to fund JointPlanning.com using banner ads provided by an ad network.

Reinshagen was using one of several popular techniques to avoid selling. It is easy to sign up with a banner-ad network that will provide your web site with banner ads, taking a commission that ranges from 15 to 40 percent.

Banner ads will not feed very many mouths. Suppose that your web site obtains 1 million page views a month, which is a very considerable level of traffic. Your revenue from banner ads sold is likely to be on the order of $5 per thousand impressions. Even assuming that you sell ads on your entire inventory of page views, this means $5,000 per month. This is unlikely to cover the cost of maintaining a decent site.

Even apart from the commission that it siphons off, an ad network tends to reduce your revenue potential. A network does not know your site. The network does not know which pages are "results pages" (where people may be finished with something and are ready to go somewhere else) or "intermediate pages" (where users are in the middle of a task and unlikely to respond to an ad). The network does not know that as an on-line guitar shop, your site will be a better place for ads from record companies than from on-line stockbrokers.

At Homefair, we averaged closer to $60 in revenue per 1,000 page views. However, to achieve this, we created a variety of revenue models. Most of our income did not come from banners. Moreover, we sold our banner ads ourselves, and these sales were based on our inside knowledge of how our site was organized and how our users interacted with it.

Marketing and Branding

I subscribe to a mailing list for people involved in Internet start-ups. One of the more frequent questions is: "We are ready to introduce our product, and now we need a marketing campaign. We want to create a brand that is so powerful that we become the 'Kleenex' or 'Xerox' of our industry. Who can help us do that?"

There is no correct answer to this question. Nobody can create a marketing and branding campaign out of whole cloth. If you have customers who are raving about your product, then you can build on

TABLE 5.1   Successfully Building a Brand

The "Apple Myth" Approach	The More Realistic Approach
1. Come up with what you think is a good idea for a product or service	1. Use test marketing to develop an offering that meets a customer's pressing need
2. Develop the product or service in your garage	2. Learn by selling to customers; tune your offering until customers achieve outstanding results from using it
3. Come up with a clever marketing strategy	3. Use public relations efforts to reinforce strong word-of-mouth support for your offering

this enthusiasm to launch successful marketing and branding efforts. However, if you have not yet introduced your product, then you have no idea whether you have anything to brand.

One of my favorite examples of branding without customer enthusiasm is Pets.com. I rarely watch television, but the Pets.com sock puppet successfully imprinted itself on my consciousness. As a pure exercise in branding, my amateur opinion is that it had to be one of the most outstanding advertising campaigns of all time.

Unfortunately, the success of the sock puppet commercials did not translate into sales of pet products on Pets.com, which went out of business in November 2000. The only hot item in their on-line store was the sock puppet.

The hypothesis that you can use marketing and branding to avoid selling is based on what I call the "Apple myth." This is the myth that Apple Computer did not need to learn by selling, because its engineers produced an "insanely great" computer and the company then used clever marketing, such as its famous Super Bowl commercial, to win customers.

The "Apple myth" suggests one process for building a great brand. I would contrast that myth with what I believe is a more realistic scenario (see Table 5.1).

Whether Apple Computer itself followed what I call the "Apple myth" strategy is questionable. One could argue that in fact the company followed what I call the more realistic approach.

However, even if the myth is a reasonable approximation of what worked at Apple, it is not a description for a typical company. Most new products have to prove themselves with customers before a marketing strategy or a branding campaign can succeed. The most realistic scenario is one in which successful marketing and branding take place relatively late in the life cycle of a product. Once customers have bonded with the product, the opportunity arises to market to other customers and build a strong brand.

The danger in pursuing the "Apple myth" is its implicit assumption that communication only needs to take place in one direction. Note that in the "Apple myth" process, all communication flows either internally among the brilliant inventors or outward from the company to consumers. According to the myth, there is no need for feedback from the consumers to the inventors. In reality, doing away with consumer feedback is a dangerous strategy, particularly in the age of the Internet.

Open Source

In 1998, I met the executives of a company called Microstate, which had developed an application server. They had just released their product as "open source," which they assumed would be a great marketing coup. I took it to mean that they were averse to doing real marketing. Neither the product nor the company went anywhere.

The open-source movement in software represents still another sales-avoidance tactic. Open source has been successful in many respects, but my guess is that its market potential is much more limited than its strongest partisans suggest.

With traditional software, the user pays to obtain a license for an "executable file." This means that the computer instructions contained in the software—its source code—are hidden from the consumer, in order to keep the consumer from copying the software and reselling it.

With open-source software, the user is allowed to see all of the computer instructions. It would be simple for the user to make copies of the software to give or sell to others. Therefore, open-source software is provided to users at no charge. Classic examples of open-source software include the operating system Linux, the leading web server Apache, the mail server sendmail, and the programming language perl.

Having forgone licensing fees as a source of revenue, developers of open-source software have a variety of economic models. One model is that they earn reputations as programmers, which may increase the salaries that they can earn in the market.

Traditional software has to be sold to nontechnical users. Therefore, developers must pay attention to the needs of users who are not experts.

Open-source software is provided to users "as is." Highly skilled programmers who want to add features to open-source software can do so on their own. However, ordinary users have no leverage with open-source software. Their money has no influence, and they do not have the "right stuff" to make their own corrections or enhancements to the code.

There is no mechanism to enable open-source software to "cross the chasm" from technical users to nontechnical users. There is no communication channel from nontechnical users to developers. With traditional software, when nontechnical users ask for features, companies that respond are rewarded. With open-source software, there are no rewards for being responsive to the broader market.

Ordinary users tend to want features that developers themselves do not appreciate. The open-source approach disenfranchises those users, saving developers the trouble of dealing with them.

Not surprisingly, open source has proved to be a disappointment in markets where nontechnical users predominate. The attempt by Netscape to switch to an open-source web browser was a conspicuous and predictable disaster. People who need web browsers include some of the newest and least sophisticated computer users. They have no voice in an open-source project.

In the right context, open source is a viable model for software development. It works best in cases where the significant users are themselves highly proficient technically. In those instances, the open-source model does indeed lead to robust, useful software.

However, too many entrepreneurs and software developers find the open-source model appealing for the wrong reason and in an inappropriate context. They are attracted to any concept that allows them to ignore feedback from the broad spectrum of potential users. They try to apply the open-source model in a situation where nontechnical consumers need to use the software. In that context, the open-source process leads you to pay attention only to the users who have the highest technical prowess themselves. You fail to learn the needs of the broader market.

Feedback from ordinary customers can challenge your preconceptions. It can undermine your model of reality. Software developers need that input.

The myth is that brilliant engineers develop great products in a vacuum. The reality is that product development is an iterative process, in which you revise your offering based on feedback from customers. The selling process is critical for gathering information that you can use to refine your product or service.

Selling by Learning

Viewing selling as a learning process is helpful in more than just product development. It also enables you to sell more effectively. In other words, trying to feed your mind will lead to better results in feeding your mouth.

In my opinion, the best book ever written on selling is an unpublished manuscript authored by Michael O'Horo. Until he gets around to finding a publisher, the best place to obtain O'Horo's wisdom is at his web site, www.salesresults.com. Meanwhile, although not as plainspoken as O'Horo, Robert Miller and Stephen Heiman adopt a similar outlook in their classic book, *Strategic Selling*.

The conventional view of sales calls is that they are presentations. You march into the prospect's conference room, crisply deliver your PowerPoint slides, and march out. Supposedly, you capture a sale, although often you fail to do so.

The standard sales presentation represents an attempt to give an answer before you know the question. It is a seller's monologue, which puts the potential buyer in a position of indifference or resistance. O'Horo says bluntly: "Presentations don't make sales. They prevent sales."

O'Horo says that sales presentations are "me-centered." They focus on the seller rather than on the needs of the buyer. In addition, sales presentations tend to be "too broad and too long." Not knowing exactly what is important to the buyer, you tend to try to cover every possible benefit of your products or services and to anticipate every possible objection.

Instead of treating a sales call as an obligation to make a presentation, O'Horo recommends using it as an opportunity to learn. To focus your learning, he has a list of questions to which you should seek answers.

Twelve Questions for Client or Prospect Calls

1. What problem needs to be solved, or what opportunity does the client wish to exploit?
2. How important or valuable is the problem or opportunity in the client's eyes?
3. What tangible results will the company receive if the problem is solved?
4. What personal/emotional benefits will the client receive?
5. What is the cost of doing nothing? What losses or pain will the client experience if the problem isn't solved?
6. What obstacles will impede us?
7. Within what time, budget or political limitations must we solve the problem?
8. How will our service solve the problem and deliver the promised benefits?
9. Why should the prospective client believe that our solution would work?
10. What does the prospect like about our competition?
11. What prevents this competitor (especially an incumbent) from being the automatic winner?
12. What is the basis for decision among competitors?

(Source: Adapted from www.salesresults.com,
Michael O'Horo. Used by permission.)

O'Horo says that you should probe for what he calls the "action imperative." The prospective customer always has the option of doing nothing. In fact, as a netstrapper, chances are you will find that "Do-nothing" is your most formidable competitor. When you go out and try to sell, you will realize that "Do-nothing" has a market share that turns you green with envy.

The "action imperative" is the factor that will force the customer to make a purchase decision. To take market share away from "Do-nothing," you need to have the customer make the sale. In an ideal sales call, each decisionmaker in the customer's organization will articulate that the problem (or opportunity) must be solved, and solved quickly. In particular, the customer decisionmakers will:

- Identify the problem as one of the top priorities for his or her organization
- State the tangible results that can be achieved by solving the problem
- Identify the personal benefits from solving the problem
- Spell out the cost of doing nothing

When the customer has bought into the seriousness of the problem, you do not have to prove that you have the best solution. If the customer has come to the conclusion that "Do-nothing" is not an attractive option, then any solution is in play. At this point, the mere fact that you are in the room and have some understanding of the problem should be sufficient to earn the sale.

To see the value of the "selling by learning" approach, consider what happens if the conditions for selling are not met. Suppose that you were Swati Agrawal of Firmseek.com (Case No. 11), trying to convince a large accounting firm to use her services to track referrals more carefully.

- If the decisionmakers at the accounting firm do not mind referring clients to companies that do not refer back to them, then they may not view the problem as a priority.
- If the decisionmakers are not sure what they are losing by not tracking referrals more carefully, they may not view the problem as urgent.
- If the decisionmakers achieve internal visibility by working with large, existing clients, then no one may have a personal stake in improving the referral network.
- If the accounting firm has lived with a chaotic referral process for a long time, they may feel that there is no need to move quickly to change it.

If any of these problems arise, you will have difficulty making the sale. You have to find the "action imperative" in order to achieve success.

Typically, a netstrapper is trying to get a customer to take a step forward with technology. For this purpose, it is not necessary, or even helpful, to make a convincing case for your technology per se. The customer does not care about whether you are using the latest technology in the most elegant way. Customers care about whether you are saving them time and money.

To succeed, you need to know a little more about Internet technology than the typical customer, and you need to know a lot more about the customer than the typical Internet geek. A large excess of technical knowledge cannot compensate for a shortfall in customer knowledge.

For example, Trevor Cornwell of Skyjet.com (Case No. 6) needed to convince travel assistants to book charter jets for their bosses by using his service. Although his web site was powered by a fancy, data-driven application, that meant nothing to these customers. What they cared most about was service. When an executive charters a jet, he or she is expecting a certain type of jet at a certain time. By showing that Skyjet.com could meet those expectations consistently, Cornwell was able to convince executives and their travel assistants to use his service.

Selling by learning means that you understand the problems that are motivating the customer. By positioning your product or service as a solution to a pressing problem, you let the customer do most of your selling for you. When customers are comfortable that you understand their business problem, they tend to assume that you are competent technically. Your ability to echo their description of the business problem will tend to convince customers that you are capable of providing an effective solution.

Positioning by Pointing to Your Competitors

Often, netstrappers are in a position of offering a new type of solution to a customer. This is a disadvantage in some respects. If a customer is not already buying a product like yours, why does he or she need it?

One approach to dealing with this challenge is to explain painstakingly to the customer how your innovative solution works. Typically, the customer will not understand what you are talking about.

A better way to deal with an innovative idea is to tone down the novelty aspect. Instead, explain the offering as competing with an expensive, well-known alternative.

For example, Karmen Carr might position her competitive intelligence service as a "sustained McKinsey engagement where you retain your intellectual capital." Many companies respect McKinsey and other consulting firms for their advice on strategic issues. However, sometimes the consulting engagements are viewed as "hit-and-run" exercises. The customer obtains a one-shot analysis of its competitive position, but the long-run benefits of understanding the strategic outlook accrue to the consulting firm.

One trend that is attracting many netstrappers is the application service provider (ASP) model, in which you create a web-based version of software that traditionally used proprietary interfaces. However, if you try to explain to a customer that you are an ASP, they will not understand. Instead, you should try to position your offering relative to a competitor. For example, Leif Johnston (Case No. 12) describes his operations management software as "a poor man's PeopleSoft." Customers who are familiar with PeopleSoft can instantly relate to Johnston's product.

Don Britton (Case No. 8) faces a similar challenge with positioning the computer outsourcing services offered by his Network Alliance enterprise. He might try telling customers that "you hire us to replace your network administrator."

I asked my students in a class at American University in March 2000 to evaluate a start-up called Webversa (www.webversa.com). I thought that the company was fairly promising, and indeed in September 2000, it secured funding from sources that included the prestigious Capital Investors Group. However, my students did not understand the point of the company's product, which converts text to voice and voice to text.

My students correctly pointed to a problem with Webversa's positioning. It is positioned as a technology solution, but in the absence of a compelling application, it is difficult to understand why someone would use it. To address this problem, the students came up with the idea that Webversa's capability could enable you to listen to the Web on a mobile phone while driving in your car. Thus, it could be positioned as competing with a radio station.

Instead, Webversa was positioning itself (as of October 2000) as enabling you to connect to "enterprise information" using "any phone." To me, this is still vague and generic, and it still fails to identify any compelling application. My guess is that the trick to getting companies and individuals to adopt phones that access the Web will be to position those devices as competing against something that people already use, rather than positioning them as pure novelty gadgets.

When you are positioning a new product, do not tell your customers that it is unique or that you have no competitors. Instead, tell them that it competes with a well-known, successful product or service. It might be something that they already buy. Even better is a competing offering that they wish they could buy but cannot afford. Once potential customers can use their knowledge of a competing product or service to grasp your idea, then you can proceed to tell them how your offering will provide more benefits at less cost.

Intermediaries Are Bad Luck

Professor Bhide found that most successful entrepreneurs made sales themselves, rather than going through intermediaries. That is consistent with our experience with Homefair. We found that intermediaries were bad luck.

For example, one of our revenue models was to license our relocation tools to newspaper web sites, which could use them to supplement their classified advertising sections. We had relatively good success in selling this product by making "cold calls" to newspapers with on-line versions.

At one point, however, we were introduced to one of the major syndication services. Newspapers receive some of their content, such as comics, from syndicates. One of the syndication services wanted to branch into the on-line content area and expressed a willingness to sell our relocation tools for us. The syndicate asked for an exclusive deal, and we agreed to that, figuring that the syndicate had more contacts, experience, and credibility with newspapers than we did.

The syndication service was a disaster. Its sales rate was much worse than ours had been. Fortunately, we had a clause in our contract that allowed us to cancel the agreement based on the syndicate's failure to reach a minimum target. When we resumed selling ourselves, we began to bring in much more revenue from this product.

Another revenue model for us was selling our relocation tools to moving companies that had their own web sites. Many of these web sites were being built by one of the large marketing agencies that also handled the Yellow Pages advertising for many movers. We tried to use the marketing agency as an intermediary. We allowed the agency to include our relocation tools as optional upgrades to the web sites that it was building for moving companies. Once again, we were disappointed in the results.

We thought that we handled the relationships with the intermediaries reasonably well. We gave them large commissions as incentives. We educated their sales force about the tactics that we had used with success. However, we did not have good luck trying to increase our sales leverage by using intermediaries.

Rob Main's Electric Press (Case No. 4) was another company that provided some of its services through intermediaries, with mixed results. Other companies won consulting contracts with the government, and they subcontracted to Electric Press. However, not being the direct contractor meant that the revenue opportunities for Electric Press were limited.

Advertising networks, mentioned earlier in this chapter, are another example of intermediaries that tend to be disappointing. If you sell sponsorships on your own web site, then your knowledge of that site can enable you to be creative in designing programs that work better for your advertisers than straight banner ads. On the other hand, if you turn the selling process over to an ad network, it will not exercise any creativity, and the commission will further reduce your revenue. As Dirk Reinshagen found out with JointPlanning.com, an ad network will not provide sufficient revenue to make a web site truly successful.

Endorsements and Public Relations Can Be Good Luck

Many companies pitch Internet-based products to small and medium-sized businesses. Often, the potential customer does not feel qualified to evaluate the offering. This can make the potential customer quite hesitant to make a purchase.

One way to overcome this hesitancy is with endorsements. For example, at Homefair, we were selling advertising to local moving companies. However, first we obtained endorsements from major van lines such as Bekins and Mayflower. Local moving companies typically operate as affiliates or franchises of the major van lines. The endorsement of the van lines gave us a lot of credibility with the individual moving companies.

Many of the other businesses with which we dealt were organized in an affiliate or franchise relationship. Real estate agents were affiliated with major companies, such as Prudential. Local executive recruiting firms were franchises of national firms, such as Management Recruiters International (MRI). Obtaining endorsements from the national headquarters helped us in selling to the individual affiliates and franchises.

Sometimes, franchises and affiliates are not on good terms with the national headquarters. Rich Ganley found this out the hard way when he first tried to market FAS-Hotline services to the franchises of Dunhill Professional Search. Dunhill's franchises ignored the endorsement of their parent organization. In contrast, when MRI endorsed Ganley's service, the franchises responded.

There are situations where a major franchise owner may be more influential than the corporate headquarters. In other situations, a major industry consultant or trade association executive may have strong influence. It pays to try to figure out whose endorsement would be valuable for your product.

Favorable articles in the press are very helpful. For example, Brandon White saw a large and sustained increase in traffic to his WorldwideAngler.com fishing site after it was described in a popular regional magazine. Rob Main's Electric Press benefited from an article in *Forbes*. Raj Khera is another netstrapper who says that press releases and coverage were helpful in drawing traffic to his GovCon.com site for government contractors.

Press attention is important enough for netstrappers that I believe it pays to have a good public relations firm. Homefair did not spend a penny on advertising in our early years. However, in my first year, my largest single expenditure other than for web-hosting and development was for a public relations firm. I obtained the services of the leading firm in the mortgage industry, and that firm helped me to get stories in all of the major trade publications.

I also wrote an article myself for *Mortgage Banker*, the publication of the major trade association in the mortgage industry. The article had to speak generally to the topic of mortgage lenders and the Internet, with only a coy mention of Homefair. However, one could be certain that it would have a broad readership.

For a small start-up, these articles in the trade press are quite valuable. They help to establish the credibility of your company, and they are useful items to include in any marketing brochure.

Selling to Small Proprietors

Small proprietors can be difficult customers to win over. Typically, they are struggling with low profit margins, have difficulty keeping up with new technology, and are suspicious of what you are trying to sell. These same characteristics, however, make small proprietors valuable to have as customers. Once you have their business, their inertia will be your ally in keeping out competition.

Once, a young marketing executive for a start-up handed me a draft of a marketing presentation. The slides included words like "revolution" and "completely transform the industry" in large capital letters. It was filled with business-school jargon, such as "first-mover advantage."

The presentation was intended for the owners of small manufacturing companies. I pictured the typical owner as:

- Male
- In his late fifties
- Without a lot of formal education
- Making decisions on the basis of experience and instinct
- Hoping to be able to hang onto his old way of business until retirement

My guess is that nothing could have turned these potential customers off more than an inexperienced MBA coming in to talk about "first-mover advantage" and total industry transformation. Instead, what small proprietors need to hear are phrases like:

- "works with your existing way of doing business"
- "exclusive benefits for you"
- "free trial offer"

Small proprietors are very reluctant to adapt their business processes to new technology.

- Trevor Cornwell (Case No. 6) found that one of the biggest challenges with implementing his Skyjet.com reservation system for charter jets was that the owners of the charter fleets lacked the know-how and inclination to update a database with information about aircraft availability.
- At Homefair, we found that providing leads to real estate companies and moving companies by fax allowed us to reach many more customers than if we had only offered leads to firms that used e-mail.

- Bernard Brookes found that it was easier to get mental health professionals to adopt a claims-processing system if he set up the system to scan in faxed forms instead of requiring the providers' offices to enter the information using the Web.

Small proprietors are not interested in hearing stories about revolutions and change. As a netstrapper, you may believe that the Internet is revolutionary and that your service can change the world, but you need to tone down your act with small proprietors. They would like to maintain their existing business practices and systems for as long as possible. You want to position your product or service to meet their needs.

Small proprietors are looking for competitive advantage rather than for a level playing field. One of the most attractive features of our real estate advertising was that we offered real estate agents exclusive advertising rights for their city on our Salary Calculator.

Small proprietors are not ready to incur financial risks on unproven products. Neil Rosen of TheSchoolReport.com liked to sign up real estate agents for a $1 introductory offer. He would obtain their credit card number to charge them a dollar and then automatically renew their advertising subscriptions. Usually, by the time the agent realized that he or she was paying $25 a month for each county in which he or she advertised, that agent had received enough leads to become convinced of the value of the service.

Selling to the Dilbert Sector

Large organizations use a bureaucratic decisionmaking process. This makes the cost of sale very high. As Swati Agrawal of Firmseek.com (Case No. 11) discovered, with a large firm it is as time consuming to obtain approval for a free trial offer as it is to make a sale. Once Agrawal made that realization, she concluded that she might as well charge large firms right away for her referral generation and tracking services, without any trial period.

Indeed, the most common mistake that entrepreneurs make in dealing with the Dilbert sector is not charging enough for their products or services. Derek Scruggs (Case No. 10) of Distributed Bits made that mistake with his e-mail marketing system by charging a subsidy price to a Dilbert-sector customer, hoping to recoup his costs on later customers.

There are many reasons to charge high prices, including these:

- Large organizations tend to have large budgets. You need the money, and they have it. If you do not charge high prices to your large customers, chances are you will have to go to investors for money. In the end, that just gives you more mouths to feed. Instead, if you charge your large customers enough to fund the business, you have fewer mouths and more food.
- The cost of sale to large organizations tends to be high. Often, there are many people within a large organization who have the power to veto a sale. The time and energy you will spend on the sales process is long, and you need to be compensated for it. As one netstrapper put it (wishing to remain anonymous): "I have to charge them a ridiculous amount of money. It's their fault."
- A bigger monetary commitment will lead to a stronger organizational commitment. One of my first customers at Homefair was Norwest Mortgage, which at that time was the second-largest mortgage lender in the country. The unit that signed up with Homefair was overwhelmed by the volume of leads that we provided, and they shut down our relationship. Had I been paid $500,000 instead of $5,000, my guess is that Norwest would have found the staff to process the leads, rather than letting the project slide. I believe that my chances of retaining Norwest as a customer would have been higher if I had charged more money.
- You want to provide enhancements without getting into nickel-and-dime pricing. That is, you want to build in enough of a cushion in the up-front fee and ongoing maintenance fees to deal with contingencies. When the customer asks for enhancements that are a little beyond expectations, the last thing you want to do is go through another trip through the corporate bureaucracy to get approval to pay for an upgrade. Instead, you are going to want to do what it takes to satisfy the customer and eat the cost. That cost is easier to swallow if you have built an allowance for it into your initial price.

Michael O'Horo and I share a view that one of the most dangerous beasts in the jungle is a Dilbert-sector company that is "interested" in what you have to offer. For a struggling start-up, "interest" in your product is a cost driver, not a revenue driver. It means endless meetings and presentations.

I saw this from inside the Dilbert sector when I worked at Freddie Mac. Small companies constantly came in to see us with ideas for products and services. The more interesting the offering, the worse off they were. Once we became interested, we would invite them back for larger and larger meetings, with more and more participants. Soon, it would become impossible to gain a consensus for a decision, unless the decision was to build a similar capability internally at Freddie Mac.

One example of a company that got shafted by the Freddie Mac decisionmaking process was Engineered Business Systems, a small Florida software company that built systems to support mortgage underwriting and credit-report processing. I brought the company to the attention of a committee that was reviewing companies to support our forthcoming automated underwriting system. The committee made their representatives fly up to Freddie Mac several times for meetings. They were given a request for proposal (RFP) to which they had to respond. The RFP included over ten pages of questions from our systems division, our underwriting division, our legal division, and other stakeholders.

Ultimately, several firms responded to the RFP, and the committee forwarded two finalists to senior management for consideration. Engineered Business Systems was one of the choices. However, when senior management made a decision, they ignored the committee's recommendations and instead picked one of the large systems integration companies. That company had no relevant experience, had not responded to the RFP, and had not been evaluated by the committee. But it got the contract, and Engineered Business Systems, which had spent tens of thousands of dollars on the application process, got nothing.

As a start-up, you cannot afford to be at the mercy of a Dilbert-sector organization's decisionmaking process. Such organizations place a high value on research, and they will gladly accept free assistance from you. However, once they need to make a purchase, a completely different set of considerations may take over.

Many netstrapping firms, such as Scott McLoughlin's web-development firm, the Adrenaline Group (Case No. 2), simply refuse to participate in any process that involves an RFP. The Adrenaline Group uses a tactic that I like to call "charging the customer for your sales presentation." With a Dilbert-sector customer, the Adrenaline Group charges for an initial consultation, which the company calls "product planning."

The core of the Adrenaline Group's service is application development for products and services delivered over the Internet. However, many Dilbert-sector companies approach developers with only a vague or misguided idea for the product. This can require many preliminary meetings to define the product, after which the Dilbert-sector company might put the product requirements up for bid to anyone. Rather than write these preliminary meetings off as sales costs, the Adrenaline Group charges for them as a "product planning engagement."

One start-up with which I became acquainted was considering developing electronic commerce tools for a particular type of Dilbert-sector company. I suggested that in their initial sales call to a company, they should propose to undertake a "readiness assessment" for the customer. This "readiness assessment" would identify the gaps in the customer's business processes and technology that would need to be remedied in order for the company to be able to engage in electronic commerce successfully. The advantages of this "readiness assessment" include:

- Dilbert-sector companies value research and analysis. A "readiness assessment" satisfies this desire.
- The "readiness assessment" can be used as a basis for showcasing the advantages of the tools being offered by the start-up. It is a way of getting your customer to pay you for your sales pitch.
- The "readiness assessment" gives the start-up an opportunity to learn about the customer from the inside. This will help the start-up to fine-tune its product and its sales pitch.

The "assessment" strategy has broad applicability. In the previous chapter, I suggested that a company that offers web-based competitive intelligence might start out by charging customers for a competitive assessment.

I think you should resist the temptation to offer an "assessment" for free. For one thing, Dilbert-sector organizations can afford to pay. For another, they will probably pay more attention to assessment if they pay for it than if they obtain it for no charge.

The "assessment" tactic represents the ultimate application of the strategy of learning by selling. By contracting to do an initial assessment, you enable yourself to be paid to learn. In turn, what you learn can help you sell more and get paid more.

Case No. 10: Derek Scruggs

Derek Scruggs quit his job in January 1996 in order to launch Distributed Bits, LLC. As he recalls, "I expected to get funding by February, and otherwise I was planning to go back to my job" working for a small systems integrator located in the Chicago area. Of course, his self-imposed deadline came and went, and he had neither obtained funding nor returned to his old job.

Scruggs's original expectation that he could obtain funding in less than two months reflected a severe case of pioneer time. He took it hard that it required six months to raise money, even though by most standards this was quite fast. In July, some friends who were traders on the Chicago Board Options Exchange (CBOE) put up $50,000, with another $250,000 promised if he made sufficient progress.

Scruggs started with a very flexible view of his business. He had come away from an Internet immersion period that began on Thanksgiving weekend of 1995 with a conviction that the Internet and Java offered exciting opportunities. He drew inspiration from Hewlett-Packard and Motorola, successful companies he regards as having started out with no specific product in mind. In that spirit, Scruggs said to himself, "I don't care what it is. I just want to start something."

His original idea was to create a development tool for Java programmers. Java™ is a flexible programming language, but it can be intimidating for those of us who lack strong programming backgrounds. The tool that Scruggs had in mind would enable a less experienced programmer to "drag and drop" Java applets (small programs) into web pages.

In October 1996, the development team that Scruggs had assembled had not yet finished the tool for Java developers, but it was far enough along that Scruggs was able to provide a demo to his angel investors from the CBOE, who brought along the CBOE's web team to evaluate the product from the perspective of a potential customer. The web team was not sold on the tool, but they were very impressed by one of the sample applets that Scruggs's company had developed to illustrate their product. This was a Java chat applet.

It turned out that the CBOE web team was interested in chat because they were finding that e-mail from their site was cumbersome. Even though the web site was fairly new and traffic was only starting to build, they were fielding over 100 e-mail inquiries a day. This was causing havoc internally. There were no systems in place for routing the mail, tracking responses, and monitoring the response process. There was no way of knowing whether an e-mail had been routed to the correct person for an answer, whether it had been answered by multiple people, or whether it had been answered at all.

It occurred to Scruggs that other companies generating inbound e-mail from their web sites were likely to encounter the same issue. He thought to himself, "If CBOE is getting 100 e-mails a day, what is Yahoo! getting?"

As a result of the meeting with CBOE, Scruggs made a decision to refocus. His company abandoned the Java development tool and instead built a system to handle incoming e-mail. The system assigns e-mail to buckets, routes the buckets to the appropriate people, and tracks and monitors responses.

Two months later, Scruggs had a contract from the CBOE to develop the e-mail management system. He charged them $35,000, which he admitted was far less than the cost of development, because he expected to be able to sell the system to many other companies.

The next eighteen months produced several challenges. Product development proceeded slowly, because Distributed Bits chose to use Java rather than a more mature language such as Visual Basic. ("That was a fatal mistake," Scruggs now says.) Sales proved to be more difficult than expected, because companies were slow to recognize that they needed e-mail management capability. Competing products started to appear, from companies backed by venture capitalists. Meanwhile, Scruggs's angel investors doled out money only sparingly, making it difficult for Distributed Bits to establish a high profile and limiting Scruggs's ability to plan more than thirty days at a time. His financial worries kept him focused on the short term, like a fugitive trying to stay one step ahead of the law.

By this point, Scruggs's angel funding was starting to be a source of weakness. Up until that point, it had been a blessing. Had he obtained venture funding early, his backers would probably have insisted that he stick to his plans for a Java development tool, even after he saw that e-mail management systems were a better opportunity. His angel investors were more flexible. However, as the market matured and grew more competitive, venture-backed firms began to gain an advantage.

In the fall of 1998, relief came in the form of a strategic investment from First Virtual Holdings, which has since been renamed Message-Media. In a transaction valued at over $6 million, MessageMedia bought Distributed Bits. MessageMedia offers outbound e-mail marketing systems, for which an inbound e-mail management system provides a useful complement. Today, many companies recognize the strategic importance of e-mail marketing, and MessageMedia finds itself in a market that is so hot that it boasts its own three-letter acronym, CRM (customer relationship management).

Case No. 11: Swati Agrawal

Despite my dismissal of business plans that rely heavily on network economies, there are some concepts that fit that mold. That is, if there are only a few participants, the business has little value to its customer and supplier base. However, once critical mass is reached, the value becomes very high. These types of businesses are difficult to bootstrap, because they require an investment in acquiring a participant base.

Swati Agrawal, cofounder and CEO of Firmseek.com, launched an enterprise in which there are network economies. Her company is attempting to create an on-line marketplace and referral network for companies in the fields of law, lobbying, consulting, accounting, finance, and public relations.

Agrawal left her position with a large law firm in the spring of 1999, and she joined with another attorney, Janice Usaki, and a software engineer, Miguel Cruz, to form Firmseek.com. Although another partner joined them initially, he left in July 2000, a few months after the site was launched. This was handled straightforwardly, with the resigning partner keeping only those shares in the company that had vested. However, these "early divorces" always take an emotional toll.

Today, when a company, particularly a start-up, needs accounting or legal services, the process of finding them can be time consuming and error prone. After I interviewed Agrawal, I met with a start-up founder who mentioned that his next appointment was with an accountant—and he had already interviewed two others. When I started Homefair, I was totally clueless about how to find an accountant or an attorney. I fired my first attorney in less than two weeks, because he was taking too many days to return my phone calls.

Agrawal herself was disappointed that when she wanted to file for a patent, the first law firm she contacted agreed to do the work but then said it wouldn't be possible to start on it for another month. She points out that had her service been operating, it would have enabled her to specify faster turnaround as a criterion to include in a request for proposal.

For the customer of these business services, Firmseek.com offers a way to specify requirements and preferences. The site enables you to convey your proposal to a list of companies that meet your criteria.

For service providers, Firmseek.com provides a mechanism to obtain clients and track referrals. In the business services market, referrals are an important source of business. For example, an attorney may recommend a public relations firm. However, no one tracks these referrals. Your company may be referring clients to an accounting firm that in turn refers all of its clients to your competitor!

Eventually, Firmseek.com expects to collect listing fees from service providers. In exchange for these annual fees, firms will be allowed to participate with the site and use its tools for referral tracking and locating RFPs from public entities (these are obtained by Firmseek.com from government web sites, using an automated search tool). However, until volume picks up, it is difficult to charge for participation. Firmseek.com offered free trials to its earliest customers, and only in July 2000, a few weeks before our interview, was Agrawal starting to charge service providers.

Agrawal found the process of getting firms to agree to a free trial to more difficult than expected, particularly with large firms. "It was taking as much time to get agreement as it would have to make a sale," she says ruefully. In part because of this insight, Agrawal and her colleagues decided to accelerate their plans for charging firms.

I think that start-ups frequently learn the lesson that the sales process with large companies is expensive because of the bureaucracy. That tendency, combined with the fact that the large company is cash rich and the start-up is cash poor, argues for having the start-up company try to obtain revenue as early in the process as possible.

Because Firmseek.com has the chicken-and-egg problem of requiring a large base of service providers to be valuable to buyers and a large base of buyers to be valuable to service providers, it might be a natural candidate for venture capital financing. However, Agrawal had found venture capitalists skittish. They have been seeing a large number of business-to-business marketplace concepts, and at this point venture capitalists only are interested in those that have proprietary tools.

One subtle differentiator for Firmseek.com is its focus on referral tracking. This can be as challenging to explain to service providers as it is to venture capitalists. It combines marketing with information technology. It cannot be described in terms of anything that service providers currently buy.

I asked Agrawal whether she had been able to come up with a way to position the referral-tracking feature in relation to some existing marketing avenue or software. She gave the charming entrepreneur's answer: "No, but it's a great idea. You've really got me thinking . . ."

Case No. 12: Leif Johnston

Leif Johnston was an early employee of Proxicom, which now is a prominent web-development consulting firm. He joined the company in November 1995. Interestingly, Proxicom itself began as a product company, but it migrated toward consulting, in response to the strength of demand in the market. In those days, you might think you had an application for, say, web-based chat rooms, but the people with money to spend could never "get" the point of your "cool tool." Consulting, on the other hand, everybody understands. As a business person, you go where the revenues lead you. In particular, Proxicom charted an "up-market" course, correctly judging that the biggest profit opportunity in web consulting would be working for Fortune 500 companies.

In 1997, between the shift in business model toward consulting and the rapid growth that the company enjoyed, Proxicom was caught with inadequate internal management and controls. In Johnston's terms, it was "hit or miss" whether a project would succeed (another former employee of that era confirms this assessment). Amid the chaos, projects would sometimes fail to be delivered. In other cases, the schedule and requirements would be met, but the cost of the project would far exceed Proxicom's fixed-price bid, resulting in a loss.

Johnston was assigned to develop systems to address Proxicom's internal management processes. He designed a web-based solution that enabled Proxicom to bring its business back under control.

As Johnston was helping Proxicom improve its operational management, it occurred to him that other companies must face similar problems. He began to think in terms of a generic solution, and he negotiated with Proxicom to leave the company to pursue this idea as a product.

From the very beginning of his new enterprise, ResourceCompany.com, Johnston used consulting as a revenue source. Although he left Proxicom in March 1998, he worked for the company as a consultant until July 1998, while he was starting his own company.

Johnston's main product, called Ops Manager, is designed for small consulting-type companies that charge based primarily on labor time and are mobile and geographically dispersed. The challenge for these companies is that with a lot of work done outside a central office, important administrative functions such as project management, time and expense reporting, and human resource management become difficult to coordinate. Things start to slip through the cracks in these areas, thereby crippling the ability of the COO to stay on top of the company.

To address this problem, Ops Manager offers a web-based solution for controlling business operations. Functions that you would perform on a desktop in a central office are instead provided by Ops Manager on a web server, from which they can be accessed by any computer with an Internet connection and a browser.

However, this description often fails to convey to managers what the software does. It's a lot easier to get a handle on it when Johnston calls it "a poor man's PeopleSoft." This is a classic illustration of the tactic of positioning your product by relating it to a well-known competitor.

Your tendency will be to spend hours trying to explain the unique features of your product or service and why they would be so valuable to your customer. But the customer just never seems to get it. Instead of trying more elaborate explanations, it is easier to point to an existing product that is well established and describe your product as doing the same thing, but more effectively for this market niche. Using this tactic, you get into the customer's head right away.

For Johnston, doing consulting at the same time he was developing the product was helpful in a few ways:

- It enabled him to maintain momentum, even without funding (he received a minimal $20,000 angel investment at the start).
- It enabled him to stay close to the market. He picked up new ideas while solving customers' problems.

Obviously, the time Johnston spent consulting was time that he could have spent developing the product. Version 1.0 was released in the spring of 1999, and if Johnston had been able to focus on it full-time, he probably could have had it ready several months sooner.

In fact, however, an earlier introduction might have met with frustration. It would have been difficult to sell the product on a site-license basis, because the size of the up-front fee would trigger difficult approval processes at most companies. Recently, the market has begun to accept a "leased application" concept, whereby buyers pay a monthly fee to use a web-based application rather than paying a fixed license fee. Johnston's offering is ideally suited to this model. He has gotten a fair amount of marketing mileage out of the fact that some of his corporate partners, including Microsoft, have featured his software as showing the practical implementation of concepts that are in their strategic vision.

One problem that Johnston probably did not anticipate was the effect that consulting would have on his exit strategy. If the perfect crime requires a clean getaway, then mixing consulting with product development is not the way to commit the perfect crime. Johnston plans to sell ResourceCompany.com to a strategic investor. However, potential buyers do not know how to evaluate the company. His financial statements include revenue from product sales, revenue from consulting to customize the product for particular companies, and revenue from consulting unrelated to the product.

In my view, for a product company, consulting is beneficial only to the extent that it enables you to improve your product. A consulting engagement is helpful if it does one or more of the following:

- Helps you understand better the customer's needs relative to your product

- Helps you assess the strengths and weaknesses of competing products
- Increases your knowledge of business terminology in your key target market
- Helps you to understand work flow in your key target market
- Gives you insight into customers' priorities for features of your product

The consulting engagements to avoid are those that are distractions. A distraction means that you do not learn anything that helps you to hone your product. Johnston, a self-described "problem solver" and "idea person," took on too many projects that were intrinsically interesting. He found himself stimulated to develop a business idea to solve generically the problem he encountered in a consulting engagement. Thus, he lost time not only in consulting itself but in trying these new business ideas as well.

The moral is that you need to be able to resist distractions if you are going to try the approach of using consulting revenues to support a product-company start-up. If you are the type who can become fascinated by any interesting new problem that comes along, then consulting can be dangerous to your company's health.

One reason that Johnston's consulting engagements were not complementary to the product is that his philosophy was to not talk about a software product until it was nearly complete. He was adamant against selling vaporware.

I asked him, "By not talking about the product to customers, didn't you take a big risk that you would misconfigure the product?" He laughed and said that indeed he had gotten burned, particularly with the second release of his product, which flopped because it was too feature-rich and complex for the users. Too late, he realized that rather than load the product with features, he would have been better off selling a plain generic product and charging for customization.

When you have a software product that targets the small-business market, you have to be particularly careful about the specialized needs of different customers. It may seem to you that a solution to every minor business problem is within your grasp. However, you often underestimate the degree to which seemingly small enhancements affect the complexity of your software. You think that adding just a few lines of code does not cost a lot, but in the long run it turns out to be very expensive.

Case No. 13: Brian Lloyd

Not everyone who becomes an entrepreneur does so by making a specific choice. For some people, the process is gradual and almost accidental.

Brian Lloyd started his journey to becoming a netstrapper in the 1970s. He was a programmer working for the Public Broadcasting System, and he hacked into the ARPANET, the predecessor to the Internet funded by the U.S. Department of Defense. "If you knew the phone number, you could get on the network," Lloyd says.

Eventually, military security was upgraded, and Lloyd was disconnected. In 1982, he conceived the idea of a communications server that would allow individuals to dial in and connect to the Net. However, he had no idea how to go about obtaining backing to create what we now would call an Internet service provider (ISP).

In October 1989, Lloyd left the Washington, D.C., area for San Jose, California, in order to increase his chances of making contacts with entrepreneurs in the data communications arena. He hooked up with Telebit in Sunnyvale and helped them to develop the first commercial server that would allow individuals to connect to the Net.

Lloyd only started his own company because he was forced to do so. Late in 1991, he talked to people at BARRnet, one of the first Internet hubs. Because they were bound by the Stanford University pay scale, they could not bring Lloyd on staff at an appropriate salary, so he formed Lloyd Internetworking and provided services to BARRnet as a consultant.

At one point, in 1992, having written a guide for the California Department of Education explaining how to connect to the Internet, Lloyd was contacted by representatives of a high school, who asked him for a connection. He provided them with a connection to BARRnet by way of his house. Soon, a local computer club heard about this connection, and its members started calling and asking for Internet connections. "Poof! Now I'm an ISP," Lloyd recalls.

By 1996, Lloyd Internetworking had eleven employees and three business models. It was a small ISP, a consulting firm and a networking troubleshooter for several high-end clients, and a developer of

PPP and TCP/IP embedded software. "We did whatever we needed to do to bring money in the door," Lloyd says, "but we didn't have the resources to keep doing all three things, so the partners decided that it was time to sell off the ISP part of the business."

At this point, Lloyd decided that it might be a good time to be acquired. He made a pitch to Livingston Enterprises, a leading manufacturer of servers for ISPs, that his consulting and services expertise was a good fit. In fifteen minutes, they had a deal. Lloyd Internetworking divested itself of the ISP business and sold its consulting unit to Livingston. Eventually, Livingston was sold to Lucent, so that Lloyd wound up with what he describes as "nearly enough Lucent stock to retire. I mean, you could retire on what I have, but maybe not quite in the style to which I wish to become accustomed."

As a potential entrepreneur, you have many opportunities from which to choose. For example, Lloyd could have pursued software development or consulting, or he might have made a strong push to build up his ISP. He had the sense to realize that the consulting business offered a route to wealth without the risks and management headaches associated with the other paths.

Often, I see people try to launch businesses that are extremely complex, with multiple potential points of failure. They try to attack a market where the customer adoption is a challenge *and* supplier logistics are a challenge *and* the software needs leading-edge functionality. Instead, try to identify a market where there is only one critical challenge and that challenge is a good match for your expertise.

Lloyd also recommends making an early effort to line up customers. This helps to ensure cash flow. Moreover, the attempt to obtain customers is a good test of the quality of your offering. As Lloyd puts it, "If you can't line up any customers up-front, maybe you don't have a viable business model."

SIX

Designing and Promoting Your Web Site

As a netstrapper, the design of your web site can make or break your company. It is easy to go wrong. Many web sites belonging to famous corporations are terrible examples from a design perspective. Most web-design consultants are dangerously misguided in their thinking. A few years ago, there was a best-selling book on "designing killer web sites" that might have better been titled "designing suicide web sites."

I wish that I could point you to Homefair as an example of the kind of web design that I recommend. However, now that we have sold the site, the design has evolved away from what I regard as best practices.

One web-design consultant whose views I respect is Jakob Nielsen, author of *Designing Web Usability*. If anything, Nielsen is even more frustrated than I am over the poor design of most web sites. For example, in May 1996, he wrote an article called "The Top 10 Mistakes in Web Design." Three years later, he updated the article and found that those mistakes still persisted. See Nielsen's web site at www.useit.com.

Nielsen is very pragmatic in his views of web design. He is not applying arbitrary aesthetic judgments. Instead, he looks at the site's effectiveness. For example, in his article at www.useit.com/alertbox/990516.html, called "Who Commits the 'Top 10 Mistakes' of

Web Design," he points out that none of the ten most popular web sites uses frames. (Frames allow a web designer to create a split screen on a page. As a designer, you can find many uses for frames. As a web surfer, you almost always dislike them.) Any site can choose to use frames (and many do), but if the ten sites with the most web traffic do not use them, that certainly should give one pause.

Probably the first step in developing a flair for web design is to become a regular web user. The more experience you have with the frustrations of poorly designed sites and the pleasure of usable sites, the better your design instincts will be.

To gain the type of experience you need, conduct an exercise with a specific purpose. Try to find the answer to a question, or try to purchase a particular type of product. Monitor your behavior as you conduct these exercises. Most people find that they lose patience with sites that are slow to download or present confusing interfaces, regardless of how attractive the sites might be from an artistic perspective.

Successful web-site design requires that you do the role reversal. A good web site is designed from the perspective of the visitor.

The Key to a Good Web Design

Almost all consumers who arrive at your web site do so by choice, with a particular purpose or expectation in mind. The typical consumer arrives with two questions paramount:

1. Can I find what I am looking for here?
2. Can I trust what I find here?

The key to a good web design is to provide visitors with encouraging answers to those two questions as quickly as possible. Most consumers give you less than a minute to indicate a positive answer to those questions. They give you less than five minutes to validate an initial positive indication.

These simple facts have many implications, which will be spelled out below:

1. Avoid "splash" pages or pages with large amounts of graphics
2. Do not force users to register for your site
3. Assume that your visitors will scan your pages

4. Include a call to action
5. Create an e-mail newsletter
6. Use standard navigation schemes
7. Label navigation links in a consumer-friendly way
8. Include a search box on your pages
9. Use outside links to fill "holes" in your content
10. Minimize the steps needed to use your site
11. Encourage consumer feedback and give personal, prompt responses
12. Articulate a clear, compelling promise to consumers
13. Include a complete description of your company and its people

1. Avoid "Splash" Pages or Pages with Large Amounts of Graphics

For some reason, there are designers who like to force consumers to view a fancy graphics page and click on the word "enter" before showing them any information. This means that by the time a consumer actually makes it to your home page, you have lost at least half of the one minute available to you for offering a positive indication that you have what the consumer wants. Splash pages are pure artistic indulgence. They are guaranteed to reduce your web site's traffic and effectiveness.

You want the consumer immediately to begin to grasp the content of your site. A large graphic at the top of the page causes the same problems as a splash page. Some consumers will lose patience waiting for the graphic to download, and those who stay will have lost precious time.

Assuming that you do not use splash pages, you should also be conservative about using graphics on normal pages. Large graphics at the top of the page force your readers to scroll down before they find any of the content they are seeking. Once they scroll down, they may lose sight of navigation information or other important features near the top of the page.

2. Do Not Force Users to Register for Your Site

Some people think that requiring registration will allow them to collect demographic information that makes their site more attractive to advertisers. I am not saying that no one is willing to register to receive content. However, you may lose most of your traffic by requiring registration. At one point, Homefair required consumers to register in order to access our comprehensive reports on cities, including cost of living, tax rates, crime information, and so forth. However, close to 90 percent of the people who visited this part of our site left without registering.

The irony is that you can probably get more registered users from an "opt-in" registration system than you can from forcing people to register. Consumers will register if they trust your site and they can see that you will provide them with benefits from registration. For example, Amazon.com offers tailored recommendations to registered users.

If you owned a brick-and-mortar business, would your policy be to strip-search anyone who tries to walk into your store? Requiring user registration is the on-line equivalent.

3. Assume That Your Visitors Will Scan Your Pages

Think like a direct-mail solicitor when you design your pages. When you receive a solicitation in the mail asking you to contribute to a cause or subscribe to a publication, you do not sit down to read every word carefully. You scan the solicitation to see if it holds any interest. As Nielsen points out, web users also scan rather than read.

A good direct-mail piece uses questions and bullet points that work quickly to motivate you to pay attention. Those same devices are effective on the web. If you use long paragraphs, as in a book or newspaper story, consumers will have difficulty determining whether your site has what they are looking for. Once they lose patience, they will give up and click somewhere else.

Most web pages are too crowded and busy. Web designers appear to be tempted to cram as many graphics, links, and special effects on a page as they possibly can. For the user, going to the home page is like arriving at a baffling intersection, with dozens of signs pointing in every direction, and having no idea whether any particular sign indicates a road, a city, a business, or a traffic rule.

4. Include a Call to Action

Another element of direct-mail solicitation is a "call to action." You are invited to "pledge now" or "return the response card today." A good web page also has a call to action. It could be a link that says to "start here" or a button that says "add this item to your shopping cart."

Joseph Murgio's OnProject.com (Case No. 15), which helps people use the web to collaborate on projects, demonstrates the use of a clear call to action. On the right-hand side of the home page, set off by white space, is the phrase "It's simple—Try it now." The user then sees four simple boxes to fill in, and then the phrase "Be more effective!" next to a button labeled "Enter" to submit the form.

Many web pages have a "call to action" that is not built-in by design. A prominent link may induce people to click, regardless of whether it is the most appropriate place for them to go next. For example, if you put a "search" button at the top of your site, most visitors will start by using that button. If you want them to start by browsing instead, move the search function to a location further down on your page.

Often, your web site is only part of your Internet strategy. Your most effective selling may take place via e-mail. Accordingly, issue a "call to action" to the visitor to send you an e-mail. Mike Covel's Turtletrader.com (Case No. 16), which provides information and software for financial speculators, issues such invitations in many places throughout the site. When you dive into the site and read an article, you are invited to e-mail if you disagree with the article or if you want more information about the topic being discussed.

One of the most pathetic mistakes on a web site is a statement that says "Check back for further updates." What that says to the visitor is: "We have wasted your time by bringing you here without the information you want. Now we invite you to waste more time by coming back and checking to see if we ever get around to providing what you are looking for."

Instead of saying "check back," invite the visitor to send you an e-mail with questions. In the short run, you can respond to the e-mail and create a satisfied customer rather than a disappointed visitor. In the long run, what you learn about customers' needs will help you to flesh out the content on the page.

5. Create an E-mail Newsletter

Consumers are often reluctant to transact with a web site on their first visit. The challenge is to get them to return. Among Internet pundits, "stickiness" refers to the ability of a web site to keep customers on the site and get them to return.

For example, with Homefair, we were aware that the point at which we attracted consumers was when they were just beginning to undertake research about a possible relocation. However, the point at which consumers had value to our sponsors was during and after relocation. How could we keep consumers coming back to our site in the meantime?

The best way to maintain an ongoing relationship with your visitors is with an e-mail newsletter. This is better than having your user "check back" with you for a variety of reasons.

- It is costly and time consuming for consumers to keep checking your web site.
- The consumer's schedule for checking your site may be suboptimal. The consumer may look for something either too early or too late.
- By not having a newsletter, you miss an opportunity to deliver advertisements that consumers are likely to read. Consumers read and respond to advertisements contained in e-mail newsletters much more than they do to banner ads on web pages.

Raj Khera (Case No. 17) of GovCon.com and MoreBusiness.com, two sites for small-business owners, had this to say about e-mail newsletters:

This is by far one of the best things you can do on your web site. It not only helps to drive return traffic, but you can also make money by selling advertising sponsorships within the newsletter. We did this quite successfully with GovCon and now with MoreBusiness.com, generating thousands of extra dollars each month. If you have demographic info on your readership, you can attract even higher rates since you'll be able to deliver a very targeted audience. You can even create two or more sponsorship placements and charge differently for each based on positioning (we charge the most for our top spot and then reduce the rates by 30 percent for the next spot). In fact, one of our Fortune 500 advertisers is using our newsletter to get subscriptions for theirs.

How much money can you make from doing this? Going rates are about $75–$300 per thousand readers and depend largely on your demographics and on the media buyer you're negotiating with.

There are a variety of opinions about newsletters. Some people think that a newsletter with a "tip of the week" is helpful. Personally, I prefer to see newsletters that offer time-sensitive information, such as industry news or announcements of new web-site content.

Another issue concerns the length of a newsletter. Some people are adamant that newsletters should be only one or two paragraphs. I am willing to plow through longer newsletters, although I do agree that once you go beyond a page you create usability challenges.

Yet another issue is whether links to web pages within newsletters are helpful. Some experts say that putting links in e-mail messages is a mistake, in part because not all e-mail software supports them. Personally, I appreciate links in moderation.

If you are finding that you want to provide people with a lot of content or many links, then I recommend a newsletter that combines web and e-mail features. The web version can contain all of the content and links. The e-mail version is short, and it links to the longer web version. The e-mail version contains a summary of what is on the web version.

The biggest pitfall with a newsletter is that readers can get in the habit of filing the newsletter away without reading it. This usually happens because people are deluged with more newsletters than they have time to read. Most newsletter owners publish their newsletters too frequently. My personal view is that an e-mail newsletter that arrives only occasionally but that always has important content will get my attention.

One of my favorite examples of a good e-mail newsletter and companion web site is Hillary Rettig's Technocopia.com. The newsletter arrives relatively infrequently, and when it comes, it contains interesting information about issues related to wiring and gadgetry for the home. The interesting content and infrequent schedule combine to make it irresistible reading.

At the bottom of every e-mail newsletter, explain how to sign up for the newsletter and how to sign off. If the newsletter is forwarded to me, I want to know how to sign on. If I lose interest in the newsletter, I want to know how to sign off.

Never send e-mail to someone who is not expecting the e-mail. Unsolicited e-mail, or spam, is not something with which any reputable business would be associated. You must not buy an e-mail list. You have to build an e-mail list from the bottom up, by soliciting on your web site, at trade shows, or at conferences.

Your web site is not the only tool you have for building a reader-ship base for an e-mail newsletter. Collecting business cards is an-other powerful technique. For example, Neil Rosen of TheSchool-Report.com wanted to obtain a list of real estate agents in order to be able to send them e-mails. He went to a conference of real estate agents and set up a booth. There, he offered to take any real estate agent's photograph, using a digital camera. He promised to e-mail the photos to the agents. They were quite happy to give Rosen their e-mail addresses!

6. Use Standard Navigation Schemes

There are three standard types of navigation schemes:

- Tabs across the top of the page, which are used to show ma-jor categories
- A "navigation bar" down the left-hand side of the page, which is used to list specific features and articles on the site.
- A "portal style" menu, where underneath your content you put a list of links that includes major categories and subcate-gories.

Each navigation scheme has its strengths. Before I left Homefair, we were using all three schemes on every page.

Tabs across the top can help an experienced user of the site navi-gate quickly. For example, if I go to Amazon.com looking for a CD, I can start by clicking on the "music" tab.

Side navigation bars list the main features of the site in a narrow column, usually running down the left-hand side of the screen. The side navigation bar is very helpful for giving the user a sense of con-text. According to Jennifer Fleming, author of *Web Navigation: De-signing the User Experience,* it is important when you are using a site to know "where I am, where I came from, and where I am going." A well-designed side navigation bar can provide this information, par-ticularly if it adjusts as the user moves around the site.

As of the winter of 2000–2001, Swati Agrawal's FirmSeek.com (Case No. 11) was using this approach in each of its main sections. In the "law" section, for example, the user sees subcategories such as "browse firms" and "create RFP," as well as other main categories such as "consulting" and "accounting." If the user switches to a dif-

ferent main category, the menu of subcategories becomes the one relevant to the new main category.

"Portal style" menus allow the user to see deeper into the organization of your site. The classic "portal" menu is Yahoo!, which lists
major categories, such as "Arts and Humanities," along with sample
subcategories, such as "Literature" and "Photography."

As a child, you used to play a game where you told your friend,
"You're getting warmer," as the friend got closer to finding a hidden
object. As long as consumers feel that they are "getting warmer," you
can trust them to stay with your site and click through until they find
what they want. The key is to have a good relationship between what
consumers would expect, based on the way a link is labeled, and what
they actually find behind the link. "Portal style" menus are effective
because they convey the "getting warmer" sensation to the user. If
the category is not self-explanatory to a particular user, the sample
subcategories usually overcome the problem.

Some sites might use all three navigation schemes. Others might
use just one or two. It depends on the complexity of the site and the
variety of your content. Therese Haar's FarmerLink.com (Case No.
14) web site, which helps farmers sell produce directly to consumers,
has tabs at the top as well as a more portal-style set of links in the
lower part of the screen.

7. Label Navigation Links in a Consumer-Friendly Way

When we designed Homefair, we tried to anticipate what the consumer would be looking for. Our major categories were described as
"Buying your First Home," "Obtaining the Best Mortgage,"
"Choosing Where to Live," "Organizing Your Move," and so on.
Try to imagine the questions that a consumer will be asking, and then
present your site in a way that minimizes the effort needed to find
the answers. Avoid vague categories, such as "resources" or "info."

Many sites turn their navigation schemes into guessing games.
They rely on graphical icons that are confusing. Or they take their
site metaphors too seriously. With something called "The Homebuyer's Fair," we could have tried to get cute by calling our main sections "Rides," "Refreshments," and so forth. However, this would
have been of no help to our users.

An example of a scheme that is easy to understand is the side navigation bar on Joseph Murgio's onProject.com. The choices are:

- User login
- Our Services
- Online Demo
- Try it now
- Pricing
- Company
- Partners

I am confident that I can guess what is behind each of those "doors," and I believe that most people would feel the same way.

8. Include a Search Box on Your Pages

Consumers visit search engines so often that many of them have come to expect a search function wherever they go on the Web. I will admit that at Homefair we never featured a search box. Instead, we relied on consumers using our navigation areas. However, this is an item that has become so standard that my guess is that in recent years our failure to include it hurt us with some consumers. Even someone as opinionated as Jakob Nielsen will tell you that if a certain design feature has become standard, your failure to conform can be a usability flaw.

Therese Haar's FarmerLink.com has a search box at the top. Suppose that I come to the site to search for a farm in Gaithersburg, Maryland, where I can buy tomatoes. I can type in "tomatoes Gaithersburg," and a list of relevant farms will come up. Many consumers are used to interacting with web sites in this way.

Have your web team install a search box, and test it to make sure that it works properly with keywords that a typical user might try. However, be careful about featuring your search box too prominently, unless you want consumers to treat the search box as their "call to action."

9. Use Outside Links to Fill "Holes" in Your Content

Not every site can have everything that the consumer expects. For example, at Homefair, consumers expected to see listings of homes. We did not have these, but we did offer a "Find a Home" section with links to other sites. This was a win for us. Consumers who wanted to see listings were going to leave our site anyway. Rather than have them leave feeling angry that we had wasted their time, we wanted them to go away happy that we had helped point them in the right direction. Eventually, we were able to earn revenue from our "Find a Home" feature by selling the most prominent positions on the page to sites that valued our traffic.

Many people cannot stand the thought of "sending traffic away" by providing links to other sites. However, you must realize that you do not have a choice. If your site does not have what the consumer wants, it is a given that the consumer is going to try a different site. If you provide a link that helps consumers find what they need, then you can retain some control and goodwill. If you do not help them, they will leave anyway, and they will be less likely to return to your site.

10. Minimize the Steps Needed to Use Your Site

Some sites have ten-question forms where they put one question on each screen. With all of the mouse-clicks and pauses in the process, most consumers will leave before they finish. Try to minimize the number of screens a consumer must click through in order to accomplish what they want on your site.

For example, when I looked at the iMove.com site in September 2000, I thought that it took too long to get to the point. The opening page was fine, with a well-stated mission ("Take control of your move") and a clear call to action (a link labeled "Start here.") However, once you clicked on "Start here," things became sluggish. First, you were asked whether you were moving within a state or between states. After you clicked on your choice, you came to a page that asked you to choose whether you were shipping household goods or an automobile. Once you clicked on "household goods," you were asked to select either a professional mover or a do-it-yourself move. Once you selected "professional mover," you received a long list of facts and observations about professional moves. Buried at the bottom was a "call to action" to contact a professional mover.

Most users are going to leave the site before they have completed this long and unnecessary sequence. As a designer, you want to make it possible for people to race through the preliminaries and get straight to the point.

11. Encourage Consumer Feedback and
Give Personal, Prompt Responses

As a netstrapper rather than a bureaucratic organization, you have the freedom to engage in honest, personal discussions with the consumers who visit your site. Many corporations take weeks to respond to consumer feedback, and what they send is often useless, sanitized PR-speak. The fact that you are a human being and not a corporate sheep is an advantage—make sure that you use it!

You want to interact with consumers as individuals. When I designed Homefair, our comment form always was one click away. My e-mail address was listed on the comment form, as well as on other pages on the site where people often seemed to have questions.

Unless I was on vacation, I answered every comment within twenty-four hours. Most comments were answered within minutes. There are few things that impress a consumer as much as getting a personal answer back at 10 A.M. on a Sunday morning.

As a web user, I find it very annoying when I leave a comment on another site and get a response weeks later. By the time I get such a response, I have typically forgotten all about the site visit, and I certainly do not bother to refresh my memory.

I responded politely and quickly to negative comments. The nastier the comment, the faster the answer. Occasionally, a management recruiter would lose a placement because the candidate would run the cost-of-living comparisons on our site and decline the offer. Naturally, the recruiters were not too happy when this happened, and they sent the most vicious comments. I would immediately send a response offering to explain the results to them over the phone.

Sometimes I would be overwhelmed with comments on a particular topic, such as a new application on our site that confused many users. These comments were a call to action to provide clearer directions or to change the interface.

User comments gave us a clear indication of what consumers wanted. For example, we received many comments from consumers with questions about school information. This led us to develop a relationship with TheSchoolReport.com. At first we linked to their site and shared revenue, and eventually we merged with the company.

There is a famous Sherlock Holmes story in which a clue is not hearing a dog bark. By reading all consumer comments, I also was able to listen to "the dog that didn't bark." For example, there was a period when pundits were recommending that every site needed to offer a chat area. However, not one consumer comment ever implied an interest in having a chat area on our site. We chose not to jump onto that fad.

I believe that a consumer with whom you have had e-mail contact is much more valuable to you than an ordinary web-site visitor. A consumer who gets a prompt, personal response from a web site feels empowered and satisfied. You gain the trust that is so critical in the Internet medium.

If you are overwhelmed with customer feedback, that is wonderful. If it is negative feedback about your web site or business, then you need to fix what is broken. If you get too many "stupid questions," then you need to feature a "frequently asked questions" page.

Do not fall into the trap of viewing customer feedback as a "cost" or a "problem." Feedback means that consumers are taking ownership of your web site. The more this happens, the more popular your site becomes. Because electronic word of mouth is so important in bringing traffic to your site, my position is that responding to consumer questions or comments is the lowest-cost marketing strategy available to a web site.

12. Articulate a Clear, Compelling Promise to Consumers

Another advantage of being human rather than a corporate sheep is that you can stand for something. A clear mission statement can make this plain to your visitors. For example, the top of Therese Haar's FarmerLink.com home page says, "Connecting the Local Farmer to their Customer."

When I started the Homebuyer's Fair, the home page said, "Our mission is to give you the information you need to help you keep more of your own money when you buy a home." I believe that this is a good example of a simple, authentic, effective mission statement. I felt that I could back up this promise with my knowledge of mortgage finance. I believed that consumers could save thousands of dollars by learning to shop intelligently for mortgages rather than passively accepting the offer of a lender to whom they were referred by a real estate agent.

It is important on a web site to speak with an authentic voice. Consumers want to connect with real human beings, not corporate spokespersons. See *The Cluetrain Manifesto*.

Note that the mission statement speaks to the needs of consumers. We did not say, "Our mission is to be the relocation portal of the Internet." That might be an enticing mission for investors, but it means nothing to consumers.

In our original mission statement, note the double possessive— "your own" money. The idea was to reinforce to consumers that they had something to lose by ignoring the information on our site.

After Homefair was bought by Homestore.com, one of the things that our new corporate owners did was take down the mission statement. As of this writing, the home page greets you with a legalistic warning that use of the site implies agreement with a set of "terms and conditions." Instead of starting with a promise to the consumer, the web site asks you to make a promise to the company.

13. Include a Complete Description of Your Company and Its People

The downside of being a netstrapper instead of a well-known corporation is that you have no brand equity. Internet visitors are properly suspicious about the motivations and qualifications of the people who put up web sites. The way to address this issue is to provide descriptions of your company that are honest, open, and comprehensive.

For articles that I wrote for Homefair, I included my byline, which was linked to a description of my background. People who wondered about my qualifications to provide opinions and analysis could read about my education and experience. This helped them to decide whether or not to believe the articles.

It is standard for a web site to include a link that is labeled "about us" or "about our company." Established enterprises, such as Intel or Dell, do not need this section (although they typically have it), because we know who they are and what they stand for. As a netstrapper, you do not enjoy instant brand recognition, and the consumer is going to arrive at your site with very legitimate questions about whether you can be trusted to be honest and competent.

Whenever I visit a site for the first time, I always spend time in the "about us" section. Sometimes it provides all of the information I want, but often it falls short. Here are the questions to which I expect to find answers:

- What is the history of your site? Who started it, and when? What were the major events in the evolution of your company?
- How do you make money? If this is not explained clearly, then I am going to assume the worst—that you surreptitiously gather personal information and feed it to telephone solicitors.
- Who are the major executives in your company? How does their background give them credibility with me as a consumer?
- How can I get in touch with people at your company? My respect increases when the company's top executives are willing to provide their e-mail addresses in the "about" section. This shows that they are not afraid to let me speak to them directly.
- Who likes your site, and why? Some sites list the awards that they have won, which is okay. I am more impressed by individual comments and testimonials. Quotes from magazine reviews also serve to enhance credibility.

Revising Your Design

Web-site design is something that is never finished. You are always under pressure to improve the site in terms of content, organization, and commercial effectiveness. The only site that is left alone is a site belonging to a company that is brain dead.

However, one thing to be careful about is making revisions unscientifically. When you revise your site design, you should be able to state an objective and measure whether or not that objective was achieved. Your web server will capture valuable information in its "log files" about each page request that comes from a consumer. There are many programs available that will analyze your site's traffic logs.

Moreover, we found traffic analysis so important at Homefair that we built our own logging, tracking, and reporting systems. These enabled us to monitor events that would not be captured by ordinary logs and log-analysis programs. We evaluated changes to our site on the basis of statistical reports.

When you reorganize your site's navigation, you are trying to increase consumer traffic to certain sections. Before you make a change, note the ratio of traffic in the target section to traffic to your site's home page. After the change, see how this ratio is affected.

When you are trying to drive traffic to sponsors, experiment with different approaches. For each experiment, measure the results. We found that the most effective way to encourage consumers to click through to sponsors was to insert a text-based "call to action" on the final page of a calculator. For example, when consumers calculated the maximum mortgage for which they would ordinarily qualify, beneath the results we included a message saying, "In order to contact a lender, click here."

Among the ratios that we watched at Homefair were:

- Leads generated per page view. For example, when we launched our city reports program, we found that fewer than 15 percent of the people who clicked on the first page of the tool ultimately filled out the form to be contacted by our sponsor. Every time we changed the city reports order form, by rewording it, by adding or deleting fields, or by changing the mix between optional and required fields, we examined the effect of the change on the percentage of people who filled out the form. For our other tools, we noticed that this ratio rose considerably if we entered consumers who filled out contact forms in a drawing for a $1,000 prize.
- Advertising click-through rates. At first, most of our banner advertisers canceled their campaigns quickly. Our renewal rate was terrible because our click-through rate was terrible, meaning that consumers did not bother to click on the banner ads on our site. While click-through rates tend to be disappointing everywhere, ours were way below average because of the sequential nature of much of our content. People did not want to interrupt what they were doing to go look at an ad. We found that we could raise click-through rates considerably by placing ads on pages where consumers were finished with a particular task. This solved our problems with sponsors and renewals.

Web-Site Promotion

Most people have the wrong idea about web-site promotion. They assume that there is some wonderful trick that you can use to bring traffic to your site. Or they think that spending a lot of money on advertising is a way to build a popular web site.

In his book *Selling the Invisible*, Harry Beckwith makes a point about marketing services that I believe also holds for web sites.

> In this popular view, marketing means taking what you have and shoving it down buyers' throats. "We need better marketing" invariably means "We need to get our name out"—with ads, publicity, and maybe some direct mail.
>
> Unfortunately, this focus on getting the word *outside* distracts companies from the *inside*, and from the first rule of service marketing. *The core of service marketing is the service itself . . .*
>
> Think of the times when you have received extraordinary service. How much more did you end up spending with that company? How many people did you tell about your experience? How much did they spend?
>
> No, you cannot get a precise figure, but it is a *huge* figure. And it's all in that company's bank.
>
> First, before you write an ad, rent a list, dash off a press release—fix your service. (pp. 3–5)

All of these comments from Beckwith apply to a web site. Because consumers can tell one another immediately by e-mail about good and bad experiences on the Web, the quality of your web site must be addressed before you can turn your attention to promotion. In fact, the most important tactic for promoting your web site is to make it a site worth visiting.

- Provide consumers with valuable information and applications.
- Enable consumers to find the valuable content on your site. Follow the design principles discussed in the previous section and in Jakob Nielsen's book, *Designing Web Usability*.

If your site adds little value to the consumer or is poorly designed, then heavily promoting your site will, at best, put your failure under a magnifying glass.

When you think that your web site is ready for launch, find people in your target audience and invite them to visit. Then ask them, "Would you recommend our site to a friend?"

The answer should come back, "Yes, I've already recommended your site. It's terrific." If there is any less enthusiasm, then you need to rework your site. If someone who represents your target audience is indifferent to your site, then there is no point in attempting any of the tactics that follow.

Assuming that people in your target audience rave about your site, the following tactics can help to spread the word:

1. Encourage Consumer Feedback, and Give Personal, Prompt Responses

This is the same as point 11 under "The Key to a Good Web Design," earlier in this chapter. Much of the traffic to a web site comes from electronic word of mouth. It comes from people sending e-mails to one another about a site, or linking to a site from their own site, or mentioning a site to an on-line discussion group.

Responding to e-mail is a competitive advantage. According to an article in the *Industry Standard,* "Only about one in three e-mail inquiries about a company's product or policies gets a response." This means that, on average, every company turns off two out of every three of its most promising Internet customers. By aiming for a 100-percent response rate, you can demonstrate superior customer service.

Also, I should reiterate that personal responses to consumer feedback are an advantage that a netstrapper has relative to a corporate web site. Large corporations typically give form-letter-like responses, and these often take days or weeks to deliver. You want to take advantage of your freedom to reply quickly and in plain language.

Because word of mouth is so important on the Web, there are huge "butterfly effects," as Beckwith calls them. You never know when a quick response to a comment or question could lead to someone recommending your site to thousands of other people. It is worth repeating that responding to consumer questions or comments is the lowest-cost marketing strategy available to a web site.

2. Pay Yahoo! to Evaluate Your Site

Yahoo!, which is the most important directory on the Web, has a service called "Business Express," for which you pay $200. For this fee, Yahoo! provides expedited consideration of your web site and a guaranteed decision within seven days about whether it will include your site in the directory.

Assuming that your web site is valuable to consumers, eventually Yahoo! will probably include it in its directory. However, seven-day turnaround is worth paying for. You want to start drawing traffic from Yahoo! as soon as possible.

3. Submit Your Site to Other Popular Search Engines

Apart from Yahoo!, popular directories include Netscape Search, AltaVista, Excite, Hotbot, Lycos, www.go.com (formerly Infoseek), and About.com. You can read about the search engines at www.searchenginewatch.com, particularly in the "reviews, ratings, and tests" area.

However, do not let yourself become too mesmerized by the topic of search-engine placement. It is not worth racking your brains to deal with that issue. Moreover, it can be a waste of money, or downright dangerous, to pay an unknown party to "help" you with search engines. Sometimes, these services do more harm than good, because their manipulation tactics are recognized by the search engines. Before you hire a third party to help with search-engine placement, do an extra amount of due diligence on that company by checking out as many of its references as possible.

4. Encourage Linking from Other Sites

Find other sites that are in your same virtual community. One way to find such sites is to go to search engines, type in keywords related to your site, and see which web sites come up. Those are sites from which you want links.

For example, at Homefair, we offered information that was valuable to people considering relocating to a new city. This ties in closely with the job-search process. Therefore, we sought links from all of the major job-search sites.

Usually, when you want a site to link to you, it makes sense for you to provide a link back in return. At Homefair, because we wanted job-search sites to link to us, we set up a "Find a job" section on our site where we could provide a list of links to job-search sites. That way, we were offering a link in return.

If you go to the search engine www.altavista.com, you can count the number of links to a site. For example, if I do a search for "link:www.familypoint.com," it comes back and says that there are 839 pages found. This means that there are 839 sites with links to Joseph Murgio's web site, www.familypoint.com, a site that facilitates family communication. The large number of links to his site is a positive indication that it is well ensconced within the web community. In contrast, Bill Baker's HireRight.com web site only has 63 links coming into it, according to AltaVista. Given that HireRight.com is in the employment and job-search category, which has an extensive and well-developed community on the web, this is an alarmingly low figure.

5. Co-Brand with Other Sites

The most sophisticated way to encourage links from another site is to offer co-branding. With co-branding, you set up a version of your content that is consistent with the look, feel, and navigation of the partner site. For example, with Homefair, our typical co-brand included several of the attractions on our site, with a very brief drop-down menu connecting those sections. We eliminated our ordinary navigation schemes, which were the tabs on top, the side navigation bar, and the portal-style menu underneath our content. Instead, our partner's navigation scheme went into play. For example, for purposes of the co-brand, we would copy our partner's side navigation bar.

When consumers are on a partner's site, they may click on a link that takes them to your content. However, it will appear as if they never changed sites. This enables the co-brand partner to maintain control of traffic. However, you can insert your logo on your pages. We used a small graphic that said, "powered by homefair.com," which helped to reinforce our brand.

When you co-brand, you should monitor your placement on the other site. We found that by advising our partners on better placement of links to our content, we could increase our traffic considerably.

Dan Cunningham's 507Media company (Case No. 23), which provides consumers with the ability to book bands for events, has a strategy that is based entirely on co-branding. His intention is to offer 507Media's applications through other sites, such as WeddingChannel.com.

6. Shamelessly Promote Yourself

At one time or another, Homefair was mentioned in nearly every major newspaper and many magazines. These stories in print media were very helpful. Consumers are bewildered by the enormous number of web sites, and they have no idea where to find the most useful and reliable content. Articles in the press that recommend sites are very influential.

Public relations firms can assist you with getting the story out about your web site. Partners can be helpful as well. Every time you set up a co-brand partnership, you should issue a press release. This helps to cement the partnership, and it may gain some coverage.

When real estate companies purchased advertisements on our sites, we sent their local newspapers a press release announcing the arrangement. Any time a real estate company gets coverage in the local paper, they are happy. Typically, if a paper ran the story, the real estate company felt that it had already received its money's worth from buying an ad on Homefair.

When something positive happens to your company, let everyone know about it. Dan Cunningham points out how important this is when you seek funding. As he puts it: "Every good thing about your company should be the saber-rattling that gets the investors to the table in the first place. If you're close to a term sheet with a investor, everyone else on your list should know. Got a speaking engagement at a conference? An e-mail should go out to everyone with a possible financial interest in your company showcasing how you're such an 'expert in the field.'"

Good publicity helps you cement relationships with partners, particularly if your partner is included in the press coverage. It builds momentum with investors. And it adds traffic to your web site.

7. Encourage Other "Sneezers"

Seth Godin's *Ideavirus* introduces the concept of a "sneezer," which is someone who helps to spread an idea. In addition to print media, there are other sneezers who can help your web site.

- People who distribute influential e-mail newsletters in your subject area
- People who moderate large e-mail discussion groups in your subject area
- People who speak frequently at conferences and conventions

If your consumers rave about your web site, then there is a good chance that these "sneezers" will also like it. They have the ability to let a lot of other people in your target market know about your site. Cultivate relationships with these people. Find out what you can do to help them, so that you can then encourage them to help you.

8. Note Your AOL Traffic

Many people are aware of the large amounts of money that some sites pay to be featured on America Online. However, AOL is a very consumer-focused company. AOL staff noticed that a lot of their customers were finding their way to Homefair, so they were very happy to arrange a co-brand with us that involved sharing revenue, rather than a payment from Homefair to AOL.

Use your log analysis statistics to keep an eye on your traffic from AOL. Also, pay attention to the comments you receive from AOL users. If AOLers tend to be happy with your web site, then you are in a good negotiating position with AOL to discuss arrangements that will increase your traffic from AOL.

Conclusion

It is a remarkable fact that most web sites are unsatisfactory. In many cases, the concept is not compelling to the consumer. Even when the concept is compelling, the execution in terms of web design can be flawed.

Another fact is that when a web site is unsatisfactory, promoting that web site is futile. You may be able to buy first-time visitors, but you cannot make them like what they find. You cannot force people to stay on a site that disappoints them.

These facts should be really comforting to netstrappers. It means that the strategies that are available to companies with large budgets, including Dilbert-sector companies and venture-financed firms, are not particularly effective. The playing field on the Web is a lot more level than it appears. Although many other companies have marketing budgets that are bigger than yours, they will burn through their money in futile attempts to promote lousy web sites.

With the Web as crowded as it is today, it seems as though it would be difficult to make a web site stand out. Although this is true, the primary reason that most sites will not succeed is that they deserve to fail. They offer nothing new or compelling to consumers. The world does not need another site that provides mortgage quotes, so do not expect your web site to be popular if that is all you offer. On the other hand, sites such as Napster or www.blogger.com (a site for helping maintain personal journals called web logs or "blogs") or Dialpad.com (long-distance telephony using the web) have enjoyed tremendous success based on word of mouth.

Your challenge is to develop a compelling web site. If you can do that, then the tactics laid out in this chapter should enable you to compete effectively.

Case No. 14: Therese Haar

On the wall of her home office, Therese Haar has posted her key operational milestone for FarmerLink.com, a web site where farmers pay a small fee to advertise directly to consumers. She wants to achieve 10,000 "hits" (consumer visits to the site) per month.

One year after FarmerLink.com launched, with $5,000 spent on the business, Haar had yet to achieve her objective. However, she plans to keep plugging away, at least through the year 2001.

Haar works as a project systems specialist for Honeywell at NASA's Goddard Space Flight Center. Occasionally, she has needed to take a leave of absence in order to spend more time taking care of her children. During one such leave of absence in 1999, she listened to a radio show that described "Community Harvest," a project that tried to provide direct access to farm produce for poor consumers. Haar decided that the Web might provide a vehicle to allow farmers to increase their direct sales of produce.

That summer, Haar talked to several farmers as well as officials in the Montgomery County, Maryland, Department of Economic Development Agricultural Services. She found them enthusiastic about the concept of FarmerLink.com, so she went ahead and launched the site.

At first, Haar was thinking in terms of a sophisticated site, perhaps even including a shopping cart. However, this would have required farmers to provide updated information on prices and availability. Most farmers feel that their business keeps them too busy to provide the required updates. Instead, working with Montgomery County's Farmer Association, Haar designed a simple template for a web page that a farmer could use to help consumers learn how to contact the farm and obtain produce. This straightforward "Yellow Pages" style of advertising helps the farmers to boost sales.

Haar went back to Honeywell in October 1999, about the time that FarmerLink.com was launched. This means that she can only pursue her business on evenings and weekends. Haar says that approaching FarmerLink.com this way is somewhat "isolating." It limits her ability to spend time talking with farmers, for instance, at agricultural conferences. Also, she needs to make an ongoing effort to meet other entrepreneurs, in order to gather fresh ideas. On the other hand, treating FarmerLink.com as a spare-time project means that her "burn rate" is effectively zero. (In venture capital, the "burn rate" is the amount of money that a business loses per month during the period when it is not yet profitable.) Thus, even though she suffered from pioneer time and was overly optimistic about how quickly she could achieve her operational milestones, she is not forced to go into debt in order to stay in business.

Haar sees other companies taking advantage of farmers by charging them a lot more money to develop Internet sites that draw less traffic. By maintaining her credibility, she expects to outlast the competition and be in a leadership position in her niche as the market for on-line produce sales develops.

Case No. 15: Joseph Murgio

In 1998, when Joseph Murgio was ready to start FamilyPoint.com, he needed an experienced web developer for a partner. Be careful what you wish for.

While working for Hewlett-Packard, Murgio had seen the potential of computer-based communications to help workers in different locations to stay in touch with one another. The idea of Family-Point.com was to provide families with these tools using the Web. FamilyPoint allows families to share photos, assemble group calendars, create discussions, and participate in live chat sessions with one another.

Early in 1998, Murgio raised $150,000 to start FamilyPoint.com, while he still worked for HP. He put up $20,000 himself and obtained the rest from friends, family, and coworkers, each of whom put in an average of $15,000.

Murgio searched for a company to develop his web site, and he came across WorldLinks.com. In addition to providing experienced developers, this company was able to handle web hosting and was

also willing to waive labor charges in exchange for a 25 percent equity stake in FamilyPoint.com.

Murgio thought that he had found exactly what he needed. They
were able to launch the site at the beginning of the summer, and he
still had most of his $150,000 to spend on marketing. He hired Be-
yond Interactive and other small on-line marketing firms to place
banner ads. They found that banners on "targeted" sites worked no
better than generic ads, so they placed ads on the lowest-cost sites
available.

Murgio, whose background was in technical sales and marketing,
had a simple economic model for FamilyPoint.com. The years 1998
and 1999 were the heyday for the strategy of "eyeball aggregation,"
in which sites were going all out to maximize their traffic, as measured by page views and registered users. Investors were valuing
membership-oriented web sites, such as FamilyPoint.com, at $50 per
person who joined.

Once Murgio had tuned his ad-placement strategy, he was able to
obtain members for $1.50 each ($3 per new member, but each member on average invited another person to join). He was creating value
using the simplest possible strategy—buy low, sell high. In fact, at
this point, he did not even worry about monetizing his membership
base by selling advertising on the site. He just focused on growing
traffic.

In the fall of 1998, someone from Scripps Ventures sent Murgio an
e-mail asking if he needed any funding. "I didn't know I needed
money," Murgio recalls. He still had about half of his original stake
in the bank. However, when Scripps put together a term sheet, Murgio realized that with the Scripps capital, he could increase his marketing efforts and acquire members more quickly.

By January 1999, FamilyPoint.com had 500,000 members and was
the 117th-most-visited site, according to Media Metrix, a leading rat-
ing service. Other venture capitalists, notably CMGI, were throwing
their support behind competing sites. Figuring that they were in a
race to dominate the family communication market, Murgio and
Scripps Ventures sought another round of funding, bringing in additional venture capital firms.

The process of obtaining the second round proved to be very long
and intense. Murgio's partner became a major liability at this stage.
Murgio had begun to regret the partnership shortly after launching
the site, but he was far too entangled by then, given the partner's eq-

uity position and the fact that the partner was responsible for every technical aspect of FamilyPoint.com, from hosting to development. "He held us hostage," Murgio recalls.

Previously, the partner's difficult personality had only caused problems with developers. Now, he began to grate on the venture capital firms that Murgio and Scripps were trying to bring on board. The partner even caused one of the firms to back out completely. Finally, the funding round closed in late summer 1999. Although FamilyPoint.com was valued at $6 million in this round, by the time it closed, Murgio describes the result as "a lot of dilution for not a lot of money."

Even before the second round of funding closed, FamilyPoint.com had received acquisition feelers from three publicly traded web sites: About.com (formerly The Mining Company), TalkCity.com, and iVillage.com. All three of these sites were attracted by several features of FamilyPoint.com's membership base:

- Its rapid growth rate
- The "stickiness" of the application, meaning that consumers spent several minutes there
- The fact that 65 percent of its members were women, a demographic group that many advertisers were seeking to reach

Ultimately, iVillage.com bought FamilyPoint.com in a transaction valued at more than $25 million. However, before any deal could come to fruition, the frustrations with his partner reached such an intense level that Murgio resigned and left his company. He retained about 10 percent of the equity, and he was quoted in the September 1, 1999, press release announcing the transaction. His stock in iVillage.com was not registered for 180 days after the transaction, by which time its value had fallen by nearly 50 percent. Nonetheless, Murgio became a millionaire when he sold most of his iVillage.com shares.

Murgio's success with FamilyPoint.com was bittersweet. He was gratified that his original angel investors received nearly $250,000 for each $15,000 they had put up. "I really liked making my friends rich and my family rich," he says. He was very pleased to describe the 5–10 e-mails he received each week from families expressing their gratitude for the communication tools his site offered. However, he was traumatized by the ruthlessness with which he felt his partner had treated him and many of the web site developers.

As early as June 1999, Murgio was already planning a new venture that would be free of bitter entanglements. He founded OnProject.com, a site designed to bring his experience with group collaboration to the world of small projects. It combines some of the technical project-management tools that can be found in traditional project-management software with some of the group scheduling and discussion tools that are found on the Web.

Murgio was attempting to ride the trend toward applications that are rented over the Internet. However, he has found that this "application service provider" model is not catching on as rapidly in the marketplace as it is in the press. He believes that for now the best revenue model for OnProject.com is to license the software for internal use by companies. The companies themselves will host their internal versions of OnProject.com's tools, which will be tuned and customized to meet particular needs. The company Ernst and Young is among those interested in this customized model.

Murgio's marketing plan for OnProject.com is focused on advertising on e-mail lists targeted to project managers. In my opinion, advertising on e-mail lists is one of the smartest marketing strategies on the Internet today. I myself subscribe to very few newsletters, but I read the e-mails that I get from them carefully, including the advertisements. This is in contrast to banner ads on the Web, which most of the time I do not even notice because I am so used to tuning them out.

Murgio is using the lessons that he learned from FamilyPoint.com. He again started with angel investors, because he was pleased with how that turned out. This time, he raised $300,000, including $50,000 of his own money. In January 2000, he raised his first venture round. He says he had almost fifty venture capitalists in his Rolodex from his FamilyPoint.com business, but his desire to forget that venture was so strong that he used a completely different investor, Anaconda Capital. For the January round, OnProject.com was valued at $11 million, and as of the time of our interview in September 2000, Murgio saw the potential to have the company acquired for $40 million in the not-too-distant future.

This time, Murgio is not using a partner for development. He is hiring his own developers. He is determined not to be held hostage again.

Case No. 16: Mike Covel

One definition of a netstrapper would be an entrepreneur who achieves without venture capital what well-funded Internet competitors fail to accomplish. Mike Covel fits that definition.

Conventional wisdom is that consumers are not comfortable buying high-end products (other than personal computers) on-line. But one of Covel's companies, Turtletrader.com, sells a course for financial speculators for $1,000. The course comes in the form of a manual and a CD-ROM.

Conventional wisdom is that Internet retailers require massive advertising campaigns in order to attract consumers. But Covel's other company, HomePharmacy.com, was selling over $60,000 of goods a month with not one penny spent on advertising, going head-to-head against competitors with advertising budgets in the tens of millions.

His story begins in the summer of 1996, when two phenomena converged. One was that he was no longer employed (he had previously worked at a hedge fund). The other was that the Web had emerged as something he could see as "the greatest distribution channel ever."

He launched Turtletrader.com in October 1996. Although at that time he paid only $20 a month in hosting fees, he did pay $4,000 to an HTML programmer to convert Covel's writing into about fifteen pages of content for the site, along with a handful of graphics. Soon, Covel was kicking himself over that expense, because by then he had taught himself HTML and realized how little effort was involved in putting text into that format.

For the first six months, Covel did not make a single sale, and his back was against the wall. "If I didn't sell this product, I was gonna go broke," he says. Still, he stuck to his $1,000 price point, and gradually the sales began to come in, first in a trickle and eventually in a flood.

In the early months, what helped Covel maintain his morale was the feedback that he received from the site. His visitor logs showed people coming from many countries. "We knew right away that we were going to be a global company," he notes. Seeing this trend led him to include examples of how the Turtletrader approach would work in Singapore or Germany. In fact, his first two orders came from Germany and Austria.

Another form of feedback was e-mail directly from visitors. Covel was meticulous about answering e-mail, and he soon found that the speed at which you answer a question is almost as important as the answer itself. People who sent questions or comments to Turtletrader.com discovered that behind the site was a real person who was willing to take the time to respond individually and specifically to their inquiries. Covel believes that a substantial percentage of his sales come from customers who have received personal e-mail somewhere along the way.

The site has grown over the years, so that now it has about 400 pages of content. It is well worth visiting if you are looking for ideas about web design.

In my experience, when people come to a web site, they really want to "get behind the curtain" and interact with your company. Covel invites this. He does not stop with the standard "contact us" page. In many of his articles, after a highly technical or controversial statement, he will say, "Do you need more information to clarify (or back up) this point? E-mail me right now." I have not seen any other site that encourages e-mail from visitors in such an engaging way.

The Turtletrader.com site is rich in information and light on graphics. Jakob Nielsen would be proud. It is also filled with little touches that provide comfort to users understandably wary of spending $1,000 on-line. In addition to the links to favorable articles in the press, Covel offers to send a hard copy of an article in the mail to anyone who requests the article by e-mail. In addition to testimonials from various clients, Covel lists the countries where people have bought the course. In addition to the site's privacy policy, Covel posts a specific privacy guarantee for people who sign up for the Turtletrader newsletter. On the same page that explains how to subscribe to the newsletter, there is an explanation of how to unsubscribe, thereby providing immediate relief for one of the main worries that experienced users have about signing up for newsletters. In short, Covel believes that no detail is too small when it comes to enhancing credibility with the user.

I have to admit that I am temperamentally unsuited to playing the stock market. To me, trading stocks is like playing one of those video games where the pace is too fast and there are too many things that can fly at you from out of nowhere. So I'm not in a position to evaluate his product.

On the other hand, I have a pretty high opinion of myself as a designer of an effective web site. That was my "Magnificent Seven" specialty with homefair.com. Yet I think that Mike Covel could take me to school. For usability and effectiveness, Turtletrader.com is one of the best case studies on the Web.

Shortly after he launched the Turtletrader web site, Covel started HomePharmacy.com, a site that sells drugstore products to customers. Since then, he has seen the rise and fall of several prominent venture-capital-funded firms, such as PlanetRX.com, which in 1999 spent $100 million in advertising to generate only $10 million in gross sales.

Covel takes the view that the companies that have had IPOs are not as big as they appear to be. For one thing, they have no physical assets comparable to, say, the restaurants owned by McDonald's. As Covel puts it, "If the big picture is that $1 billion in assets means a big company, and some hot dot-com has $10 million and I have $0, they're not really that far ahead."

HomePharmacy.com is generating sales at an annual rate of close to three-quarters of a million dollars, without one penny being spent on advertising. In the fall of 1999, it was the number four consumer drug site on the web, ranking ahead of CVS.

To achieve this level of visibility without advertising, Covel has mastered the art of promoting a web site. He follows the usual good practices of using relevant keywords in titles, links, and the hidden so-called "META tags" that are used to communicate with the automated search engines. He goes beyond that by participating in relevant Internet communities, such as popular chat areas and e-mail-mediated discussion groups.

With the IPO mania that prevailed at the time, HomePharmacy.com probably had a significant market value in late 1999. This evaporated with the market correction in April 2000, but the market downturn is a much more serious setback for his competitors than it is for Covel. His current outlook for the company: "We're going to get rich, but from building a great business as opposed to an overvalued IPO."

SEVEN

The Zen of Partnership

At Yahoo!, we find new partners faster than at a square dance.
There is a simple reason: Forming partnerships is our business.
—Elizabeth Collett, "The More, the Merrier,"
Context, July–August 1999 (see www.contextmag.com)

Partnerships are very important to netstrappers. As a small company, you need partners in order to be able to compete effectively with larger firms. On the Internet, partnerships are easy to establish, and they help you to bring traffic and revenue to your web site.

Trevor Cornwell's (Case No. 6) challenge with building Skyjet.com, a reservation service for charter aircraft, was that the small proprietors who run charter-jet businesses were not inclined to provide regular updates of their schedules. Without this information, Cornwell would not have an accurate picture of the capacity of his "virtual airline" and would be unable to operate his reservation system. Fortunately, he was able to work with a partner who was already compiling this information for a slightly different purpose.

Layla Masri (Case No. 21) wanted to hold down the payroll of her web-design firm, Bean Creative, while being able to handle the uneven flow of project work. She developed a network of contractors with which to work. Many small netstrappers in service businesses adopt this approach.

Mark Matassa (Case No. 18) developed PersonalReader.com, an editorial service that selects articles in topic areas. He found that other web sites were in a better position to market his service to consumers, so he began to provide his service on other web sites. These partnerships were a way of building traffic and generating revenue.

At Homefair, we saw an opportunity to obtain traffic from *USA Today's* popular web site, while the news organization saw our content as helping to make its own site more "sticky." Accordingly, we developed a co-brand, which is a popular form of web-site partnership. Eventually, Homefair had over 1,000 co-brands.

How to Be an Ideal Partner

In my view, the secret of obtaining partnerships is what I call the Zen of partnership: To get the partners you need, become the ideal partner.

This is yet another instance of doing the role reversal. If you can view the relationship from the perspective of the potential partner, you increase your chances of obtaining the partnership. Below are some more specific implications of the Zen of partnership.

1. Rein in the Lawyers

An ideal partner is one with whom you can arrive at a simple, fair agreement with minimal legal wrangling and negotiation. When you are trying to select partners on the Internet, there are many to choose from. Everyone soon realizes that it only pays to work with companies that are agreeable. No one can afford to waste time trying to deal with a company that unleashes its lawyers to saddle you with long, complicated proposals that put you on the defensive.

2. Find Simple Ways to Share Benefits

When you share revenue, try to keep formulas simple and even-handed. In many of Homefair's co-brand agreements, we shared revenue on a "one-third each" basis, meaning that one-third of the revenue was received by the site that supplied the content, by the site that brought in the traffic, and by the site that sold the advertising.

In other cases, we would have the other site host the first page of one of our calculators, while we hosted the second page. The other site would have rights to revenue from the first page, and we would have rights to the second page.

3. Pitch Your Partner's Value Proposition

An ideal partner can explain the value of the partnership quickly and clearly. As Gary Lefever of womenconnect.com (now defunct) puts it:

> Know what is important to your prospective partner and speak to it. I must have six calendar software proposals on my desk and all I hear is, "I have the fastest this, I have the best that." I don't care. I'm not a tech guy. But if you can tell me how this is going to help build my community, how it is going to increase my stickiness, my repeat visitors, or my ability to garner a higher advertising rate, now I'll talk to you.
>
> **(Source: Available: www.netpreneur.org/events/ doughnets/990722/transcript.html.)**

4. First You Dance, Then You Date, Then You Get Married

An ideal partner develops a relationship incrementally, starting with a small deal that builds trust, then deepening the partnership step by step. As Yahoo!'s Collett puts it, "We can't spend a month on grand scenarios and detailed contracts. To compensate, we start small. We regard the contract as a living document. We say, 'Hey, you send me some content that I can use on my site, and I'll send you some links that will let people get from my site to yours.' Then we take it one step at a time."

Our relationship with TheSchoolReport.com, a company with a database of information on schools that provided consumer leads to real estate agents, developed gradually, over a period of years. At first, we simply swapped advice back and forth. Then, we set up co-branded versions of sites for one another. Next, we began to think of ways to combine our content into a sort of joint offering. Eventually, we merged.

5. Celebrate Your Partnership

One way to cement a partnership is to hold celebrations. The more you celebrate, the tighter the bond becomes.

In the early years of homefair.com, my biggest blown opportunity was with the Housing Guides of America, a loose association of publishers. These were glossy print publications that provided listings of new home developments in twenty-four cities across the country. There were about twenty publishers in the association, since a few of them owned magazines in two cities.

My first week in my new office, I contacted the *Washington, D.C., New Homes Guide*, a free glossy color directory of all of the new home developments in the metropolitan area. I was fortunate to be put through to the company's database programmer, Chuck Coffey. Coffey was aware of the Internet, and he was willing to meet with me and to recommend my proposal to his boss, Charlie Browning.

I proposed the creation of a searchable, on-line version of the *New Homes Guide*, along with a contact form that could be sent to each individual builder. Browning liked the idea of the contact forms, but he wanted them going directly to the *New Homes Guide* first, so that he could be sure to claim credit. We managed to come to terms and implement the project fairly quickly.

My goal was always for Browning to help me to convince the other Housing Guide publishers to participate in my site. This would have helped give homefair.com tremendous credibility by providing searchable home listings in most major metropolitan areas. It would have helped establish homefair.com as a premier destination for consumers to view new homes on-line. This in turn would have given us tremendous potential to increase revenue as home builders began to include on-line advertising in their marketing budgets.

My dream of having every *New Homes Guide* on homefair.com was never realized. The problem was my inability to forge a relationship with Charlie Browning and the other Housing Guide publishers. At a business level, our relationship was positive in an arm's-length way. Browning was happy with the on-line version of his guide. We sent leads to the other Housing Guide publishers as well as to Browning. The fees that I charged the publishers for the leads were low enough that they were happy to renew, particularly as traffic rose every month.

The Housing Guide publishers were classic small proprietors, in that new technology represented a threat to established businesses operating on low profit margins. For that reason, my sales task was delicate. I had to present my knowledge of the Internet in a way that was not threatening.

However, in my sales approach to Browning and the Housing Guide publishers, I failed to achieve an emotional bond. I gave

Browning a fair business proposition. But what I really needed to do
was make him feel like a hero.

The *Washington, D.C., New Homes Guide* and homefair.com issued a joint press release, and we got some coverage in *Builder Magazine*. Browning was happy about that, and that should have clued
me in to his needs. I should have done a lot more joint marketing in
order to help bind our two companies.

- I should have created marketing posters for Browning to
  take to trade shows.
- I should have created screen prints for him to give to
  builders.
- Every time there was an article about homefair.com, even
  though it did not mention the *Washington, D.C., New
  Homes Guide,* I should have adapted it to produce a market-
  ing slick that said "*Washington, D.C., New Homes Guide*
  Partnership Receives Another Accolade" for Browning's use.
- I should have offered to help produce and pay for mailings to
  builders that highlighted the success of the *New Homes
  Guide*/Homefair collaboration.

Had I done some of these things, it would have made Browning
feel like a hero and a winner for having chosen to work with Homefair. If he had conveyed such an attitude to the other Housing Guide
publishers when he met with them, this would have gone a long way
in overcoming their skepticism and fear of the Internet medium.

When Homefair began to market lead-generating programs to real
estate companies and moving companies, the effort faced the same
sort of small-proprietor suspicion that I had encountered with the
Housing Guide publishers. However, my partners Rich Ganley and
Bryan Schutjer made sure that we celebrated our partnerships. When
we received good press, Ganley and Shutjer forwarded the accolades
to all of our partners and customers. This helped to reinforce the fact
that our partners had made the right decision in choosing to align
with us.

At one point, when a cable station in Oregon did a positive story
on consumers using Homefair, Ganley obtained a tape from the station, along with permission to make copies to send to all of our partners and customers. Ganley knew that if our customers felt proud of
their relationship with us, then our renewal rate would be high.

6. Co-Brand Easily

One of the most powerful ways to form a partnership on the Web is to create a co-branded site. One site uses the content of another site to enrich its traffic. Most web-content sites can use this model. For example, Dan Cunningham's 507Media planned to create versions of its band-booking software to be used by sites that offer wedding planning services.

The technical aspects of this strategy can be challenging. Your content may rely on a database that requires frequent updates. The other site may have a very complex and precise look and feel. Your technical team has to find a way to create a blended site easily. For example, in the case of Homefair, our technical team had to treat font colors and background colors as parameters that could be specified by the co-brand site, so that we could blend in with anyone's color scheme.

7. Coach Your Partners

At Homefair, we had partnerships with many of the Web's leading job-search sites. We noticed that some of the largest sites had relatively ineffective co-brands in terms of delivering traffic to our content. Other co-brands were much more productive. We looked at the productive co-brands, and we found that their placement of links to our content was much more naturally likely to lead to click-throughs. We dedicated staff to calling all of our co-brands with advice on how to place their links to our co-branded content.

8. Choose Carefully What You Won't Do

Not every potential partner is compatible. With some of our partners, Homefair could set up a co-brand in minutes by copying a few files from the partner's web site and entering a few parameters into our database. However, with other partners, the requirements were much more complex. In some cases, it was cost-prohibitive to do as the partner wished.

We made a mistake by being too accommodating to Moneymag.com. We agreed to provide our cost-of-living data rather than create a co-branded version of the Salary Calculator. The result was a nightmare. Moneymag.com never updated our data, which led to conflicts between the results on their site and the results on ours, because their site was using information that was up to two years out of date. Consumers would contact us about these conflicts, which damaged our credibility.

Moneymag.com was part of Time-Warner's ill-fated Pathfinder web site, which went through shifts of strategy and personnel on a frequent basis. Consequently, it took years for us to straighten out that relationship.

We made the opposite mistake with Yahoo!, which also wanted us to supply the data so that Yahoo! staff could create their own calculator. They, too, went through some personnel changes that prolonged the negotiations. It seemed as though this was going to be another troublesome partner, so we decided not to accommodate Yahoo!'s needs. Later, Neil Rosen, the founder of TheSchoolReport.com, told us that Yahoo! was easy to work with once you followed the company's specifications. Given Yahoo!'s market share, it would have been worthwhile for us to hire an additional programmer, if necessary, to adapt our content to Yahoo!'s requirements.

Conclusion

A netstrapper should start with the point of view that every other company is a potential partner. Some companies have access to customers who would also be interested in your offering. Other companies have information or products that you can bundle with your own.

Starting from this large universe of potential partners, you narrow down the list of companies with which you work. Some partnerships offer little potential, so they are not worth your time. Some partnerships will not work, because the goals of the other company conflict too much with your own. Finally, there are partnerships that will not work because the other partner is too difficult to work with.

Take the time to learn your partners' business models, so that you can become the ideal partner. By becoming the ideal partner, you can obtain the maximum value from your partnerships.

Case No. 17: Raj Khera

By the time the venture capital herd discovered the field of business-to-business Internet commerce, Raj Khera had already been doing B2B for three years. He had decided back in 1995 that there was a profitable opportunity in creating an on-line community for businesses.

In the spring of 1995, Khera, his brother Vivek, and Barry Friedman decided that a particular vertical market was ripe for the Internet. Government contractors, early adopters of the Internet because of its heavy use by the Department of Defense and other agencies, were hampered by the complexity and expense of obtaining relevant information. Khera abbreviated "government contractors" to Gov-Con, and started GovCon.com. He estimates that his total start-up costs were under $100,000.

Khera conceived of GovCon.com as an on-line magazine for government contractors, and his initial revenue model was to sell advertising to companies that provide services to those firms. Potential advertisers included banks, law firms, and accounting firms.

The analogy with magazine advertising implied that the key selling point would have to be solid information about user demographics. To Khera, this meant that he was going to have to induce his users to fill out registration forms, so that he would be able to collect statistical information for presentation to advertisers. Because the Gov-Con.com site was gathering information for statistical purposes only, it provided users with a strict privacy policy. No third party could receive a user's information without permission from the user.

However, it takes more than a privacy policy to encourage users to register for a site. Khera needed to provide valuable information to his audience. To do this, he paid $13,000 a year for an electronic subscription to *Commerce Business Daily* (CBD), which is a complete list of new bidding opportunities for government contracts over $25,000.

Government contractors were familiar with the print version of CBD, which cost about $350 per year for a subscription to a publication that was printed on low-quality paper, too voluminous, and hard to read. Khera provided free, instant access to CBD in a searchable format that saved users considerable time in finding relevant contracts on which to bid. The only thing users had to do to obtain this access was fill out a registration form, giving the size of their company, the business category, and a few other elements of demographic data.

Because convenient access to CBD was such a compelling application for government contractors, much of the traffic growth to the GovCon.com site came from word of mouth. Because registration was free, large contractors such as Lockheed Martin told literally hundreds of their employees to register on the site. To supplement word-of-mouth publicity, Khera also employed other popular techniques:

- An e-mail newsletter that gives registered users updates on enhancements to the site as well as important developments in the government contracting industry
- PR announcements and press releases
- Advertisements in targeted publications
- Awards to other web sites, with the recipient site encouraged to link back to GovCon.com

Based on his experience, Khera believes very strongly that on the Internet, it is critical to keep improving in order to stay ahead of the competition. For example, his company developed a service that they called "BidRadar," which was an e-mail alert service that the user could customize to target a particular category. This proved to be very popular and helped to increase both customer traffic and user registrations.

In 1995, Khera found that the segment of advertisers that fit the small-proprietor model, such as law firms and small accounting firms, had no idea what the Web was about. To help overcome their objections to advertising in this unknown medium, GovCon.com developed a sponsorship package that included a small web page with a contact form. Moreover, because GovCon.com had collected name and address information as part of the registration process, it was easy to pre-fill the contact form. When a user went to a contact form, his or her information was already filled in, and all the user had to do was submit the form.

As traffic to the site grew, Khera constantly sought out other information providers to expand the site and to obtain revenue from sales of products and subscriptions. Today, over half of the revenue of the site is derived from this source, with the remainder continuing to come from advertising.

Unlike many sites that were started in the early days of the Web, GovCon.com handled the transition to a complex, database-driven system relatively easily. This may reflect the fact that one of the partners, Raj's brother Vivek, holds a doctorate in computer science, which evidently prepared him well to lead the technical operation.

At the end of 1999, Khera sold GovCon.com to high-flying VerticalNet, which asked Khera not to discuss the terms. CEO David Coakley, who joined GovCon early in 1999, went to VerticalNet in the transaction, but the founding partners of GovCon wanted to continue to be entrepreneurs. The sale has allowed the Khera brothers to focus full-time on MoreBusiness.com, a small business portal they started several years ago that was overshadowed by GovCon's success.

Case No. 18: Mark Matassa

Mark Matassa has been in the news business for more than twenty years, since he was sixteen, and has spent most of his career as a newspaper reporter and editor. He was the political editor for the *Seattle Times*, that city's leading newspaper, before leaving to start PersonalReader.com, an editorial selection of news articles in specific categories.

Matassa brings a sense of personal mission to his enterprise. He has strong views about what constitutes value-added in journalism. He abandoned a brief stint with MSNBC in 1996 when he decided the venture did not live up to his standards for developing independent, original content.

Many entrepreneurs have a personal mission as well as a commercial goal. The stronger your sense of personal mission, the more likely it is that you will face conflicts, situations where you have to decide whether to adapt and accept ("sell out") or turn away business.

For example, I have always considered banner ads on the Web to be an abomination. Nonetheless, by 1996, we decided to adapt and accept banner ads on homefair.com, although they never became our dominant source of revenue.

On the other hand, shortly after Central Newspapers purchased homefair.com in 1997, someone with good connections on the board of our new parent company came to us with a proposal to sell a service called "biweekly mortgage conversion" on our site. I view this as a scam, and I asked to see the marketing materials. It turned out that they were deceptive and misleading, and we declined.

In January 1999, Matassa and a friend, Emory Thomas, launched PersonalReader.com. They conceived it as a smart clipping service, in which human editors would select the best stories on a topic. They then would write a short description of each story and provide a link to the article. The consumer would receive by e-mail or on the Web the list of descriptions and links.

To begin with, Matassa focused on politics and Thomas focused on baseball. Not sure how they would obtain revenue from the effort, they began by sending the collections of stories for free to friends and associates.

One of the recipients was Bob Kolasky, an editor for Intellectual-Capital.com, a popular web site for political discussions. Kolasky was getting ready to launch a spin-off called VoxCap.com, a discussion site tied to several specific issues. In July 1999, Kolasky asked if he could license PersonalReader.com for use on VoxCap. Suddenly, Matassa and Thomas had a revenue model: content licensing.

Matassa and Thomas proceeded to expand PersonalReader.com, adding categories and new clients to license their content. They expanded staff to include a full-time content manager and several freelance editor-writers.

In March 2000, Matassa was faced with another one of those agonizing decisions about personal mission. Business.com, a portal for information about business, offered to buy PersonalReader.com with a view toward focusing on business news exclusively. Thomas liked this offer, but Matassa did not. The new focus was too far removed from Matassa's original intention. As a result, the partnership split, with Matassa retaining PersonalReader.com and Thomas joining Business.com.

At our interview in August 2000, Matassa said that he felt "proud that we're still here," joking that "PersonalReader.com is the first profitable Internet company." While other Internet companies have obviously been profitable both before and since, he has a point in that the vast majority of sites trying to make money on "content" have failed to do so. By keeping costs low, Matassa has been able to eke out a profit on annual revenues of $250,000.

As of the time of our interview, Matassa was looking for funding in order to achieve more aggressive growth. My guess is that he may face some difficulty attracting investors, because of two factors:

- He does not have a strategy for what I call "standing up to the bear," that is, for charging a high price for the service. This means that in order to achieve high returns, Personal-Reader.com will need to expand its client base dramatically while controlling costs carefully, a difficult feat to pull off.
- He does not buy into the concept of an exit strategy. "Where I come from in the newspaper business," he says, "papers stay in the family a long time. Survival indicates quality."

EIGHT

Making a Clean Getaway

There is no such thing as a perfect crime without a clean getaway. Similarly, there is no such thing as a well-executed business that cannot be restructured cleanly.

Ed Vielmetti (Case No. 19) helped found MSEN, one of the most famous of the early Internet service providers. Its business success fell far short of its potential. Vielmetti believes that one of the biggest factors that held the company back was its initial partnership agreement, which gave a veto to each of the five founders. The company could not be restructured or refocused quickly and cleanly.

Netstrappers cannot afford the luxury of floundering when a crucial decision is at stake. Agreements need to be sufficiently flexible to allow for an "early divorce" on fair terms, so that one partner's obstinacy does not lead to paralysis.

A clean getaway is more than just an exit strategy. An exit strategy refers to a goal of either selling a business or taking it public. By a clean getaway, I mean that at any time after founding a company, it can undergo a restructuring or change of personnel of any kind without triggering an expensive legal case. Many of the netstrappers whom I interviewed can tell you about the personal and financial costs of a messy getaway.

191

Michaela Conley (Case No. 5) began her business with a friend. After several months, their concept of a web site to help people in the health promotions field was going nowhere and her friendship was finished.

The partnership with which Scott Mendenhall (Case No. 20) started his software company, Kolina.com, did not work. Breaking up the partnership cost the company over $50,000 in legal bills, at a time when total revenue was only $30,000.

In contrast, when one of the partners left Swati Agrawal's Firm-Seek.com (Case No. 11), a referral network for business services such as law firms and accounting firms, the departure was handled smoothly by the existing agreement.

To minimize the risk of losing a friendship, I recommend taking the steps outlined in Chapter 4, "Planning Your Business." To minimize the legal and financial costs of an "early divorce," and to make your business more flexible in general, I suggest you follow the principles in this chapter, which focus on enabling you to make a clean getaway.

To facilitate a clean getaway, your company's financial and legal agreements must be drawn up so as to anticipate important contingencies. Do not simply count on your attorney to anticipate these contingencies.

Once, when I was discussing a contingency with an attorney, he said, "Don't worry. In that case, you would have one helluva lawsuit." He thought that I would have the upper hand if the need for litigation arose.

Unfortunately, that is how too many attorneys think about contracts—they view a contract as an opportunity for one side to gain an advantage. They are trained to be advocates for one side or the other rather than as partners trying to be fair to one another. From the advocacy perspective, it does not matter how poorly the contract deals with a contingency, as long as "your" side would be in a good position in the resulting lawsuit. Maybe these advocates are good at winning lawsuits. However, the lawyers that I prefer are ones who are good at preventing lawsuits. That means designing agreements that are flexible and fair.

The contingencies for which you want to be prepared include:

- The death of a key person

Suppose that three of us are partners, and I die. My estate is going to claim some ownership of the business, even though my heirs have no expertise to offer. My partners are in an awkward position. On the one hand, they do not want to take assets away from a grieving family. On the other hand, the business cannot afford to carry a non-functioning partner.

- A new job offer

One or more of the founding partners may receive an attractive new job offer. If this has not been anticipated, the partner may still own a share of the company, even though the partner is no longer helping the company. A particularly painful experience is when the departing individual actually goes to work for a competing enterprise.

- Someone offers to buy out our company

When a buyout offer arrives, the founding partners may disagree with one another. Some partners may be inclined to accept the offer, while some may be inclined to reject it.

- A venture capitalist or investment banker proposes to merge our company with another company

The merger might be very advantageous to some of the partners, but its effect on other partners and on angel investors may be less constructive. An angel investor may be the lead investor in our company, but in the combined company, the angel's share may be small. The angel investor may not like losing control over his or her money.

- Market conditions change

You may start out with a plan to build the company prudently, using an "under-the-radar" approach. However, the venture capital market suddenly discovers your market niche, and it becomes clear that changing to a venture-funded strategy is appropriate. At this point, if your initial agreement is too messy in its ownership structure, that could preclude any deal with venture capitalists.

Useful Contract Terms

Given all these types of contingencies, there are some generic contract terms that can help give your business the flexibility that it needs. These include:

1. Regular Valuation of Your Business

Every year, your business needs to have a value established, in order to be used under various contingencies, such as the death of one partner. This valuation ought to satisfy two criteria. First, the partners should agree that the value is reasonable. Second, other parties, such as an insurance company, must be able to accept the valuation. For the latter reason, an accounting firm that is experienced with business appraisals typically must perform the valuation.

2. "Key-Person" Life Insurance for the Partners

Each partner is covered by a life insurance policy. If one partner dies, the other partners are beneficiaries of the policy. Among other things, they can use the proceeds of the policy to compensate the deceased partner's estate for that partner's share of the business, as given by the regular valuation.

3. Noncompete Clause

It makes sense for a partnership agreement to include a "noncompete" clause. Such a clause will state that if a person leaves the partnership, for up to a specified time period, such as one year, that person cannot work in a related or competing business.

4. Vesting Schedule

Another important part of the agreement should be a vesting schedule. It is particularly essential for netstrapping companies, because individual opportunities and markets are so fluid. Personnel changes in the first few months of an Internet start-up are quite common.

To prepare for this contingency, four of us might form an equal partnership, where each of us owns 25 percent of the company. However, we might agree that our shares vest at the rate of 1 percent per month, until after two years and one month we become completely vested. That way, if I leave after six months, I am entitled to 6 percent of the company rather than 25 percent.

5. Mutual Buyout Agreement

With a mutual buyout agreement, any partner or combination of partners can offer to buy out the remaining partner or partners. However, whatever valuation of the company is embedded in a buyout offer must be acceptable as a sale.

For example, suppose that you and I are 50-50 partners, and we have a mutual buyout agreement. If I offer to buy you out for $150,000, then my offer implies that I value the entire business at $300,000. You have the choice of either accepting my offer or buying me out for the same valuation. If you decide to buy me out rather than accept my offer, then I automatically have to accept your buyout.

This mutual buyout agreement ensures that I will be fair when I make you an offer. If I make a lowball offer to you, it can backfire because you have the right to force me to accept that same lowball valuation.

Suppose that a third party offers to buy our company for $500,000, but you do not want to accept the offer. I might offer to buy you out at a valuation of $500,000. At that point, you have to either put up or shut up. You have to either find a way to buy me out at a valuation of $500,000 or accept my offer. If you truly believe that $500,000 is "cheap," then you will try to find financing to buy me out.

6. Hybrid Debt or Equity

Convertible preferred stock is a hybrid instrument that combines aspects of debt with aspects of equity. Debt with warrants is another such instrument. The point of using hybrid instruments is that they enable you to retain your common stock, which gives you more flexibility.

The problem with issuing common stock is that it can create a fragmented ownership structure. It is hard to run a company with many competing constituencies looking over your shoulder.

Even though the founders may retain a majority of the stock, they have a fiduciary responsibility to each minority shareholder. This means that they have to be appeased when you are considering a transaction that will restructure your company, such as splitting off a subsidiary. If anyone does not believe that his or her interests are adequately protected in the restructuring, you may face a legal challenge. One entrepreneur who was trying to do a spin-off told me that he had thirty shareholders, and he needed to call each one to explain the purpose of the restructuring.

The problem with debt is that it may not match the need of the start-up for long-term financing. Typically, when you obtain your first round of financing, you want to keep your first-round investors on board for the second round. With debt, the second-round investors almost always have to buy out the investors from the first round. This will require a larger cash layout on the part of the second-round investors, and therefore it will restrict the set of potential second-round investors.

With hybrid instruments, you have the option at the second round of issuing common stock to the first-round investors to replace the securities that first were issued to them. For example, each share of convertible preferred stock issued in the first round might trade in for one share of common stock in the second round. The nice thing is that the terms for this conversion have been laid out on the day that the convertible preferred shares were issued. This means that you do not have to go through a protracted negotiation with the first-round investors in order to determine the number of shares they will receive.

Many founders are leery of giving up more than 50 percent of the company, because they do not wish to lose "control." I do not share that concern. When Central Newspapers owned 80 percent of Homefair, that worked out very well for us. They were great to have on the team. Moreover, our contract stipulated that even though we were minority shareholders, our partnership team had a veto over any financial restructuring of our company.

I would be much more concerned about a situation where you own over 51 percent of the company but have many minor investors with diverse interests. Under those circumstances, you may have "control," but you also have fiduciary responsibility and legal exposure. When the founder of a company that sold training videos in the dental industry wanted to develop a web-based subsidiary, he was somewhat hamstrung by the need to gain approval from over two dozen shareholders.

I believe that you should try to limit the ownership in your company to people whom you really would like to be owners. In my view, the owners of a company are a team that has to play well together. The problem with handing out equity is not what you give up in terms of financial control. What I worry about is losing the necessary cohesion in your ownership team.

Built to Last?

At the height of Internet mania, *Fast Company* had a cover story that raised this controversy: "Built to Last or Built to Flip?" The issue is whether it is ethical to start a company with the intention of selling it quickly.

I believe that *Fast Company* misstated the controversy somewhat. I would have phrased the issue as: "Built for profits, or built for fools?" It appeared to me that some of the companies that went public were designed to take money from foolish investors rather than to develop into legitimate, profitable businesses.

My opinion would be that as long as you build for profits, you can build to last *and* build to flip. You can create a valuable, long-term business, but at any time you may choose to merge, restructure, or sell.

If you choose not to flip your business, that is fine. However, paying attention to the issues that were raised in this chapter can give you the option to flip, which means greater flexibility and fewer legal hassles when new opportunities arise.

Conclusion

The problem of forging the right type of ownership agreements is tricky. Arrangements that are too poorly specified can lead to personal bitterness and legal wrangles when something goes awry with the partnership. On the other hand, agreements that are overly rigid and preclude restructuring can hamstring your company. You need to be able to adapt to new market conditions and take advantage of new opportunities.

In the dynamic netstrapping environment, you are likely to go through a sequence of agreements. At each stage, try to design an agreement that will get you through the next set of contingencies, one that allows for a smooth transition to the next stage of your company's structure.

Case No. 19: Ed Vielmetti

In late 1991, almost two years before I had even heard of the Internet, Ed Vielmetti and two of his coworkers at a small options trading firm in Ann Arbor, Michigan, had been talking for about a year about ways to turn their interest in the Internet into a business. At the time, the Web did not exist. The Internet tools that were closest to mainstream were e-mail and Usenet News (Internet discussion forums).

The vision that Ed Vielmetti, Tim Endres, and Owen Medd had was for a company that would sell Internet access to businesses. They started MSEN (the acronym had several evolutions, all starting with "Michigan" and ending in "Network") in their spare time in Medd's basement, using an old Sun workstation and "fast" 9600 baud modems, and they piggybacked on their employer's Internet connection. Their first customers were friends and former coworkers. They used local organizations, such as the Sun users' group, to spread the word about their Internet connection service.

In 1992, angered by their employer's decision to pay retirement funds as an annual bonus rather than in cash, they quit their jobs and tried to make MSEN a viable company. They now needed their own Internet connection, which was not easy to obtain in those days, because the academic and governmental organizations that dominated Internet access were hostile to commercial firms. Finally, MSEN was able to obtain a connection through PSInet through a leased line to upstate New York. Total revenues that year were under $100,000.

The year 1993 was the most exciting one for Vielmetti. He and his coworkers helped set up one of the first commercial Internet enterprises, the Online Career Center, which was later bought by Monster.com. On their own, the MSEN team bought a satellite dish and developed software to download Reuters news feeds into Usenet Newsgroups. Vielmetti was quoted in a *New York Times* article about the growth of the Internet, and *Forbes* magazine also published an interview with him.

By 1994, demand for Internet access was surging. MSEN could not keep up with the growth. Its billing system was in chaos. Its operational infrastructure was inadequate. Some of the people who formed competing Internet service providers were MSEN customers who had become so frustrated with MSEN's busy signals that they decided they could deliver better quality themselves.

For the past year or so, the company had been hamstrung by an agreement that gave five partners (the three founders plus two financial backers) equal authority, including veto power. Now, critical decisions needed to be made, and no one had the power to make them. It seemed as though the process of evolving from a hobby to a business was too stressful for the founders to handle. Relations among the principals were so strained that the only way out of the logjam was for one of the partners to buy out the rest, for $45,000 apiece.

It may seem remarkable that someone who was in the right business at the right time could have come out so poorly. To me, Ed Vielmetti's experience illustrates some very common issues that trip up entrepreneurs.

1. Visionaries Have Difficulty with Focus

Because they were so early, there were many interesting opportunities available to the MSEN team. It appears to me that they tended to attempt to exploit new opportunities before they had solidified any particular business. Nobody wanted to mind the store.

Entrepreneurs in general, and technical entrepreneurs in particular, get bored easily. Your attention gets drawn to something that is technically challenging, such as the Reuters News feed project. Meanwhile, something as mundane as installing new capacity or keeping up with billing and collections is neglected. If none of the principals has the temperament to mind the store, then it is imperative for a growing firm to hire an operations manager who can keep the business under control.

2. Agreements Outlive Their Usefulness

Business conditions change. Before you sign an agreement, ask yourself whether the escape clauses are satisfactory. Also, it is a good idea to have the business appraised every year. Such an appraisal can help you determine a fair price for a buyout if the partnership needs to break up.

3. Somebody Has to Be the CEO

It may seem idealistic to give every partner a veto. However, in reality, it is a recipe for disaster. If there is enough trust among you to justify a meaningful partnership, then you should be able to agree on a CEO.

Case No. 20: Scott Mendenhall

Scott Mendenhall and his sister, Kelly, wrote their first business plan while still in college at the University of Notre Dame. He describes the idea as a sort of "web-based Nintendo," which would combine the Web with TV. This was 1994, and they quickly realized that the concept was way beyond their ability to execute.

Mendenhall graduated in 1996, and he started working as a web developer for the company that evolved into Proxicom. He began as a webmaster, but he graduated to become the youngest project manager at the company. On the side, he also started his own company, Kolina, to do web development for smaller companies. At first, Proxicom encouraged this, but eventually he was asked to sign a noncompete agreement, and he had to back off.

Mendenhall knew that "working for somebody was never going to be my bag," and he was ready to venture out on his own as early as the fall of 1997. However, at that time, Proxicom hired Nancy Goldberg to do sales, and Mendenhall stayed on in order to have the opportunity to learn from working with someone he regarded as the first sophisticated salesperson he had ever met. When Goldberg left Proxicom in February 1998 to join Cybercash, Mendenhall soon resigned, along with two colleagues, to pursue Kolina full-time.

Mendenhall, like many netstrappers, went through what I call an "early divorce." Within a month, personality differences led his partnership to dissolve. This resulted in litigation that took over a year and was "not pretty," as Mendenhall put it. He estimates that the legal bills mounted to $50,000 for a company that had only brought in $30,000 in revenue.

In June 1998, Mendenhall and his sister reconstituted the company as Kolina Technologies. The operating model at the time was to spend 25 percent of their time doing consulting, 25 percent on overhead, and the remaining 50 percent on product development.

The conventional wisdom is that the best way for a technical company to lever its skills is to sell products. The theory is that for a product company, sales are not tied to the number of technical staff, as they are for a consulting company. This means that compared with a service company, a product company can achieve large revenues with a lower head count.

However, the theoretical advantages of a product company are offset by the disadvantages. Research and development expenses can be lost completely if the product never makes it to market. The company's success may depend on marketing capability, while its core competence is technical.

By late 1999, the Mendenhalls realized that the disadvantages of a product focus outweighed the theoretical advantages. They decided to focus on technical consulting. Their particular skill was in the "middleware" component of web sites, where the pages that users receive are controlled from databases. Once they became a web-development company, Scott Mendenhall says, "the floodgates opened" and demand for Kolina's services soared. They rapidly tripled their staff. As of our interview in September 2000, it appeared that revenues for 2000 would be nearly quadruple their 1999 sales.

Although the company is now focused on services, Mendenhall continues to seek "home-run capability." One approach is to work for start-ups at lower fees in exchange for equity. Mendenhall refers to this strategy as making technology investments. In fact, his accountant has recommended that Kolina create a separate entity, Kolina Ventures, to track the performance of these investments.

For accounting purposes, Kolina Technologies (the consulting arm) will book the forgone fees as receivables from Kolina Ventures (the venture arm), which will acquire the equity in the start-ups. Assuming that the equity becomes valuable, Kolina Ventures will pay its bills to Kolina Technologies and still show a profit.

Another approach that Mendenhall is trying in his quest for a home run is building a network of consulting companies with complementary capabilities. Calling itself the Lode7 Alliance, this group is sharing leads and enhancing its ability to compete for larger projects.

Mendenhall is cautious about these home-run strategies. He points out that it is important not to lose focus on the core consulting business.

I asked Mendenhall to articulate the most important lesson he learned from the period when salesperson Nancy Goldberg was his mentor at Proxicom. Mendenhall answered that he came away with the idea that in sales, "it's all about the relationship." If you can provide outstanding customer service, then a small project can lead to a larger project as well as to referrals to other companies.

Mendenhall applied this lesson when he was given a tiny project by BBC-America. This first assignment netted Kolina less than $4,000. However, it led to a relationship that now brings in more than $20,000 a month. BBC-America also recommended Kolina to PBS Video (part of the Public Broadcasting System), a relationship that expanded to include PBS on-line and the PBS information technology department.

A strong relationship tends to reduce the sensitivity of the client to price. If you have proven your capability to deliver a system that satisfies the customer's needs, the client will be reluctant to try a different supplier simply because that supplier promises a lower rate.

When you hear me say that entrepreneurship is a contact sport, you may think that the only way to play is to attend networking events and that the best way to keep score is by counting the business cards you collect. However, that is not the way that Scott Mendenhall sees it. He says that while he has been an active participant in local networking events, "we have gotten zero business from that channel." Mendenhall instead believes that the best opportunities for taking advantage of contacts derive from depth rather than breadth of relationships. Customer satisfaction and attention are the keys to his approach to playing the contact sport.

NINE

How to Resolve Some Typical Dilemmas

Dilemmas Often Encountered by Start-Ups

Every start-up faces its own unique set of problems. However, there are many dilemmas that affect a large proportion of netstrappers. This section helps you to deal with these typical dilemmas.

1. Jump In with Both Feet or Take Your Time?

Therese Haar (Case No. 14) had left a lucrative software-project management position to form FarmerLink.com, a web site designed for farmers who sell produce directly to local consumers. The site was popular with consumers and farmers, but the business was a long way from profitability. How much longer should she keep it up before returning to the safety of a regular paycheck?

Kristen Jones was on the other side of this dilemma. She had an idea to start a web site for young lawyers and law students looking for jobs. However, she did not want to leave her job until she had obtained funding. Ironically, I ran into her at a networking event where the speaker said that investors want to see a high level of commitment on the part of the entrepreneur, and therefore they are loath to provide funding to someone who has not quit his or her job.

The dilemma that Jones and Haar were facing is a common one. Should you be aggressive or cautious? Should you jump in with both feet or take your time?

Many netstrappers begin gradually, keeping their day jobs and starting their under-the-radar businesses in their spare time. Raj Khera (Case No. 17) began GovCon.com, his web site for government contractors, in his spare time. Layla Masri (Case No. 21) started her web-design firm Bean Creative in her spare time. Both ultimately proved successful.

The dilemma is that you can suffer from being either too cautious or too aggressive. If you are overly cautious, you will miss out on an opportunity. If you are overly aggressive, your business may fall victim to pioneer time; that is, you do not allow enough time for the business to succeed, and when your aggressive self-imposed goals and deadlines are not met, you fold prematurely.

In general, I believe that in deciding whether to leave your job to start your own company, it is better to err on the side of being aggressive. The worst thing that can happen if you leave your job is that either you have to come back later and ask to have it back or you have to find another job elsewhere. While those outcomes are not pleasant, they are not the end of the world, either. For example, Jones should not be worried about finding new employment if her business fails to take off.

However, in Haar's case, I believe that some caution was in order. A major challenge with FarmerLink is that the farming community is very slow to embrace the Internet. She could have the right idea for the year 2001 or 2002, but if she made an all-out make-or-break effort in the year 2000, she may be out of business before the market develops for her.

I recommended to Haar that she take a job, preferably part-time, that provides her with some financial support but allows her to maintain FarmerLink.com. She will not be able to put as much energy into FarmerLink as she might like, but she can continue to build on the momentum that she has created.

Without intending it, I followed that course with homefair.com. I had started so early, in 1994, that the market was nonexistent. Suffering a classic case of pioneer time, I came to my self-imposed one-year deadline without having achieved profitability. I went back to work at Freddie Mac, my previous employer, and I expected to sell or fold

Homefair. However, my wife, Jackie, urged me to keep Homefair going, because she knew that I enjoyed the Internet business.

Although in retrospect I should have stayed with Homefair, it turned out that I had a sufficient head start that I was able to keep the site going by working nights and weekends. Soon after I returned to Freddie Mac, I found my critical partners, the Arizona relocation company that was able to translate our traffic into revenues by selling real estate companies the opportunity to obtain leads. Within a year, my partners had made the business promising enough that I arranged to scale back to part-time work at Freddie Mac. Within another year, when Central Newspapers invested in Homefair, I quit the Freddie Mac job for good.

In trying to resolve the dilemma of whether to jump in with both feet, the key question is: Will your market wait for you?

If the answer is "yes," the market will wait, then your approach should be cautious. It is more important to be able to stay the course than to get a fast start. This was my situation in 1995, and I believe that it was Therese Haar's situation in 2000.

If the answer is "no," then you should move aggressively. If you wait, then start-ups that appear to be competitors are bound to emerge. Lacking your own market presence, chances are you will overestimate these other firms. This will lead you to be even more hesitant. Eventually, you will give up completely, without having even made the attempt.

2. Pay in Equity or in Cash?

Like just about every business founder, Joseph Murgio (Case No. 15) needed to conserve cash. So when he needed to build the first version of his FamilyPoint.com web site, a community portal for families, he offered equity to his technical consulting firm. As a result, he became entangled in a bitter relationship.

This illustrates one of the hazards of using stock and stock options with employees and suppliers. You may be in a generous mood as you start your company, but you might regret it later as reality intrudes.

These days, all sorts of people who work with start-ups are willing to take some of their compensation in equity. You can trade stock for office space, legal services, accounting, advertising, consulting advice, public relations—there seems to be no limit. But are you wise to do this?

There are two advantages to paying in equity rather than cash. The first advantage is that you conserve on short-term dollars. The second advantage is that you align your interests with those of your service provider. With web developers, for example, you have less risk that they will deliver a shoddy product and say, "That's what you specified in the contract. If you want us to improve it, you will have to pay for another project." Instead, with equity in your company, the developers will be more focused on having the final product be successful.

However, there are at least two disadvantages to paying in equity rather than cash. One disadvantage is that in the long run you may end up paying much more for the service. Some routine accounting work that would cost $1,200 could turn into a $1 million giveaway. Of course, if this happens, it means that your company's stock is worth hundreds of millions, and you may not care.

The second disadvantage is that you may limit your subsequent flexibility. Very often, start-ups need to be restructured. You create a new company, either as a spin-off or by folding the first company altogether. At this point, the more shareholders you have, the more complicated and challenging it is to restructure.

For example, when I joined with the Scottsdale group of Rich Ganley, Bryan Schutjer, and Steve Ziomek, we did not bother to undertake a valuation of my company or the Homebuyer's Fair web site. We simply dissolved my company and formed a new company to run the web site, with each of us owning a one-fourth share.

Before this transaction, I owned 100 percent of my company. Suppose instead that I had obtained legal services by giving my attorney a share of equity, say 2 percent. Now, what would I owe the lawyer? Because this was a completely new company whose main value was going to be created in the future by the effort of our team (hence the division into one-fourth shares), I would not have felt that the attorney was entitled to a 2 percent share of my stake. Since the transaction with the Scottsdale group effectively valued the assets of my company at zero, one could argue that the attorney would be entitled to 2 percent of nothing. But would you really want to say that? To a lawyer?

The situation could easily become more complicated. For example, suppose that the new company, rather than giving me a 25-percent share, had given me an "earn-out" (a payment based on the next year's earnings) or paid me a salary. When I dissolve my first company, are the shareholders entitled to a proportion of the earn-out? Are they entitled to a proportion of my salary?

Because of the potential for subsequent transactions to create unexpected issues, my recommendation is to avoid giving away equity. Instead, try to use creative alternatives to help conserve cash and foster alignment with suppliers.

One alternative to giving your suppliers equity is to give them convertible preferred stock. This stock may convert to common stock. However, our company has the option of paying off in cash instead.

For example, suppose that my start-up incurs legal expenses of $4,500. I might negotiate an agreement where today I pay the attorney $500 in cash, and for the remaining $4,000, I offer preferred stock. The preferred stock has a dividend rate of 4 percent per month, until it is either converted to common stock or redeemed by the company for cash. In six months, if our company converts the preferred stock to common stock, the attorney will receive $4,960 in common stock. Alternatively, we can pay the attorney $4,960 in cash at that time.

The advantage of convertible preferred stock is that it does not force a complicated ownership structure on later investors. The next round of investors will have a choice of either cashing out the preferred shareholders or allowing their equity to convert to common stock. This allows the new investors to clean up the ownership structure should they choose to do so.

If I had my choice, I would use convertible preferred stock with employees and technical consultants rather than giving them stock options. It is fair to both you and your suppliers. It allows your suppliers to share in the upside should your company prosper. However, it limits their upside, due to the fact that they may be paid in cash rather than allowed to ride your stock price all the way up.

Thus, the right answer to the question of whether you should pay in cash or pay in equity probably is: "Neither." Ideally, you should pay using convertible preferred stock. If your suppliers will not accept this kind of arrangement, then my advice is to lean toward cash. Your new company needs the flexibility to restructure itself in unforeseen ways in the future.

3. Focus on Market Position or on Profitability?

Some of the most famous Internet start-ups have wrestled with the trade-off between profitability and market position. For example, when Netscape went public, its executives felt pressured to deliver profits. Critics argue that in the business market, Netscape over-priced its products and shortchanged quality, to the detriment of its long-term market position.

In contrast, Amazon.com was vehement in its determination to focus on long-term market position. The company's shareholders were exhorted to accept huge losses as part of this strategy. Critics believe that the result will be to saddle the company with debt obligations, adding to the shareholders' risks while cutting into their returns.

You do not have to be a large, publicly traded company to be confronted by these issues. We ran into this problem at Homefair.

We had always focused on profitability. Moreover, our agreement with our major investor, Central Newspapers, was much like an earn-out, with the partners' future payments tied to earnings over the next three years, with near-term earnings weighted more highly.

Meanwhile, in 1999, the stock market's "dot-com euphoria" was on the upswing, and several of our competitors were obtaining venture capital and dolling themselves up to go public. This meant that they were making all-out plays for market share, at almost any cost. We found that investors were valuing Internet companies largely on the basis of market position. Experts were talking about "price per registered user" and predicting a shakeout of companies that were only number two or three in their market niche.

We discussed with our parent company the fact that focusing on short-term profitability could lead us to lose market share to aggressive, venture-funded upstarts. Central Newspapers in turn talked to investment bankers, who advised our parent company that the value of our company would be greater if we maintained our position of market leadership.

Accordingly, Central Newspapers set up two funds that we could use for investments that would enhance our market position. This included a branding campaign and enhancements to our web site's infrastructure. One fund, for really long-term investments, did not count against our profits at all in our "earn-out." The other fund, for medium-term investments, was amortized rather than expensed, which eased its impact on the "earn-out." When we believed that a project belonged in one of these two buckets, we would, with the approval of a committee from Central Newspapers, finance the project out of one of the funds.

As it turned out, our parent company earned a very high return on these funds. We had barely begun spending them when the opportunity arose for Central Newspapers to sell our company to Homestore.com at a huge profit.

In our case, we did a number of things that I believe were a healthy way of handling the trade-off between market position and profitability.

- We had outside investors (Central Newspapers and their investment bankers) validate our view that market position was valuable.
- We set up a separate accounting mechanism for investments designed to enhance our long-term market position. This was particularly important for us in relation to our earn-out. In contrast, when Don Pickering (Case No. 1) sold his web-design firm Cosmix.com, he sacrificed a lot of personal returns by taking a longer-term approach to managing his company in spite of his earn-out provisions. Even if you are not under the gun of an earn-out, setting up a separate account for long-term investments will enable you to provide a clearer picture of the state of your company and give you an incentive to track the performance of projects aimed at enhancing your market position.
- Within our long-term investments to enhance market position, we identified specific projects with specific objectives. Again, this strengthens accountability. Also, it will allow you to articulate to current and potential investors your approach to building your market position.

4. Outsource or Do It Yourself?

When I first started my business, I asked my accountant for a suggestion about where to find a bookkeeper. Instead, he recommended that I keep my books myself, using a computer program.

It took me forever to set up the program, which in 1994 still had a pre-Windows interface. Moreover, even when I had the program working, I sometimes made mistakes, and these were very difficult to undo.

Obviously, I would have been better off going with my initial instinct to outsource my bookkeeping. What threw me was the fact that an expert—*my accountant*—was suggesting that I do it myself.

In fact, it is quite common for professionals to make these sorts of recommendations. You can get quite a surprising amount of advice to do things yourself.

- Many lawyers question the need to use an attorney to develop documents for such routine start-up activities as incorporating or filing for a patent. "It's just boilerplate," they will say.
- News reporters will tell you that they are much more interested in stories that come directly from the CEO than in press releases that come from public relations firms. Hence, you will be advised to handle your own PR.
- Web developers will tell you that it is very easy to learn HTML and JavaScript™.
- Graphic artists will tell you that it is easy to scan in artwork and save it as Internet-ready images.

I have come to realize that when you are looking for help that is considered routine within a particular field, an expert will tell you to do it yourself. This is because the expert is paid for custom work and thinks that anyone can handle routine "boilerplate." Thus, you get the advice to do it yourself—advice that you will be only too tempted to take.

My recommendation is that you outsource routine work—to low-cost service providers. Maybe a paralegal can take care of your first incorporation document. Maybe a high-school student can do your first graphics. Maybe a part-time bookkeeper can handle your accounting in the first year.

However, try to avoid the trap of doing unimportant work yourself in order to save cash. In the start-up phase, your time is the company's main asset, and you need to deploy that asset to its most valuable uses.

There are two aspects of your business that as a start-up you must not even consider outsourcing:

- Sales
- Web-site design

You cannot outsource sales without sacrificing a necessary opportunity to learn. As an under-the-radar company, you have an unproven offering without an established market. Until you develop a customer base and a reputation, only you will be able to sell your product or service. Remember, Professor Bhide found that among the successful start-ups he studied, 88 percent of the founders sold directly to users.

By web-site design, I mean decisions about what should appear on each page. Details about color and graphics can be a joint decision between you and a web-development firm. You cannot outsource website design because your web site represents your sales effort on-line.

A consulting firm cannot design your web site, because it knows nothing about the business. Many consulting firms say that they solve this problem by conducting an intensive interview with the business. My thinking is that if your business can be understood in a few hours of interviewing, then you probably do not have a meaningful franchise.

Although you may never write a line of code or draw a single graphic, you must be in charge of the design of your web site. You can outsource the implementation, but not the design.

5. Seek Funding Early or Late?

One of the most difficult dilemmas is choosing when to seek funding. I interviewed several entrepreneurs who felt they could have built their businesses more effectively had they sought funds sooner. However, there were also some who regretted their early funding. For example, in retrospect, Trevor Cornwell (Case No. 6) feels that his first $100,000 for Skyjet.com, the on-line reservation system for charter jets, cost him too much. My guess is that Brandon White (Case No. 22) took too much money too soon and would have been better off growing his WorldwideAngler.com fishing site more slowly. As it is, he may have too many mouths to feed relative to the size of the market.

There are two main advantages to obtaining funding early. One advantage is that your company can grow faster and achieve its operational milestones more quickly. The other advantage is that you are in a better position to overcome pioneer time. Without funding, pioneer time can lead you to reach your pain threshold and give up on your business too early.

There are two main disadvantages of early funding. One is that the time you spend trying to obtain financing detracts from your ability to execute your business. The other is that early funding gives you some very expensive mouths to feed. Although funding gives you more time to dig out, it means that you start out deeper in the hole.

In principle, the question of when to take funding can be answered in terms of economic theory: You should take funding whenever the internal rate of return is greater than the cost of funds. For example, if the investor is looking for a rate of return of 100 percent and your internal rate of return is 200 percent, then you should take funding.

This economic theory is almost certainly correct, even though it may be challenging to apply in the real world. It is worth understanding how the calculations ought to be made, even though the variables seem to be almost impossible to pin down in practice.

To calculate the internal rate of return for investment, compare the value of the company twelve months from now with and without funding. For example, suppose we project that without funding our company will be worth $500,000 in one year. However, with $1 million in funding today, we believe that our company will be worth $3.5 million in one year. In that case, $1 million today makes a difference of $3 million a year from now. A difference of $3 million represents a gain of $2 million over the $1 million in funding, or a 200-percent rate of return. That is our internal rate of return.

If we could get $1 million as a loan with an interest rate of 100 percent, we should take the loan. A year from now, we will owe $2 million, but the value of our company will be $3.5 million. On the other hand, if investors want to see a 500-percent rate of return, our projections do not support that.

Because the rate of failure in start-ups is very high, it is not unusual or unreasonable for investors to demand returns of 500 or 1,000 percent. Suppose you invest $100,000 each in ten start-ups and nine of them fail, with each failure costing you 100 percent of your money. If the tenth business succeeds and is worth $1.1 million, delivering a 1,000-percent return, then your average return is only 10 percent ($100,000 on an investment of $1 million).

Typically, investors in start-ups seek their high returns by taking equity rather than making loans. Nonetheless, the concept of a rate of return still matters. As an entrepreneur, you might be willing to undertake an enterprise where the internal rate of return is only 100 or 200 percent. However, investors will not be willing to take equity in those cases. If there is a 90-percent chance that your company will fail, then the upside needs to be much higher than a 200-percent rate of return in order to justify the investment.

Calculating the internal rate of return on investment is a challenge. It requires that you estimate the market value of your company in one year in a highly uncertain environment.

Another approach to making the decision on obtaining funding is to use a rule of thumb. My rule of thumb is that you should take money only when doing so will help your business achieve a positive cash flow within six to twelve months. If you cannot achieve positive cash flow within twelve months, even with funding, then you are going to dig yourself into a very deep hole. In that case, it might be better to stay in a shallower hole longer than get into a deep hole sooner.

Conclusion

All start-ups face difficult choices. Most of the dilemmas you face will be issues that cannot be anticipated ahead of time. That is what makes entrepreneurship interesting and challenging. However, the dilemmas described in this chapter are ones that you ought to think about ahead of time. Nearly every netstrapper faces the issues of when to jump in full-time, whether to pay suppliers in equity or cash, whether to sacrifice short-term profitability for long-term value, which functions to outsource, and when to seek funding.

Case No. 21: Layla Masri

How do you define success? Venture capitalists might set a goal of ten times the amount of their investment, so that a company might have to earn tens of millions of dollars a year in order to meet their objectives. On the other hand, many entrepreneurs would be satisfied just to replace the salary they gave up when they quit working for someone else.

Layla Masri, having experienced dysfunctional management behavior, downsizing, and other "perks" of corporate life, is more than
happy to have built a small web-development consulting firm that
has exceeded her financial goals and even attracted attention from
potential buyers. So far, Masri has resisted the urge to sell out. Having her own business gives her an opportunity to run a company the
way she would like rather than suffering from the arbitrary decisions
of others. "I want to be in charge of my destiny," she says.

Masri and her husband, Keith Soares, started Bean Creative in their
spare time, while they were doing advertising work at a trade association. Her background was in writing, his in graphic design. They had
wanted to start their own business for a while, and in the past they
had talked about forming an all-purpose creative shop that handled
print media as well as the Internet. However, by the time they were
ready to launch in early 1997, the Internet had reached the point
where it made sense to focus solely on that medium.

In order to build a portfolio, they literally gave away their first
web site, to a friend who wanted one for his tile business. Their first
paying client, who found them in the Yahoo! directory while searching for a local web-design firm, was "a typical first client," says
Masri, meaning that the client took advantage of the fact that Bean
Creative was new and needed to build a reputation.

The first year was difficult. To earn business, Bean Creative had to
offer fixed-bid terms, which meant committing to doing a job for a
fixed price. At times, this was disadvantageous. In one particular instance, their client paired Bean Creative with another company that
was supplying back-end technology for Bean Creative's front-end design, and the process of getting the pieces to fit together proved to be
very time consuming relative to the revenue the project brought in.

Still thinking of Bean Creative as a sideline, Masri took a job with
an advertising firm. Early in 1998, the firm called a group of employees, including Masri, into a meeting and told them that they were being "downsized." At this point, Bean Creative had enough work to
cover about six months of Masri's salary, and she decided that it was
time to try to put all of her energy into her own business.

Later that year, Soares was also "downsized," but he took another
job, because the monthly fluctuations in income from Bean Creative
were still making the couple nervous. His new job happened to provide Soares with an opportunity to become more familiar with the
type of programming that is needed for data-driven web sites. Within

six months, Bean Creative was able to win bids on more expensive projects, and Soares was finally able to join his wife full-time.

Today, Bean Creative charges for business on the basis of hours worked rather than using fixed-bid pricing. This helps to reduce the tension that can arise in a fixed-bid environment when the client asks for a reasonable enhancement that was not included in the original specification. Masri says that fixed-bid contracts would be particularly unwieldy today, when web sites are more complicated than they were a few years ago. For budgeting purposes, clients are given an estimate of the work that will be needed to complete the project, but estimates are not binding.

Bean Creative does no advertising. Its business comes from a combination of word-of-mouth referrals and potential contacts finding their site on the Internet. Masri's marketing strategy includes getting listed in specialized directories of web-design firms. For positioning on major portals such as Yahoo!, she makes sure that the search engines know about Bean Creative's geographic location, because clients often want to work with a company that is local to Washington, D.C., including its Virginia and Maryland suburbs.

The strategy of building a portfolio ultimately paid off. Customers can come to Bean Creative's web site and see examples of work done for the company's client base, including *National Geographic* and Carnival Cruise Lines.

One mistake that Masri wishes they had avoided was taking on clients with whom they did not have a good working relationship. The end result was often a site that Bean Creative did not even want to show in its portfolio. Masri and Soares have learned to be selective in who they accept as a client.

As of my interview with Masri in August 2000, business had expanded to include three additional employees, as well as a number of freelancers who are brought in to staff projects as needed. No longer needing to subsidize clients in order to build a portfolio, Masri said their profit margin had risen to 50 percent of sales. They had already met their financial goals for the year, including tripling their income from 1999.

Case No. 22: Brandon White

As crowded as the Web has become, it is still missing information that you would expect to find there. For example, in 1996, Brandon

White, while working on his master's degree in psychology at Washington College, was looking for information on fishing in the nearby Chesapeake Bay. He expected to find a site with fishing reports, weather information, and the types of articles one might find in a regional fishing magazine.

When White, an avid angler, did not find the fishing information that he expected, he began to think in terms of creating his own web site for fishermen. He had no idea how to build a web site, so he started to hang around the computer center at Washington College. He befriended the best undergraduate computer whiz, Tom Gattone, and recruited him as a partner, albeit a skeptical one.

In order to pay Gattone a salary, White took a part-time job at a spinach farm, using his wages from that to fund initial development. In March 1997, they were up and running as ChesapeakeAngler.com. The site included:

- Articles about fishing in the area
- Fishing reports about where fish were biting
- Fishing regulations
- News from local sources, such as Maryland's Department of Natural Resources
- Weather reports
- Tides
- A message board system for fishermen to pass along tips to one another

White was offering a total solution to a fisherman's problem, which is how to catch more fish.

Within three months of launch, his site was favorably reviewed in a regional magazine. With that write-up, plus word-of-mouth publicity, traffic to the site and activity on the message boards increased. Fishermen from outside the region found the site, and they started asking White if he could provide similar information for their locations.

White's revenue model was advertising, from companies that sell boats, tackle, or travel information for avid fishermen, as well as other companies that would want to advertise to this demographic. This was a challenging group of businesses to convince to advertise. Most owners of tackle shops rejected the concept of Internet advertising, but a few took the view that "This is going to be big." Among the businesses that did choose to advertise, those that provided information such as fishing reports were more successful than those that merely used the type of ad that would appear in the Yellow Pages.

By the summer of 1997, White decided to attempt to expand the site to include additional regions. Gattone was now sufficiently impressed to invest $25,000, as did Brennan Starkey, White's boss at the spinach farm. White quit both the job and his graduate work to devote full time to his fishing site. By January 1998, he and Gattone launched WorldwideAngler.com, which added coverage in the northeastern United States and Florida.

In 1998, White began the process of locating potential investors. Reading a business magazine, White noticed that a photo of a man who had just invested in a venture capital firm showed him holding a fishing rod. Using the Internet, White looked up the man's address and wrote him a letter. The following Wednesday, the man called and said, "Give me a term sheet by Monday." At that time, White had no idea what a term sheet should contain.

Unfortunately, the venture capital firm was one that funds firms in the late stages, whereas White's firm was at the seed stage. However, his interest was now piqued. White's grandfather had a friend whose son was Mark Walsh, who played a major role in the formation of VerticalNet, an early entrant in the B2B arena (business-to-business markets on the Web). Walsh said that if the venture capital firm would not back White, "My friends and I will."

Meanwhile, White saw a picture in the Washington College magazine of an alumnus, Matt Weir, who did angel investing. White contacted the alumnus, who happened to have lunch with Tom McMurray, a retired venture capitalist. It turned out that McMurray was an avid fisherman, and he had been using White's web site for two years. Weir gave White's phone number to McMurray.

Shortly thereafter, White received a phone call. "Hi, I'm Tom McMurray. I was with Sequoia Capital. You may have heard of us. We funded Yahoo!, Cisco, Apple . . . I want to come see you tomorrow." White said that would be okay.

When McMurray saw White's office, in the spare bedroom of his apartment in Easton, Maryland, he said, "Is this really how you're operating? . . . Don't worry, this is how we found Cisco." They went to lunch, and at the restaurant McMurray turned over a placemat and outlined the business.

After lunch, White took McMurray fishing, and McMurray caught a fish on his first cast. "That's when I had him hooked," White jokes.

On the boat, they agreed on a valuation for the business, and Mc-Murray committed some of his personal money and agreed to serve on the board.

At this point, White went back to Mark Walsh, who was floored that White had landed McMurray from Sequoia. He joined up and also brought along Gene Quinn, who brought expertise in sports, media, and on-line marketing.

Finally, in May 1999, White completed his initial round of funding, with a total of $1 million. Investors even included the man whose photo White had seen in the business magazine back in 1998 (he persisted with the contact, even meeting the gentleman in Florida). Shortly before the round closed, he received a call from Frank Bonsal of New Enterprise Associates, giving WorldwideAngler.com another famous investor.

Today, WorldwideAngler.com employs fifteen people. Its content covers all fourteen fishing regions of the United States, as well as five regions overseas. Only some segments of the fishing community use the Web ("It might still be too early," White concedes when assessing his business.) However, the site gets a healthy 1.3 million page views a month. In a niche where much of the growth is still in the future, this is a strong base from which to build.

If these could be monetized at a rate of $50 per 1,000 page views (not an unrealistic goal for a targeted site), its current page views would translate into $65,000 a month. However, one challenge for WorldwideAngler is the fact that the fishing-boat industry, which is the most promising source of sponsorship revenue, is undergoing a downturn. This may reduce the ability of WorldwideAngler to monetize its page views.

I asked White to explain how he was able to build up such strong site traffic even though in two years they have spent less than $100,000 on marketing. He mentioned the following factors:

- Understanding your audience. WorldwideAngler takes the view that its visitors want to catch more fish and have a better fishing experience. The site is designed with those goals in mind. This in turn leads to word-of-mouth traffic. Just as fishing lures spread from fisherman to fisherman by word of mouth, the recommendations of other fishermen are the most powerful form of advertising for WorldwideAngler.com.

- Use of viral marketing. For example, WorldwideAngler offers inexpensive promotions, such as a wrapper to put around a drink can, to people who recommend the site to five friends.
- Use of public relations. Articles in the press are better and cheaper than advertising.
- Use of sponsored events such as picnics and fishing tournaments.
- Putting flyers on cars at fishing shows.
- Putting the web-site address on the cars and boats of WorldwideAngler.com employees.

TEN

Characteristics of Successful Netstrappers

The Ideal Netstrapper

Do you have what it takes to be a netstrapper? That's a good question, and I wish I could give you a scientific answer. That is, I wish I could give an answer based on statistical analysis of a controlled experiment. Instead, what I can offer is the impressions and opinions I have gained from my own experience, from reading books like Bhide's *The Origin and Evolution of New Businesses*, and from interviews with over two dozen netstrappers. Based on these impressions, perhaps you can compare yourself to successful under-the-radar entrepreneurs and identify areas for development.

1. Charm

It wasn't so much their music that attracted them to me at first. It was their *charm*. They were very charming people.

—George Martin, interviewed in *The Compleat Beatles*, explaining
why he agreed to produce the Beatles' first record

You have heard me say that entrepreneurship is a contact sport. Your survival depends on your ability to make the right contacts. You need to be able to open the door to customers, tap into technical talent, get advice, and coax strangers into providing funding. Even direct contacts are not enough. Some of your most valuable contacts will be people who themselves offer no help but who can supply you with other contacts.

The Internet, by expanding opportunities for communication, is making the process of acquiring and using contacts even easier. For example, to find a literary agent for this book, I sent an e-mail to author Chris Locke in Colorado with a subject-heading "ISO Literary Agent." Within hours, he sent a reply that introduced me to his agent for *The Cluetrain Manifesto*, David Miller, who works out of Boston and who eventually became my agent.

Still, because contacts are so important, geographic proximity retains value. That is why entrepreneurship is heavily concentrated, in locations like Silicon Valley.

So, if you're going to be an entrepreneur, you need to acquire contacts. But all of the contacts in the world won't do you any good unless people want to work with you. That is why an entrepreneur must have charm.

Dan Cunningham (Case No. 23) had nothing but charm going for him when he built 507Media, the company with a system for booking bands on-line for weddings and other events. He made up for his lack of capital by charming his employees into working for "deferred salary." He made up for his lack of industry knowledge and contacts by ingratiating himself with the members of the Pho List, a group of music-industry folks that meets regularly at a Vietnamese restaurant.

One key to having charm is being willing to accept advice graciously. Many entrepreneurs are too busy trying to deliver their pitch to listen to advice from customers or potential investors. They turn off their audience by becoming defensive and argumentative when someone offers advice.

When I met Jay Minkoff (the Philadelphia publisher of guides for new homes and apartments), I listened eagerly to his opinions and advice. When he quizzed me on the demographics of the Internet at the time (the summer of 1994) and pronounced, "This is an apartment market," I acknowledged his insight.

My willingness to listen and accept coaching paid off with Minkoff. Soon, he was faxing me a list of over fifty apartment-locator services around the country that were potential customers for Homefair. A few months later, I asked him if he knew some companies that I could contact that worked generically in relocation. One of the contacts he provided led me to Rich Ganley in Scottsdale, Arizona, which in turn led to the partnership that took my business from my accountant's estimated value of $20,000 to the point where we were purchased for $85 million.

Another key to having charm is to show interest in other people. I call it "doing the role reversal." Professor Bhide has a more academic way of expressing it.

> Perceptive entrepreneurs require an "allocentric" orientation: They must look at the world through other's eyes and see what others value and how they "frame" their choices. They have to be skilled at eliciting information, asking questions in an unthreatening way that encourages others to open up. They have to listen without a confirmation bias and be sensitive to the unspoken, to body language and other nonverbal cues.
>
> (Source: Bhide, *The Origin and Evolution of New Businesses*, pp. 107–108)

For example, when I conduct job interviews, I want to convey to applicants that their contributions and their career goals will be valued. I encourage applicants to ask questions. For my part, I ask questions that a career counselor might ask. (Why did you go into civil engineering? How did you go from there to becoming a software developer? Looking at this job opportunity, what excites you the most about it? What concerns you the most about it?)

This interviewing style demonstrates to applicants that their opinions matter to me. It conveys my genuine concern for their growth and career development. In today's tight job market, particularly for technical staff, to be successful in hiring you need charm.

I was charming during sales calls in that I did not give PowerPoint presentations. This was primarily because I do not know how to use PowerPoint. However, not having a slide show forced me to have conversations with my customers. These conversations enabled me to learn something about their businesses and their needs. As *The Cluetrain Manifesto* says, "Markets are conversations." Or as expert sales coach Michael O'Horo says at salesresults.com, "Presentations don't make sales. They prevent sales."

I don't think you can expect to be charming all the time. For everyone, there are situations and people that represent a challenge. You have to try to work around those situations.

For example, I often have hostile feelings toward people in powerful positions. Even though I try to hide my attitude, corporate executives can somehow sense my lack of respect. In short, I doubt that I could ever be charming to the head of a large corporate IT department.

When two of my Homefair partners, Rich Ganley and Bryan Schutjer, were negotiating the major transactions involving our sale to Central Newspapers and later Homestore.com, I never met the principals on the other side until after the deals were final. I do not remember anyone consciously saying that it would be safer keeping me under wraps. However, I think that in the back of all of our minds was a concern that my less charming self might come out if I were brought into the negotiations with the major honchos from the acquiring companies.

With the Internet, one point to keep in mind is the need to cultivate long-distance charm. E-mail is notorious as a medium for giving offense, in part because of the haste with which it can be composed and sent and in part because the distance and anonymity of the Net have fostered a cultural habit of incivility and downright rudeness. As an entrepreneur, you cannot afford any unnecessary enemies. When you use e-mail, make a conscious effort to convey charm.

2. Talent-Scouting Ability

The top challenge faced by entrepreneurs in the United States is finding and retaining quality people to work for them, according to a report released recently by the National Commission on Entrepreneurship. Obtaining seed capital is the second-biggest challenge, according to the commission's survey of more than 250 entrepreneurs in 17 cities.
—Elaine Wu, "Top Challenge for Entrepreneurs: Finding People,"
dbusiness.com, July 26, 2000

To be fair, I should point out that the survey cited above was taken over an eight-month period, some of which went back to the time when dot-com mania was at its height with investors. Today, obtaining seed capital would probably show up as a higher concern than it was during the survey. Nonetheless, the market for talent is extremely tight.

In today's economy, talent is the critical resource. If an agricultural economy's task is to allocate land and an industrial economy's task is to allocate capital, then the information economy's task is to allocate talent.

Established companies and venture-funded firms are able to hire the people with the best résumés and who seem to represent the highest quality at the least risk. In order to compete with these well-funded rivals, netstrappers have to be more creative and take more risks in their search for talent. Netstrappers who can identify talent that others miss will have an advantage. Those who overlook talent or who misread talent will struggle.

One of the best illustrations of good talent scouting was the team that Neil Rosen assembled at TheSchoolReport.com, a company that obtained information about schools and used this information to provide real estate agents with consumer leads. The Connecticut Menagerie, as I called it, was a group of the type of low-budget, highly productive oddballs you find only at companies that are bootstrapped.

The Connecticut Menagerie

> *The inability to provide compelling short-term inducements (or credible long-term insurance or payoffs) to top-tier resource providers forced entrepreneurs to make do with the second tier . . .*
>
> *In the typical VC-backed start-up, the VCs will insist that the entrepreneur recruit a top-quality team quickly. Generous cash compensation and stock options are used to attract experienced and capable personnel . . . Bootstrapped ventures cannot afford to pay such salaries; and the perceived value of equity in their companies also is low . . . [Their employees] rarely were well-educated or experienced, and many had been unemployed or dissatisfied with previous jobs.*
>
> —Bhide, *The Origin and Evolution*
> *of New Businesses*, p. 87

For netstrappers, a big challenge is obtaining top-tier performance from a team that does not necessarily have top-tier credentials. One netstrapper who did this very effectively was Neil Rosen, the founder of TheSchoolReport.com, a company with which Homefair merged in 1998.

Rosen, whose background is in teaching, knew that when people with children buy a house, one of their biggest concerns is the local schools. They want information about class size, test scores, sports, extracurricular activities, special programs, and so on. He conceived the idea of creating a nationwide database with this information and then selling the relevant local data to real estate agents on a diskette.

Meanwhile, along came the Internet, and Rosen saw an opportunity to sell the school information directly to consumers. Unfortunately, he learned as we did that consumers were reluctant to pay for information. Both Homefair and TheSchoolReport realized (not entirely independently—we were sharing ideas back and forth for years prior to the merger) that although consumers would not pay with hard cash, they were willing to provide contact information to real estate agents in exchange for receiving data. Thus, the revenue model became real estate agents paying for leads rather than consumers paying for data. Because real estate agents place such a high value on getting their name and photograph in front of people, the lead-generating package that Rosen sold the agents included a customized web-page ad on his site.

Had Rosen used top-tier resources, it would have cost him tens of millions of dollars to assemble the school information as well as develop the systems on the Web necessary to deliver the information to consumers and build the customized ads for the real estate agents. Instead, he made ingenious use of second-tier resources to obtain top-tier results.

I used to call Rosen's team the Connecticut Menagerie. This was a misnomer, because he used a database programmer based in Boston and a web-programming consultant based in New York, in addition to the staff at his office in Fairfield, Connecticut. But the term "menagerie" was hardly an exaggeration.

Rosen had his HTML programming done by a team that included a kid out of high school and a Russian émigré—people whose work could be procured for salaries of roughly half the going market rate. However, that is not unusual. Many netstrappers will tell you stories about using "a kid" or "a guy working out of his basement" for HTML coding, which does not require a true professional.

The truly amazing capabilities of the Menagerie were in the fields of research and web programming. These were the keys to Rosen's business.

My first visit to the Menagerie was at a joint meeting of Homefair and TheSchoolReport shortly after the merger between our two companies (in fact, at that time the agreement was awaiting final approval from our parent company, Central Newspapers, Inc.). At this meeting, Rosen introduced his head of research to us by saying, "And here is the person who is responsible for gathering all of our data. Who are you calling yourself this month?—she changes her name about once or twice a year—I think now she wants to be called Meredith."

In my experience, you can suspect some emotional instability if someone changes his or her hairstyle often, so you can imagine how nervous I felt encountering a person who was in the habit of regularly changing her name. And this was the most critical person in the entire operation, because "Meredith" was the keeper of the "company jewels," the massive database of school information. She had designed and molded the data-gathering operation, recruiting and training an army of housewives working part-time out of their homes to call school districts around the country. Fortunately, although she was quite a character, my worst fears—that she would go completely off the deep end, leaving us with no way to fill in for her capability—were never realized. She was indeed worthy of the trust that Rosen placed in her.

An executive of the caliber of "Meredith" was available to TheSchoolReport.com because the corporate talent-evaluation process had passed her up. My guess is that her fatal flaw in the Dilbert sector was honesty.

Although there were no wallflowers on our team, "Meredith" was particularly direct and forceful in expressing her opinions. When she opposed a project, such as attempting to create a ranking system for schools, she let us know in no uncertain terms. I think that the corporate environment tends to be fairly unfriendly to people who speak their minds in such fashion. In the Dilbert sector, if you say that you are against a project, you wind up being labeled "not a team player." In that situation, the strategy for getting ahead is to say nothing and instead to go about quietly undermining the project. Oh, by the way, did I tell you that I'm cynical when it comes to corporate politics?

Another critical component of the Menagerie was Rosen's primary computer consultant, Paul Delano. The match between Rosen and Delano was ideal. Rosen had no computer background at all, and the features he would request for systems made them extremely complex. Delano was very well trained and talented, and he took pride in building elegant, flexible systems. More important, Delano was a business novice and committed himself to fixed-bid contracts that embodied serious underestimates of the work required to complete the projects. The result of all of this was that Rosen obtained a flexible, feature-rich system at a bargain price.

Unfortunately for me, by the time the merger took place, Paul Delano had figured out how to stand up to the bear. He was asking us for $150 an hour, and even that was only if his time freed him up from commitments to customers who were paying him still higher rates.

Rosen was a volcano of ideas. He was fiercely controlling. The expectations that he set and the demands that he made were unrealistic and outlandish. But in people like "Meredith" or Paul Delano, he managed to find the rare individuals who could realize the unrealistic and deliver the outlandish at a discount.

One of the factors that made the Menagerie work was that there were some elements present to maintain sanity. Rosen's wife, Roseann, brought her soft-spoken, calming presence into the office on a part-time basis. And the company controller, Tina Diaz, was a solid, reliable operations manager, willing to put in as much overtime as was needed to make sure that the Menagerie executed the fundamentals of billing and collection.

The odd man out in the Menagerie was David, who had been brought in by Rosen's investors as CEO shortly before our merger discussions got underway. David was a first-tier resource, an alumnus of Dartmouth, Harvard, and McKinsey. Those credentials alone will practically get you funding from a venture capitalist. Still, he was not a netstrapper. A few months after the merger closed, he left. However, we did not feel that losing him was anything to worry about. Given the choice, we were much happier to have retained "Meredith" in the Menagerie!

Your challenge is to obtain first-tier performance, using second-tier resources on a third-tier budget. For example, Trevor Cornwell (Case No. 6) built the first version of Skyjet.com, his reservation system for charter jets, using a software developer from Hungary who charged only $5 an hour. This illustrates the type of talent scouting that a netstrapper must often do.

On the other hand, when I asked netstrappers to talk about mistakes that they regretted, several of them, including Mike Covel (Case No. 16) and Don Britton (Case No. 8), listed poor personnel decisions as being their biggest errors. There are few things more debilitating in a small start-up than a hire who turns out to be unable to perform up to expectations.

My guess is that talent scouting is so important that in the future it will be done scientifically, using computer models that correlate the results of personality tests with outcomes in various employment situations. Companies like Microsoft and Capital One do this today.

For now, we evaluate talent intuitively. As a result, two managers will use approaches that seem to be totally different, even contradictory. For example, Aleksander Totic, principal engineer of Epinions.com, was quoted as saying:

> When it comes to hiring, I'm still in the Netscape mode. If during a job interview someone asks more questions about business than engineering, he or she doesn't get the job.
>
> (Source: Quoted in "Netscapees," *Forbes*, September 4, 2000)

When I interview technical staff, I take nearly the opposite view from Aleksander Totic. If a technical applicant were to ask me penetrating questions about the business, I would regard that as a strong plus.

Given these differences in approaches for evaluating talent, I cannot say that any one method is best. I do believe that there is some evidence that favors being systematic by putting each candidate through the same interview process. I believe also that the evidence favors having 360-degree interviews, where potential colleagues and subordinates as well as the potential supervisor are given an opportunity to interview the candidate. In addition, having all of the interviewers meet afterward for a group debriefing has been found to be a good practice.

3. Information Sponges

Some netstrappers are Ph.D.s, and some are GEDs. Regardless, they read avidly, forward useful articles to others, and appreciate receiving information that is forwarded to them. With the pace of innovation today, people who cannot accept the need to retool themselves and learn new skills will be unable to operate effectively in the leading-edge zone where netstrappers work.

An information sponge is someone who constantly seeks to learn both from reading and from experience. Bill Baker (Case No. 24), founder of HireRight.com, a company that provides employment-screening services, fits that mold. He loves to make a concentrated effort to learn everything he can about a new technology opportunity. He was able to identify a need for faster, more reliable screening of job candidates. He figured out which databases he would need to access in order to meet that need.

Scott McLoughlin (Case No. 2), who founded the Adrenaline Group, is another example of an information sponge. When he started his business, he read several books on marketing and entrepreneurship. He then set out to apply the ideas from his reading to the challenge of developing his company. For an information sponge, knowledge is meaningful if and only if it can be applied.

It is important to be an information sponge because of the speed with which you have to make decisions. In 1997, we were having problems with our Netscape server, and we finally concluded that the situation was not going to be remedied. At that point, we had to choose between going for a Microsoft-based solution or a solution based on Java servlets. Both approaches posed risks. Microsoft's server operating system, known at the time as Windows NT™, was not considered reliable enough for our requirements. However, Java servlets were new and untried.

This is the type of decision that most corporations will take months to make, requiring white papers, specification comparisons, studies by consultants, and so forth. We did not have that luxury. My partners and I wanted the situation resolved in two weeks or less.

Fortunately, as an information sponge, I had taken an eight-week night course in Java in 1996, which gave me just enough exposure to give me confidence that it made sense as a language for server applications. When Dirk Reinshagen, our consultant, reported his initial positive impressions of Sun's JavaWebServer™, we adopted it. Our server performance improved dramatically as a result.

Although netstrappers are information sponges, they are not information gluttons. They tend to be fairly focused in terms of their information gathering. They are interested in what they can absorb and apply, not in what they can collect and store. For McLoughlin, *The E-Myth Revisited* was an important book because it caters to his situation. As a skilled technician trying to start a business in his specialty, McLoughlin fit precisely into the intended target audience for that book. Entrepreneurs in different circumstances might see no reason to read it.

Before Homestore.com and I parted company, their people wanted to put me on a project to do background research on the characteristics of the household furnishings industry. They were looking for articles about industry trends, information about market shares of different vendors, and so forth. I guess they were trying to assemble supporting documents for an initiative in that field. I did not see how the information that we were supposed to gather could be used for anything other than filler in a business plan. None of the information was critical to making the go or no-go decision on the initiative. A netstrapper would not waste time collecting it.

Netstrappers must be comfortable operating in an environment of ambiguity. To me, this means focusing on the information that is going to make a difference to your decision. People who are uncomfortable with ambiguity either tune out information that challenges their preconceptions or else go overboard in gathering irrelevant information, leading to "analysis paralysis." The information sponges absorb what they need—no more, no less.

4. Ability to Stand Up to the Bear

You are going to need revenue. In order to get enough revenue, chances are at some point you are going to have to propose to a customer a price that represents an outrageously high markup over your costs, and you will have to make that price stick. I call this "standing up to the bear."

I once read somewhere that when you meet a bear in the woods, you should not run away. The bear is too fast for you. Instead, your best chance is to stand up tall and show the bear that you are not intimidated. If you can pull it off, the bear will not bother you.

I don't know whether standing up to the bear really works in the woods. I can't say that I'd ever want to try it. But I've always wanted to use it as a metaphor.

Just as most of us instinctively run from the bear, I think that most of us are too quick to reduce our pricing to something that will just cover our costs. I don't know the psychology involved—it could be guilt, fear of rejection, or eagerness to please. In any case, economic theory notwithstanding, we seldom maximize profits.

When I think of maximizing profits, I think of Rich Ganley (Case No. 3) quoting Prudential a price of $200,000 for a project that would have cost us about $25,000. Moreover, Prudential management knew that its existing processes did not fit well with the leads that the company was going to receive from consumers using our web site. Ganley told Prudential executives to expect a low conversion rate until Prudential learned the nuances of dealing with customers over the Internet. He said that they should think of trying to work the leads as going to school and to treat the $200,000 as "tuition." That's standing up to the bear.

I think of Mike Covel (Case No. 16), who sells a course manual and CD-ROM to financial speculators on his Turtletrader.com web site. He stuck to his price of $1,000 even after almost six months of not making a single sale. That's standing up to the bear.

On the other hand, I think of Derek Scruggs (Case No. 10) of Distributed Bits running low on cash after he developed an e-mail management program for the Chicago Board Options Exchange and charged them less than his cost. At the time, he hoped to recover the cost on later sales. He ran away from the bear, and the bear got him.

Based on a few limited cases, one is tempted to leap to the generalization that it's the entrepreneurs who have tasted bankruptcy or come close to doing so who are the best at standing up to the bear. Ganley and Covel fit that description. The entrepreneurs with the lowest thresholds for personal financial pain, including Layla Masri, Rob Main (Case No. 4), and myself, seemed to have the least aptitude for standing up to the bear. Masri's web-design company BeanCreative.com ultimately succeeded, but she and her partner spent a long time eking out a part-time living as they charged customers low prices. Electric Press, the web-development and hosting service that Main helped found, never achieved as much as its more aggressive rivals in the field. It was only his second business, eFed.com, that brought him a big success.

Operating in environments where customers have no idea what constitutes a reasonable price, the timid approach is to charge . . . a reasonable price. Doh-oh!! That is not profit-maximizing behavior. Under those circumstances, you should be trying to get away with charging *unreasonable* prices.

5. Beginner's Mind

In his study of successful entrepreneurs, Professor Bhide found that

> [B]esides lacking business or managerial experience, entrepreneurs often have limited knowledge of or contacts in the industry they enter . . . About 40 percent of the Inc. founders I interviewed had no prior experience in the industry in which they launched their ventures, and among those who did, the experience often did not seem deep or well rounded.
>
> (Source: Bhide, *The Origin and Evolution of New Businesses*, p. 36)

Many netstrappers also enter markets in which they begin with limited knowledge or contacts. For example, Dan Cunningham's company developed a web application for the music industry, even though his background is civil engineering.

Perhaps the best example of "beginner's mind" is Trevor Cornwell of Skyjet.com. He knew nothing at all about the charter-jet industry, but he happened to notice that a business associate had a plane that spent a lot of time on the ground waiting between trips. A venture capitalist would not have picked out Trevor Cornwell as the right person with the "domain expertise" to execute a business plan to create a virtual airline out of the charter-jet operators, but he did it anyway.

Can it be that when it comes to domain expertise, ignorance is bliss?

You can put a positive spin on ignorance and naïveté by using the phrase "beginner's mind," which comes from a treatise on Zen Buddhism. The term suggests a freedom from the constraints of too much expertise.

For example, in June 1999, I met with several veterans of the moving industry to discuss a web site that would allow moving companies to make competing bids for household shipments. One challenge to implementing a bidding model for household moves is that moving companies typically send out estimators to the home in order to have an idea of the weight of the shipment. To deal with this problem, the industry people thought in terms of training consumers to carry out the process that an estimator would go through in filling out what the industry calls "cube sheets."

Instead, "beginner's mind" led me to propose that they attempt a completely different method of estimation, using the demographics of the household (such as income, number of household members, and length of time in residence) as well as characteristics of the house, such as number of bedrooms. The formula from the estimate could be derived from a statistical analysis of actual moves.

As of this writing, we do not know whether a statistical estimator will be sufficiently accurate to meet the need. Should it work, however, it will be much simpler than teaching consumers to do "cube sheets," and it will not be as subject to manipulation by the customer. This illustrates the advantage of beginner's mind. It was the person who came into the meeting knowing nothing at all about the moving industry who proposed an innovative solution to one of the most vexing challenges with the new business idea.

6. Ability to Focus

Professor Bhide's data show that 88 percent of entrepreneurs credit their success to extraordinary execution of an ordinary idea, with only 12 percent claiming to have started with an extraordinary idea. If success depends on execution, then execution depends on focus. However, focus is not the strong suit of the typical visionary.

Bhide's study predates the Internet, which has increased the value of visionary ideas. However, my guess is that even with Internet businesses, fewer than half of the founders are visionaries.

Among the founders that I interviewed, certainly Bill Baker is a visionary. He has started several companies that led the way in personal computing and the Internet. Another visionary is Don Britton (Case No. 8), who sees that small businesses have difficulty maintaining their computer networks and that the technology has arrived to enable such businesses to turn these problems over to remote third parties.

Visionaries have the ability to see and exploit the "killer trends" that can help to power a business. Bill Baker saw the personal-computer revolution and the potential for word-processing software back in the 1970s. Don Britton sees that as the cost of bandwidth falls and the cost of technical talent rises, small businesses will find it increasingly economical to outsource completely their computing services. To the extent that starting Homefair made any sense, it was because I saw the power of the Web as a commercial tool.

Visionaries also have the ability to foresee and overcome key tactical obstacles. On September 15, 1940, England stood alone against Germany, and its battle for survival was at its climax. It was the heaviest day of fighting in the air war known as the Battle of Britain. On that day, of all things, Winston Churchill was envisioning the eventual amphibious assault to retake Europe. For that purpose, in commenting on the proposed budget of the Royal Navy, he indicated his preference to shift resources toward the building of landing craft, to carry troops from the sea to a beach. *Landing craft*. They came in handy on D-Day, nearly four years later.

Unfortunately, visionaries also tend to be distractible. Churchill's military staff viewed him this way. Often, they ignored his requests, expecting or hoping that his mind would shift elsewhere. Only if he asked for a project repeatedly were they convinced that he was not going to forget about it.

A fictional visionary is the character Toad, in Kenneth Grahame's children's classic, *The Wind in the Willows*. In one scene, Toad's new horse-drawn carriage has been rudely thrown into a ditch by an automobile. Toad's friends expect to find him outraged, but instead Toad sits in a state of peace, blissfully imitating the sound of the car's horn. The new form of transport has captured Toad's imagination.

In my first supervisory job at Freddie Mac, I inherited an employee who was much like Toad. This Toad was a computer programmer, and a talented one at that. But he was very distractible. One day, for reasons known only to himself, he was wandering through the tape library in the computer center in the basement of the building, and he pulled down a couple of tapes, curious to read the labels. It turned out that they contained mortgage data that had been missing for years and given up for lost. Eventually, the tapes he found were used to restore that data, a coup that earned the "project of the year" award in the IT division. Three cheers for distractibility.

On the other hand, you could never give this Toad an assignment with a deadline. If he had a report that was due to the CEO that afternoon and an interesting new piece of software arrived, he would play with the software and forget about the report.

I think that distractibility is what venture capitalists hate about visionaries. The venture capitalist wants to see focused execution against a plan as badly as I wanted to see my computer programmer produce the report for the CEO. If the visionary is unable to exercise sufficient discipline, then the relationship with the venture capitalist will not work.

I would tend to sympathize with venture capitalists in that I believe that a visionary's distractibility must be kept under control in order for a business to be successful. After Homefair purchased TheSchoolReport.com, one of the things that made it difficult for me to get along with Neil Rosen, its visionary founder, was that he kept launching new initiatives at a rate that I thought was unsustainable. My concern was that he did not have the focus to see an idea through to profitability before he became captivated by his next brainstorm.

I had the task of trying to consolidate and integrate the databases and web sites of our two companies, which put me in the position of being the person who had to say "no" when Rosen undertook a new project that I did not think we could handle. I started telling friends that it was Karma: in my previous life, I had done so much complaining about IT bureaucrats that I had come back as one.

If you are a visionary, it may be necessary to fight a constant battle with yourself in order to manage distractibility. Force yourself to become a list maker. Write down goals, set deadlines, and commit to schedules. Distractible visionaries tend to resist such practices. If you cannot adopt them yourself, then find someone who can help you. Look for a person with strong project management experience.

If you are a visionary, then your drive to achieve has to be sufficient to overcome your distractibility. If you cannot focus, you cannot succeed.

Conclusion

My guess is that if you have all of the characteristics listed in this chapter, then you already are a successful entrepreneur. Most of us have weaknesses in one or more areas. To identify your areas for development, you might ask yourself the following questions:

1. (Charm) How often do you receive offers of help and advice from others?
2. (Talent scouting) How often have you hired someone who succeeded in spite of flaws or inexperience?
3. (Information sponge) How many new ideas have you tried to apply in the last month?
4. (Ability to stand up to the bear) How often have you sold something at a price way above marginal cost?
5. (Beginner's mind) When was the last time you suggested a solution for a problem outside your area of expertise?
6. (Ability to focus) Is it typical for you to commit to achieving specific goals, and do you track your progress toward those goals by using schedules and milestones?

This quiz can help you identify the type of people who will make an effective team. It is difficult for one individual to have all of these characteristics. When you choose a partner, someone who has some of the qualities that you are missing will contribute more than someone who shares your weaknesses. Eventually, you will want to have a team that has all of the characteristics of successful entrepreneurs.

Case No. 23: Dan Cunningham

When I first interviewed Dan Cunningham of 507Media Group, he was looking for the funding he needed to complete the execution of his business plan. Meanwhile, he had gotten remarkably far by using what I might call the three C's: contacts, charm, and credit cards.

507Media is developing a web application called Agent507, to be hosted on other sites, that will allow consumers to book musicians for events such as weddings, bar mitzvahs, and company parties. On the sites that carry Agent507, you will be able to review music and video clips, read biographies, read reviews, check availability, and book the band. The revenue model is to obtain a commission from the bands when consumers book them through Agent507.

Cunningham says that the original spark for the idea was an article he read in January 1999 about MP3 technology. Based on the article, he became convinced that the music industry was headed for some pretty big changes.

Venture capitalists place a high value on "domain expertise," which in Cunningham's case would mean experience as an executive in the music industry. Instead, Cunningham's background is in civil engineering, with an emphasis on project management. Project management is all about maintaining discipline and focus, which is one of the characteristics of a successful entrepreneur.

Cunningham tried starting his business with a partner, but that did not work out. When Cunningham really needed money, his partner said that he could contribute only his time. When Cunningham needed his partner to devote time to the project, it turned out that time was not available either.

Cunningham's fortunes improved in June 1999, when he happened to reconnect with a childhood friend, Joe Olmsted, who was with Intel at the time but took an interest in Cunningham's project. They hoped to create an all-encompassing music portal, but they lacked the capital to do so. However, they were able to go a long way toward developing what they call a fully automated talent agent, to allow consumers to shop for and book bands.

Even though he began as an outsider, Cunningham was able to use contacts to work his way up the food chain of the music industry. By the time I interviewed Cunningham in September 2000, his management team and board of advisers included about a dozen individuals with impressive credentials, including:

- The founder and former president of the music division of one of the two leading talent agencies
- A former senior vice president with Geffen Records
- An executive with experience at Warner Brothers Records
- The chief operating officer of Napster
- The agent responsible for several well-known Nashville acts

The entire team is on "deferred salary." Cunningham's ability to coax them along illustrates why I believe it is so important for a netstrapper to have charm.

Cunningham assembled this team through what he describes as a slow, methodical process of networking, gradually expanding his circle of contacts one step at a time. His favorite story is about making contacts at the "Pho (pronounced 'fuh') List."

It seems that there was a man named Jim Griffin who left Geffen records to start his own music-technology consulting firm. Soon, he was besieged by phone calls. (At this point, my mental juke box starts to play Joni Mitchell's "Free Man in Paris" as background music.) Finally, in May 1998, Jim told a few people, "I don't have time to talk to you, but every Sunday I go to this Vietnamese restaurant for *pho* (soup). You can meet me there and we'll talk."

The first week, four people showed up at the restaurant. The next week, a few more showed up. By August 1999, attendance was up to forty. Eventually, there were over 100 people involved, and if you wanted to deal in the cutting edge of music and technology, you had to attend, or at least get involved in the mailing list that the meetings spawned. Cunningham managed to join the invitation-only group, and many of his contacts came from the Pho List.

Armed with these strong connections in the music talent-agency market, Cunningham says that it has been relatively easy to obtain bands to supply 507Media with talent. Musicians and regional talent agencies have been very receptive.

One of the major challenges for 507Media is to get in front of customers. Developing and promoting the company's own web site as a distribution channel would mean spending time and money trying to compete for traffic. Instead, their approach is to embed their application on other sites such as WeddingChannel.com, a site that helps people plan weddings. Cunningham says that eventually he would like to be part of the more well-known site in that space, theknot.com, but for now the number-two site is more motivated to deal quickly.

The other major challenge is funding development of the business itself, including Agent507. Having "maxed out on four or five credit cards," Cunningham had six employees working on deferred salary. What this meant was that for a period of sixty days, the staff would not be paid. After sixty days, if Cunningham obtained his funding, the staff would get paid. If he did not obtain funding, then either party could choose to end the relationship. Employees also received some equity in exchange for taking this risk.

Cunningham even convinced an outside web developer to do much of the initial development for next to nothing, in exchange for receiving larger payments upon funding. When funding did not materialize as quickly as hoped, further development of Agent507 had to be suspended.

As of our interview in September 2000, Cunningham's charm had taken him about as far as he could go. With a little more funding, he could launch the product. Without it, 507Media would have to close up shop.

Case No. 24: Bill Baker

How long are you prepared to wait in order to get venture capital funding? Does twenty-three years sound reasonable?

For Bill Baker, twenty-three years was how long it took. In the meantime, he had created several well-known, successful businesses.

In 1977, at the dawn of the personal-computer revolution, he founded Information Unlimited Software (IUS), which developed EasyWriter™ for Apple and then for the IBM PC. After IUS was sold to Computer Associates in 1983 for $10 million, Baker founded Island Graphics, which developed a number of popular graphics programs for Sun workstations. This company was sold to DiNippon Screens in 1989 for $11.5 million.

After working for a few years as a marketing consultant for another successful start-up, Baker started to focus on the Internet in 1992, and he got the creative urge once again. He founded California Software, which developed InterAp, a single application that integrated all Internet applications. In those days, to use the Internet, you had to have separate applications for e-mail, file transfer, web browsing, and chat. In addition, you needed a special program to connect a PC to the Net.

Although InterAp was a good idea, there were a several other companies that had identified integrated Internet client software as an opportunity. Two of these companies, Netscape and Microsoft, took a particular interest in capturing this market. By the time it had its product ready, there was not much in the way of market share left for California Software, so Baker sold most of his company to Stac (now Previo) and morphed the remainder into HireRight.com.

The original concept behind HireRight.com, which was founded in 1994 but really got going in October 1995, was to be an end-to-end solution for corporate recruiters, from a résumé database all the way to delivering the employee's first paycheck. As Baker saw it, hiring is a major decision that is highly error prone and begs to be improved by information, which the Internet facilitates.

HireRight.com's ambitious effort was initially funded by $2 million from Stac, amounting to 20 percent of the company. This was actually part of the agreement by which Stac acquired California Software for $10 million. Later, Baker provided supplemental funding in the form of preferred stock and loans totaling another $6 million.

By the time HireRight.com launched in June 1997, the on-line recruiting market was crowded. A few market leaders, notably Monster.com, had established very strong market positions. HireRight.com did not have enough market power to gather the job and résumé listings needed to realize the "end-to-end" vision.

However, what HireRight.com had that the other recruiting sites lacked was an efficient tool for the job-application prescreening process. This is the process where the employer checks your background to verify that you have no criminal record, worked where you say you worked, went to school where you say you went to school, and so forth. HireRight uses Internet technology to do this rapidly and at low cost, for customers such as Cisco.

I suggested that perhaps HireRight.com waited too long to talk to customers. Baker agreed that this probably was a mistake, which resulted in the company developing a lot of features for which it could not subsequently recover its costs. However, he points out that customers are now starting to see the potential benefits of comprehensive end-to-end hiring solutions rather than the fragmented structure that exists on the Internet today.

Even though the prescreening application falls short of Baker's original end-to-end vision, a successful working product was sufficient to draw the interest of institutional investors. In the summer of 2000, Baker closed a deal with a venture capitalist whereby investors repaid his $4-million loans, bought out Stac's $2-million stake, and put another $7 million in the company. Thus, after a twenty-three-year career as an entrepreneur, Baker finally received institutional funding.

As a founder of successful companies, Baker would seem to fit the profile of someone who would easily find venture capitalist backing.

Therefore, I was very curious to find out why he found it difficult to get funding. He listed the following reasons:

- Venture capitalists tend to be afraid of "idea people." They prefer a management team that is strong in terms of execution and attention to the details of running a company.
- The market opportunity has to be very big. If they do not see a $1-billion market cap, they lose interest.
- They consider a 5x return a failure. That is, they will not put in $10 million if they think that their investment will be worth "only" $50 million in a few years.
- They do not want to leave the entrepreneur in control of the company. Even though they might not technically have more than a 50-percent ownership, they may insist that the entrepreneur reserve shares for employees and other investors. Moreover, regardless of the ownership share, the venture capitalist will insert provisions that restrict the entrepreneur's decisionmaking ability.

I can certainly understand Baker's point of view, given his negative experiences in the past. However, I believe that for most entrepreneurs, it would be a mistake to shun venture capital money because of the control issue.

I can certainly believe that there have been instances in which a founder lost control of a business to venture capitalists with results that were disastrous for the business. However, I suspect that the opposite occurs much more often. That is, when the venture capitalists and the founder are at odds, it is the venture capitalists who have the sounder business strategy. Venture capitalists tend to be veteran entrepreneurs themselves. They have a more objective and experienced perspective than the typical founder.

I think that if you are debating whether to seek venture capital, the "control issue" should not be a factor. There is no doubt that venture capitalists can make major changes to your vision, strategy, and execution plans. However, this should help your business, unless you have chosen a venture capitalist out of desperation or carelessness.

It seems to me that it ought to be pretty easy to avoid getting into a bad relationship with a venture capitalist. Before you sign on (preferably before you even contact them), try to talk to the founders of some of the companies in the firm's portfolio. Listen to how they describe their experience, and make sure that it sounds comfortable for you. As with any other important relationship in your business, a little due diligence can go a long way.

Another question it occurred to me to ask a serial entrepreneur like Baker was: "Why do you keep doing it?" Obviously, he had made enough money from his first business to retire. What motivates him now?

His response was interesting. As Baker sees it, he has had two opportunities in his lifetime to participate in revolutionary developments. First, he participated in the early days of the personal computer. Next, he was involved in the Internet.

As a matter of fact, Baker's next goal is to get into biotechnology. He makes this transition sound easy. He says, "DNA is just software, right? It's just another computer language."

He has taken a course in bioengineering. He has started a lab in his house, and he will buy mail-order kits to do experiments.

Case No. 25: Lisa Martin

Lisa Martin, the founder of LeapFrog Solutions, Inc., is not a visionary. When she speaks, she does not shower her listeners with "new-economy" buzzwords. Instead of a trendy networking event for twenty-somethings, her starting point for making contacts was the local Chamber of Commerce. She does not have a technical background.

Interestingly, of all of the netstrappers that I interviewed, Lisa Martin had the easiest time meeting her revenue goals and achieving success. Martin's secret is that her background is in marketing and sales. That experience enables her to estimate the time and effort involved in making sales, to develop and implement marketing plans for her company, and to make realistic revenue projections. Knowing what to expect in terms of revenue in turn helps in budgeting for expenses.

In contrast, someone who has never closed a sale is not in a position to make revenue forecasts. It is second nature for someone with sales experience to set targets, calculate the number of customers to contact, estimate the time to close, and predict the closing rate. Meanwhile, the rest of us have to learn to think in those terms.

Professor Bhide found in his survey of successful entrepreneurs that in 82 percent of the cases, the entrepreneur was the main person conducting early sales. In another 10 percent of cases, the entrepreneur was heavily involved in those sales. In only 8 percent of the cases was the entrepreneur "somewhat involved" in early sales. Based on these results, Bhide concluded, "Effective face-to-face selling is critical for entrepreneurs" (*The Origin and Evolution of New Businesses*, p. 108).

I would not discourage you from netstrapping if you have no sales experience. However, in that case I would recommend that you not waste a lot of time on your initial business plan. Planning without sales experience is a bogus effort. Once you have undertaken some initial sales attempts, then you will be in a position to create a meaningful plan.

Early in 1996, Martin left her position with Image Communications, a marketing communications firm. Initially, she left to join a smaller firm that was focused on marketing communications for trade shows, but she maintained a consulting relationship with it as a project manager for one of its large accounts. Martin soon fell out with her new company, because it was comfortable staying in copy writing, while she wanted to become more involved with the Web.

In July 1996, Martin formed LeapFrog Solutions. Her idea was to blend traditional marketing communications with web-site development and Internet marketing. To keep expenses down, LeapFrog spent its initial years as a "virtual company," with its members working out of home offices and communicating over the company's server.

Martin joined the Fairfax County Chamber of Commerce, a move that led her to many helpful contacts. Early in 1997, LeapFrog landed an important initial contract to develop part of the "extranet" for Mobil Oil. Mobil's dealerships buy products, from signs to gas pumps, through Mobil's catalogs. The print versions of these catalogs are expensive to produce and to maintain. Mobil engaged LeapFrog to put these catalogs on the Web, so that they could switch to an electronic ordering system.

Before the opportunity with Mobil presented itself, LeapFrog had never built a database-driven commerce site. LeapFrog's experience was in front-end web design, but with potential customers like Mobil, Martin realized that "people expect us to know the back end."

She judged that demand for database-driven web sites was going to continue to expand, so she decided that LeapFrog would develop the capability to meet customer expectations in this area.

Martin has worked assiduously to cultivate new contacts. Her involvement with the Chamber of Commerce led her to the Northern Virginia Technology Council, which offers a program called Mind-Share for what it calls "techpreneurs." Not only did Martin gain knowledge from participating in the monthly sessions of this nine-month program, but she also added three new clients from among her classmates!

As of the fall of 2000, LeapFrog had moved from "virtual" to real office space, where six people worked full-time. At the time, the firm also employed about ten contractors, although the plan was to increase the ratio of employees on staff to contractors.

Growth in revenues has been so strong that Martin at one point considered the option of taking on investors and perhaps eventually attempting to expand to the point where the company could go public. However, she decided that as a profitable company, they did not need capital, and as a service business, they did not have a compelling story for scaling to the size of an IPO.

When I asked Martin to list her biggest mistakes, nothing popped into her head. Eventually, she mentioned that she had stuck too long with an accountant who was not paying attention to the firm's rapid growth. As a result, at the end of one year, the accountant waited until one week before the deadline before informing Martin that a tax payment was going to have to be $70,000 higher than anticipated. Another mistake that Martin cited was allowing an attorney to nearly cost her a contract by inserting clauses that were objectionable to the client but that Martin was willing to drop.

Netstrappers frequently run into minor frustrations and disappointments with attorneys and accountants. Part of the problem is that netstrappers' requirements in terms of speed and flexibility can be unusual, and many lawyers and accountants fail to adapt their business practices. Another problem is that as an entrepreneur, you are so pressed for time that you select an attorney or an accountant quickly in order to put the decision behind you, at the risk of being careless about whom you pick.

ELEVEN

The Future of Netstrapping

The idea that dot-coms are dead, or that the new economy is an illusion, looks to us like the same herd analysis that so recently led people to think that on-line retailing could replace the shopping mall . . . there remains an enormous amount of vibrancy and opportunity and entrepreneurial creativity in the Internet Economy. It just takes independent thinking to find it. And that's how it should be.

—Jonathan Weber, "The Power of the Herd,"
Industry Standard, November 6, 2000

Weber's point is particularly relevant in the under-the-radar sector. Netstrappers are largely insulated from the storms that have buffeted the venture capital community and captivated the media. The purpose of this chapter is to help reinforce Weber's point that the entrepreneurial opportunities remain excellent, particularly under the radar.

Do Netstrappers Need the Stock Market?

As you read this, where is the Nasdaq? 5,000? 1,000? It makes relatively little difference to a netstrapper.

Most netstrappers are surprisingly hostile to the stock market. For example, Mike Covel, discussing his HomePharmacy.com, proudly says, "We're going to get rich, but from building a great business as opposed to an overvalued IPO."

When we sold Homefair to Homestore.com, we were adamant that at least half of the proceeds be paid to us in cash. Naturally, Homestore.com would have preferred to pay us in stock. However, our attitude was that we were not about to trade a profitable business built with years of effort for assets that would be subject to the vicissitudes of the stock market. Ultimately, we were paid in a combination of cash and stock, and I can say that the cash has retained its value.

Many of us who choose to become entrepreneurs do so in order to try to take charge of our own destiny. Instead of relying on other companies and other management teams, we are betting on ourselves. From this perspective, trading our company for shares that represent a small ownership stake in someone else's company feels like a step backward.

To a venture capitalist, taking a company public is a cork-popping occasion, the ultimate reward for a successful investment. On the other hand, to an entrepreneur, it represents a threat to one's autonomy. The value of your company, which previously seemed to be something under your control, is now in the hands of a capricious casino.

I have always had some doubts about the role of the stock market in the Internet economy. Historically, the stock market emerged as an institution to help solve the major challenge of the industrial economy, which is to mobilize and allocate capital. I believe that the biggest challenge posed by the Internet is allocating talent. I cannot predict what institutions will emerge to serve that need, but it would not surprise me to see that what develops over the next twenty years as the ultimate talent allocation system bears little resemblance to the Nasdaq or the New York Stock Exchange.

The intensity of Internet mania on the stock market took me by surprise. The first major Internet IPO was in August 1995, when Netscape went public. The day after Netscape's IPO, I wrote, "The romance between the Internet and Wall Street cannot last."

For more than four years, this stood as the worst of several poor prognostications I made about the Internet. However, in the year 2000, sentiment began to shift, and the Internet stocks lost their magic.

Until then, venture capitalists had a nice little scam going. They were able to do a lot of fund-raising on Wall Street. But now it seems that investors are getting tired of giving to the nonprofits for which the venture capitalists raised funds.

In contrast, many netstrappers were pleased by the stock-market correction. Their view is that with some rationality restored to the market, the focus will be on business fundamentals. There will be less pressure for artificial consolidation based on overvalued companies using their stock as currency to buy out their competition. Also, fewer companies will be provided with resources for extravagant marketing campaigns. This will make for a more level playing field, which will give businesses that are fundamentally sound a better chance of success.

However, a weak stock market represents something of a mixed blessing for under-the-radar entrepreneurs. It poses a challenge with respect to exit strategy. Rob Main, Raj Khera, Joseph Murgio, and I are among those who sold our companies to publicly traded firms. In a bear market, you may not be able to sell your company as easily, and you may have to stay with your business longer.

I believe that most netstrappers would rather build a solid enterprise than try to make a fortune by fooling stock-market investors. Certainly, the focus of this book is on creating a real business. If you identify a genuine market need and create a company that meets that need, then I believe you will achieve the success that you deserve, regardless of how the stock market behaves.

Overall, I would advise you to make the netstrapping decision without regard to the performance of the stock market. Even in the 1930s, there were successful start-ups, and I doubt that we are going to revisit those awful days. I believe that the environment for starting a business under the radar will continue to be favorable.

Filling the Vacuum

Earlier in this book, in Chapter 3, "Room Under the Radar," I explained the striking contrast between the target valuation of the entrepreneur and that of the venture capitalist. I pointed out that it is plausible for an entrepreneur to be satisfied with a business that might reach an ultimate value of $5 or $10 million. On the other hand, venture capitalists insist that for a new enterprise to be worth funding, it must have the potential to be worth at least $1 billion.

This gap in objectives between the entrepreneur and the venture capitalist is an anomaly. As a student of economics, I do not see this vacuum persisting. If the under-the-radar zone is rich with profit opportunities, then people will choose to fill it.

I believe that it is plausible that most of the wealth that will be created in the Internet economy will be in firms with a value of less than $1 billion each. If that is the case, then the venture capitalists are like the proverbial drunk looking for his lost watch.

In the classic joke, a drunk looks for the watch under a lamppost, which is not where he dropped it. When asked why he is looking under the lamppost, the drunk replies, "That's where the light is." Venture capitalists are searching for wealth in the form of $1-billion companies because that is their lamppost, even though it may not be the best place to look. The best place to look may be in companies that successfully capture niche opportunities rather than in companies that overextend themselves by trying to attack the broadest possible markets.

I doubt that Netscape, Amazon, or Homestore (the company that bought Homefair) were helped by their broad ambitions. Netscape lost an opportunity to dominate a lucrative business in web servers while it pursued grandiose strategies that in theory were supposed to bring down Microsoft. Amazon did not try to solidify a profitable business selling books but instead made large investments in auctions, sales of drug products, and other dubious enterprises. Homestore was in an excellent position to provide technology to real estate professionals and consumers, but instead it defines its mission as providing "everything for the home." This leads Homestore to compete in many areas where other companies might be expected to have an advantage.

Andrew Zacharakis, an assistant professor at Babson College, wrote in the summer of 2000:

As John Taylor, director of research at the National Venture Capital Association, told me during a recent meeting, for the last couple of years "everybody's [been] looking to hit the home run, but those bets won't pay off for much longer." Instead of the home run mentality, people need to revert to the idea of hitting singles and doubles.

(Source: "Let the Good Times Roll?"
Babson Bulletin, Summer 2000)

This comment suggests a scenario in which venture capital funds that continue to reach for spectacular billion-dollar prizes will be unsuccessful. Companies that are more modest in their ambitions will be the winners.

If the billion-dollar companies become harder to find, then venture capitalists will have to adjust. Venture capitalists are too competitive and results-oriented to continue to put money where it will not be profitable, while ignoring better opportunities. In the future, if the most successful businesses will be enterprises operating in niche markets, sooner or later the venture capitalists will find their way into the under-the-radar zone.

In order to participate in the under-the-radar market, venture capitalists will have to operate without as many mouths to feed. They need to achieve a greater percentage of successes, so that the successes are not burdened by a requirement to offset the failures.

My guess is that among the changes that will take place in the venture capital process are the following:

1. More Specialization

Today, venture capitalists aim for glamorous reputations. They want to be associated with "hot" companies. At times, it appears that every venture capitalist is chasing the same deals.

Going forward, venture capitalists may become much more specialized. An individual firm may devote all of its funds to a single market, such as supply-chain management for restaurants. Individual investors would diversify by putting their money into several different funds rather than looking to the venture capital firm to provide a broadly diversified portfolio.

2. The Scientific Method

The venture capital process is designed to solve a statistical problem. Venture capitalists operate in an environment in which there are a large number of "bad draws" (businesses that will fail) relative to the number of "good draws" (new businesses that will succeed). The venture capitalist's task is to select from this environment a portfolio that will include at least one or two good draws out of every ten businesses that are funded.

This sort of statistical problem lends itself to two types of errors. The first is passing up a "good" company. The second is funding a "bad" company.

Entrepreneurs tend to fault venture capitalists for making many errors of the first type—passing up a good company. An entrepreneur thinks, "I have a great idea here. The venture capitalists are really stupid, because they are not funding it."

In fact, the reverse is more likely to be the case. That is, venture capitalists are probably backing too many bad ideas for every good idea that they support. My guess is that the biggest potential for improvement among venture capitalists is to become even more discriminating.

Despite the drop in the Nasdaq, venture capitalists remained committed to romantic criteria for evaluating new concepts:

> It's when you meet some guy and, after half an hour, you decide the laws of physics have been suspended, the laws of economics are out the window, and this thing is really going to work.
>
> (Source: Derek Proudian of Ironweed Capital,
> quoted in "Unconventional Wisdom from a
> Trio of True Believers," *Business Week Online*,
> February 5, 2001)

Given that theirs is a statistical problem, it would be surprising to see venture capitalists continue to rely heavily on gut feeling and human judgment ("You had me at 'Hello'"), without subjecting more of their hypotheses to statistical testing. For example, venture capitalists insist that "domain expertise" (knowledge and experience within a particular industry) is a critical component of a business team. Meanwhile, Professor Bhide found that about 40 percent of successful entrepreneurs were quite inexperienced in the area of the business they founded. Although this does not prove conclusively that venture capitalists place too high a weight on domain expertise, it suggests that a scientific examination of this topic would be useful.

Imagine if we had a historical database of the performance of thousands of start-ups. Suppose that we had information on the characteristics of the entrepreneurs (including their level of domain expertise), the rate at which the enterprise was projected to burn cash, the point at which the business was projected to achieve profitability, and so forth.

With a historical database, we could use statistical analysis to examine various hypotheses regarding the factors affecting the rate of return on capital invested in start-ups. Perhaps it would turn out that in a large sample, with other variables taken into account, domain expertise would indeed emerge as a critical factor. On the other hand, domain expertise might turn out to have little or no power in predicting business success.

Venture capitalists would consider this hypothetical research project to be preposterous. Experts in any field rarely believe that a statistical model could replace their human judgment. However, we have seen it happen.

- In *Interface Culture*, Steven Johnson tells the story of how "a relatively obscure English professor at Vassar, Don Foster" used a statistical model to determine that the author of the anonymous book *Primary Colors* was *Newsweek* columnist Joe Klein.
- In August 1997, an Othello match (Othello™, whose trademark is currently owned by Pressman Toys, is a board game, somewhat like Go or chess) was arranged between a computer program, Logistello, and Takeshi Murakami, considered one of the best human players of all time. The computer, using methods based on statistical modeling of a large database of past games, crushed Murakami, six games to none. (The author of Logistello, Michael Buro, has a web site at www.neci.nj.nec.com/homepages/mic/mic.html. The match is described there.)
- As of 1990, nearly all home-mortgage loan decisions were made by human underwriters using rules of thumb, such as a requirement that the mortgage payment be no more than one-third of the borrower's monthly income. By the year 2000, statistical credit-scoring models based on past default experience were making these decisions more accurately and allowing people with less income to qualify for larger loans.

In each case, the human experts did not believe that what the computers were doing was possible. I am particularly familiar with the Othello example. The leading computer programs are not taught any of the strategies and tactics used by humans, and humans are convinced that the computers are "wrong," even as they proceed to lose to them. Rather than imitate humans, the computers compare two positions statistically—based on the average score achieved in a similar position in the historical database of Othello games. As a result, the computers make moves that occasionally seem bizarre but turn out to be sound.

My guess is that a statistical model to predict business success would make decisions occasionally that venture capitalists would find bizarre. However, if one could assemble a sufficiently large body of data, one could construct a statistical scoring system to evaluate entrepreneurs and business models. I suspect that such a system would pick better portfolios than does the current human process of sifting through business plans on the basis of "gut feel."

Conclusion

The future under the radar looks bright. Regardless of what happens to the stock market, opportunities exist for profitable businesses on the Internet that can be launched without requiring venture capital. If the large, billion-dollar opportunities were to dry up, as I expect they may, then venture capitalists will eventually shift away from their home-run-or-nothing strategy. To make the adjustment to hitting singles and doubles with consistency, I suspect that they will have to become more specialized and more scientific in their approach.

Today, venture capitalists have little choice but to pay attention to stock-market fluctuations, because the profitability of venture-fund portfolios depends on Wall Street valuation. However, the stock market should not be nearly as important a factor in your decision to become a netstrapper.

The decision to become an entrepreneur revolves, as it always has, on the axis of the trade-off between autonomy and security. Starting your own business means giving up some security in order to gain some autonomy.

I tend to make sarcastic comments about the Dilbert sector, but in fact I have a lot of respect for large companies and for people who work in such enterprises. Big companies provide many types of rewards to their employees, including social support as well as economic security. It is easier to maintain a life-work balance in a large enterprise, in part because it is easier for a corporation to provide business continuity when you stay away for a weekend or take a vacation.

I will still respect you in the morning if you decide that the potential rewards from netstrapping do not justify the risks and challenges. I will also respect you if you decide to attempt to start a business on a part-time basis at first, which is a route taken by many of the entrepreneurs whom I interviewed for this book.

If you have chosen to become a netstrapper, then you should not underestimate the challenges that you face. When I told my story, I said that starting a business is like going through adolescence. As far as I know, nobody has written a book that can get you through adolescence without making any mistakes. Similarly, I would never suggest that this book has given you everything you need to know to avoid making mistakes when you start your business. My hope is that it has helped you focus on some important issues and that it has increased your chances for success.

INDEX